NEWS ONLINE

News Online

Transformations and Continuities

Edited by

Graham Meikle
Guy Redden

© Graham Meikle and Guy Redden 2011

All rights reserved. No reproduction, copy or transmission of this
publication may be made without written permission.

No portion of this publication may be reproduced, copied or transmitted
save with written permission or in accordance with the provisions of the
Copyright, Designs and Patents Act 1988, or under the terms of any licence
permitting limited copying issued by the Copyright Licensing Agency,
Saffron House, 6–10 Kirby Street, London EC1N 8TS.

Any person who does any unauthorized act in relation to this publication
may be liable to criminal prosecution and civil claims for damages.

The authors have asserted their rights to be identified as the authors of this work
in accordance with the Copyright, Designs and Patents Act 1988.

First published 2011 by
PALGRAVE MACMILLAN

Palgrave Macmillan in the UK is an imprint of Macmillan Publishers Limited,
registered in England, company number 785998, of Houndmills, Basingstoke,
Hampshire RG21 6XS.

Palgrave Macmillan in the US is a division of St Martin's Press LLC,
175 Fifth Avenue, New York, NY 10010.

Palgrave Macmillan is the global academic imprint of the above companies
and has companies and representatives throughout the world.

Palgrave® and Macmillan® are registered trademarks in the United States,
the United Kingdom, Europe and other countries

ISBN 978–0–230–23344–7   hardback
ISBN 978–0–230–23345–4   paperback

This book is printed on paper suitable for recycling and made from fully
managed and sustained forest sources. Logging, pulping and manufacturing
processes are expected to conform to the environmental regulations of the
country of origin.

A catalogue record for this book is available from the British Library.

A catalog record for this book is available from the Library of Congress.

10 9 8 7 6 5 4 3 2 1
20 19 18 17 16 15 14 13 12 11

Printed in Great Britain by
CPI Antony Rowe, Chippenham and Eastbourne

Contents

Notes on contributors   vii

Introduction: transformation and continuity   1
Graham Meikle and Guy Redden

1 Journalism, public service and BBC News Online   20
Stuart Allan and Einar Thorsen

2 Managing the online news revolution: the UK experience   38
Brian McNair

3 The crisis of journalism and the Internet   53
Robert W. McChesney

4 When magical realism confronted virtual reality: online news
   and journalism in Latin America   69
Jairo Lugo-Ocando and Andrés Cañizález

5 Newsgames: an introduction   84
Ian Bogost, Simon Ferrari and Bobby Schweizer

6 The intimate turn of mobile news   99
Gerard Goggin

7 News to me: Twitter and the personal networking of news   115
Kate Crawford

8 News produsage in a pro-am mediasphere: why citizen
   journalism matters   132
Axel Bruns

9   'Comment is free, facts are sacred': journalistic ethics in a
     changing mediascape   148
     Natalie Fenton and Tamara Witschge

10   Journalism without journalists: on the power shift from
     journalists to employers and audiences   164
     Mark Deuze and Leopoldina Fortunati

11   Web 2.0, citizen journalism and social justice in China   178
     Xin Xin

12   Marrying the professional to the amateur: strategies and
     implications of the OhmyNews model   195
     An Nguyen

     Conclusion   210
     Guy Redden and Graham Meikle

Index   218

Notes on contributors

Stuart Allan
Stuart Allan is Professor of Journalism in the Media School, Bournemouth University, UK. His recent publications addressing online journalism include *Online News: Journalism and the Internet* (2006), *Digital War Reporting* (2009, co-authored with Donald Matheson), *Citizen Journalism: Global Perspectives* (2009, co-edited with Einar Thorsen) and *News Culture* (third edition, 2010).

Ian Bogost
Ian Bogost is Associate Professor in the School of Literature, Communication, and Culture, at Georgia Institute of Technology and Founding Partner, Persuasive Games LLC. He is the author of *Persuasive Games: The Expressive Power of Videogames* (2007) and *Unit Operations: An Approach to Videogame Criticism* (2008), and the co-author (with Nick Montfort) of *Racing the Beam: The Atari Video Computer System* (2009), all published by the MIT Press. He is co-author (with Simon Ferrari and Bobby Schweizer) of *Newsgames: Journalism at Play* (2010), published by the MIT Press.

Axel Bruns
Dr Axel Bruns is an Associate Professor in the Creative Industries Faculty at Queensland University of Technology in Brisbane, Australia. He is a Chief Investigator in the ARC Centre of Excellence for Creative Industries and Innovation (CCi), and a Senior Researcher in the Smart Services Cooperative Research Centre. Bruns is the author of *Blogs, Wikipedia, Second Life and Beyond: From Production to Produsage* (2008) and *Gatewatching: Collaborative Online News Production* (2005), and the editor of *Uses of Blogs* with Joanne Jacobs (2006; all released by Peter Lang, New York). Much of his work can be found at snurb.info and Produsage.org, and he also contributes to the Gatewatching.org group blog with Jason Wilson and Barry Saunders, and tweets as @snurb_dot_info.

Andrés Cañizález
Andrés Cañizález is a researcher at the Centre of Communication Research at the Universidad Católica Andres Bello (UCAB) in Caracas, Venezuela. He also serves as academic coordinator of UCAB's Program for Advanced Studies in Freedom of Expression and the Right to Information. He is also director of the Venezuelan chapter of the Press and Society Institute. He has authored and edited over a dozen books and monographs such as *Prensa y Elecciones en América Latina* (2004), *Pensando la Sociedad: Actores Sociales, Espacio Público y Medios en Venezuela* (2007), *Libertad de Expresión: Una discusión sobre sus principios, limitaciones e implicaciones* (2007), among others. He is also the editor of the journal *Temas de Comunicación*. In 2010 he was selected as a Reagan Fascell Democracy Fellow at the National Endowment for Democracy in the USA and received the Titus Brandsma International award for his work in defence of the freedom of expression in Latin America.

Kate Crawford

Kate Crawford is an Associate Professor in the Journalism and Media Research Centre at the University of New South Wales, Sydney. Her current research focuses on social media and technologies of listening. Her books include *Adult Themes* (2006) and *Understanding the Internet: Language, Technology, Media and Power* (forthcoming, with Chris Chesher and Anne Dunn).

Mark Deuze

Mark Deuze (Weblog: http://deuze.blogspot.com; e-mail: mdeuze@indiana.edu) holds a joint appointment at Indiana University's Department of Telecommunications in Bloomington (United States) and as a professor of journalism and new media at Leiden University in The Netherlands. His published work comprises seven books – including *Media Work* (Polity Press, 2007) and *Media Life* (Polity Press, 2011) – and articles in journals such as the *International Journal of Cultural Studies, New Media & Society,* and the *Journal of Media Sociology.*

Natalie Fenton

Natalie Fenton is a Professor in Media and Communications in the Department of Media and Communication, Goldsmiths, University of London where she is also Co-Director of the Goldsmiths Leverhulme Media Research Centre: Spaces, Connections, Control and Co-Director of Goldsmiths Centre for the Study of Global Media and Democracy. She has published widely on issues relating to media, politics and new media and is particularly interested in rethinking understandings of public culture, the public sphere and democracy. Her latest book, *New Media, Old News: Journalism and Democracy in the Digital Age* (ed.) is published by Sage, 2010.

Simon Ferrari

Simon Ferrari is a doctoral student in digital media at the Georgia Institute of Technology. He is co-author (with Ian Bogost and Bobby Schweizer) of *Newsgames: Journalism at Play* (2010), published by the MIT Press.

Leopoldina Fortunati

Leopoldina Fortunati is a professor of sociology of communication at the Faculty of Education of Italy's University of Udine. She is the author and editor of many books, including (with Jane Vincent) *Electronic Emotion: The Mediation of Emotion via Information* and *Communication Technologies* (Peter Lang, 2009). She is very active at the European level and is the Italian representative in the COST (European Cooperation in Science and Technology) Domain Committee ISCH (Individuals, Societies, Cultures and Health). She is associate editor of the journal *The Information Society.* She is the co-chair with Richard Ling of the international association Society for the Social Study of Mobile Communication (SSSMC). Her works have been published in 11 languages: Bulgarian, Chinese, English, French, German, Italian, Japanese, Korean, Russian, Slovenian, and Spanish.

Gerard Goggin

Gerard Goggin is Professor of Digital Communication and deputy-director of the Journalism & Media Research Centre, University of New South Wales, Sydney. His books include *New Technologies and the Media* (2011), *Global Mobile Media* (2011), *Mobile Technologies: From Telecommunications to Media* (2009; with Larissa Hjorth), *Internationalizing Internet Studies* (2009; with Mark McLelland), *Cell Phone Culture* (2006), and *Digital Disability* (2003; with Christopher Newell).

Jairo Lugo-Ocando

Jairo Lugo-Ocando is Director of Journalism Studies and a member of the Stirling Media Research Institute at the University of Stirling (UK). His research interests include media and democratisation in South America and digital technologies in the developing world. He has worked as a reporter, staff-writer and chief sub-editor for several newspapers in Venezuela and has also been correspondent for newspapers, magazines and radio stations in Venezuela, Colombia, Mexico and the United States. He has authored and edited several books and monographs including *The Media in Latin America* (Open University Press/ McGraw Hill, 2008), *ICTs, Democracy and Development* (VDM Verlag, 2009) and *Statistics for Journalists* (Palgrave, 2011) among others. He is a guest lecturer in the School of International and Public Affairs at the University of Columbia (NY, USA) and the University of Malaga (Spain), and is currently leading a research project on open source software in the newsroom funded by ORACLE/Sun Microsystems.

Robert W. McChesney

Robert W. McChesney is Gutgsell Endowed Professor at the University of Illinois at Urbana-Champaign. He is the author or editor of 17 books, including, with John Nichols, *The Death and Life of American Journalism*. His work has been translated into 25 languages.

Brian McNair

Brian McNair is Professor of Journalism, Media & Communication at Queensland University of Technology. He is the author of many books and articles on news media, including *Cultural Chaos* (Routledge, 2006), *The Sociology of Journalism* (Arnold, 1998), *News & Journalism In the UK*, Fifth Edition (Routledge, 2009) and *Journalists On Film* (Edinburgh University Press, 2010). His books have been widely translated, and he is a regular contributor to online, broadcast and print media.

Graham Meikle

Graham Meikle is the author of *Interpreting News* (Palgrave 2009) and *Future Active: Media Activism and the Internet* (Routledge 2002). He is Senior Lecturer in the Department of Film, Media & Journalism at the University of Stirling in Scotland.

An Nguyen

Dr An Nguyen is a Senior Lecturer in News Media/Journalism Studies in the School of Media, Film and Music, the University of Sussex, England. A former Vietnamese journalist and an Australian-educated scholar, he is the author of *The Penetration of Online News* and numerous papers on online journalism, online news audiences, journalism professionalism, and science journalism. He wrote this chapter when he was a Lecturer in Journalism Studies in the Department of Film, Media & Journalism at the University of Stirling, Scotland.

Guy Redden

Guy Redden is Lecturer in the Department of Cultural Studies at the University of Sydney. He is author of articles about the relationships between culture and economy, and his research interests include online gift economies. He has previously taught at Prince of Songkla University in Thailand and the University of Lincoln in the UK.

Bobby Schweizer
Bobby Schweizer is a doctoral student in digital media at the Georgia Institute of Technology. He is co-author (with Ian Bogost and Simon Ferrari) of *Newsgames: Journalism at Play* (2010), published by the MIT Press.

Einar Thorsen
Einar Thorsen is Lecturer in Journalism and Communication in the Media School, Bournemouth University, UK. He has a PhD in online journalism focusing on the BBC News website during the 2005 UK General Election, which was funded by the AHRC. His publications include *Citizen Journalism: Global Perspectives* (2009, co-edited with Stuart Allan), articles on the evolution of public service media in an online environment, and on Wikinews and the neutral point of view.

Tamara Witschge
Tamara Witschge (PhD) is a lecturer at the Cardiff School of Journalism, Media and Cultural Studies. She obtained her PhD degree from the Amsterdam School of Communications Research, University of Amsterdam in May 2007. Tamara's main research interests are media and democracy, changes in the journalistic field, equality and diversity in the public sphere, and the public debate on immigration. Her PhD thesis '(In)difference Online' focused on online discussions of contested issues. From 2007–2009 she was a research associate at the Media and Communications Department and worked on the Leverhulme Trust funded project 'Spaces of News'. This project aimed to explore the ways in which technological, economic and social change is reconfiguring news journalism and shaping the dynamics of the public sphere and public culture. Tamara is the General Secretary of ECREA (since 2008). She was one of the main organisers of the First European Communication Conference (ECC), held in November 2005 in Amsterdam and is part of ECC's organising committee (Barcelona and Hamburg). She was the Secretary of the Board of ECREA (2007–2008) and the chair of the Young Scholars Network of ECREA (yecrea.eu) from 2008–2009. She is a member of the editorial board of the international journal *New Media and Society*, as well as *PLATFORM: Journal of Media and Communication*.

Xin Xin
Dr Xin Xin is a senior research fellow at the China Media Centre, University of Westminster. She teaches graduates and undergraduates in the Department of Journalism and Mass Communication <http://www.wmin.ac.uk/mad/page-97>. Her research interests include: media, culture and society in transitional societies, particularly in China and Russia; international communication; impacts of marketisation and globalisation on media institutions; impacts of new technology on journalistic practices; propaganda, public diplomacy and international relations.

Introduction: transformation and continuity

GRAHAM MEIKLE AND GUY REDDEN

News matters. It remains the main forum for discussion of issues of public importance. It offers an arena in which journalists and media firms, politicians, other high-status sources of information and audiences come together to inform, persuade, influence, endorse or reject one another in a collaborative process of making meaning from events. But the news is changing in ways that are not yet well understood. The news environment of the twenty-first century is being shaped by both emerging transformations and contested continuities. Content, distribution channels, geographical constraints, production values, business models, regulatory approaches and cultural habits are all changing as new media technologies are adopted and adapted by users, often in unexpected ways. Established media organisations are in many cases struggling to adapt to a changed environment – even though, paradoxically, they have driven many of the changes themselves.

Consider the news coverage of the Iranian election of June 2009. Many observers expected the incumbent president Mahmoud Ahmadinejad to be defeated by the opposition leader Mir Hossein Mousavi. The announcement of Ahmadinejad's victory was followed by mass demonstrations in Tehran and a violent crackdown on protesters. Western correspondents in the city were subject to censorship and in many cases confined to their hotels, and so a crucial conduit of information from Iran became the microblogging service Twitter, augmented by other social media tools, including blogs, Facebook and text messages. Major incidents, such as the shooting dead of a young woman named Neda Agha-Soltan (see also Gerard Goggin's chapter in this volume), were relayed around the world through a complex media environment that mixed old and new – it combined the posting on YouTube of eyewitness mobile phone video of her dying in the street, a *#neda* topic on Twitter, reports on the BBC, thousands of tribute images on Flickr, dedicated Facebook groups and op-eds in papers from the *New York Times* to the *Guardian*.

1

The protests surrounding the Iranian election played out in real time on a global scale before a participatory news audience. The disputed electoral irregularity and the undisputable violence were witnessed by participants and onlookers networked worldwide through twenty-first century phenomena such as mobile phones, blogs, broadband, wireless connections and social network tools like Twitter or Facebook – as Stuart Allan (2009) observes, citizen journalism works best in times of crisis. But the protests illustrated not just the transformations in the media environment, but the continuities as well. In particular, this was also a media event that showed just how essential professional journalists remain.

The cacophony of information streaming to and from Iran, and echoing around the Internet and the established media, demonstrated precisely the value of experienced professionals who could distinguish between signal and noise, who understood the political history and context of Iran and who could help onlookers to make sense of the drama on our TV, computer and mobile phone screens. On the one hand, the mediation of the Iranian election showed how news audiences could now inform each other, cutting out the journalists in many cases; but on the other hand, it showed just what professional journalists could add to that process – at least in theory. In this case, many were dismayed by the disappointing response to events in Iran by one leading news provider. CNN's main offering that crucial Saturday night was a rerun of Larry King interviewing celebrity motorcyclists, and so *#CNNfail* became a major topic on Twitter (see also Kate Crawford's chapter in this volume).

This book examines the interplay between such continuities and transformations in the public sphere. Its twelve essays question established understandings of news in the light of change. They consider the shifting boundaries between the popular and the professional entailed by the redistribution of news functions. They critically analyse how popular digital communications reconfigure relations of production and consumption, and associated forms of cultural and political participation.

A central concept in these debates is convergence (Pool, 1983; Rice, 1999; Jenkins, 2006; Castells, 2009; Deuze, 2010). The coming together of telecommunications, media content and computing in multiple platforms, coupled with ongoing processes of industry merger, acquisition and alliance, have made possible a new digital media environment that operates in real time on a global scale. The convergence of industries and technologies makes possible certain other forms of convergence, discussed in more detail below. Each of these manifests different kinds of behaviour by those whom Jay Rosen (2006) has now famously termed 'the people formerly known as the audience'. The former audience have new options – they can access, organise, manipulate, create, collaborate on and share media content in powerful new ways.

This introduction provides one framework in which the essays in the book can be set, although readers will of course make their own connections between ideas as they read. It focuses first on how news organisations are responding to technological and industrial convergence, before tracing the impacts on the news of three further levels of convergence: the convergence of media forms and textual systems; of public media and personal communication; and of the professional and the non-professional.

Challenges for news organisations and institutions

News is, among other things, a product – news is not just found and reported, but is actively produced and marketed by organisations, whether commercial, public service or alternative in orientation. The priorities and imperatives of news organisations have shaped the news. They have shaped the principles of selection and of presentation – 'news values' – through which certain events are elevated to the status of important and others go unremarked, and in so doing have exercised an enormous claim to define reality by determining what counts as news (Galtung and Ruge, 1965; Gans, 1979; Hall, 1981; Harcup and O'Neill, 2001). Their employees (White, 1950) or in some analyses the institutions themselves (Shoemaker, 1991; cf. Bruns, 2005) have been seen as 'gatekeepers', controlling and restricting access to the conceptual arena of the public sphere (Habermas, 1974, 1989). They have set the agenda for public debate (McCombs and Shaw, 1999; McCombs, 2004), telling us what to think about, if not what to think (Cohen, 1963). Their ownership structures and commercial orientations have been shown to influence not only the content of the news, but also the commercial and regulatory contexts in which media firms operate (Herman and Chomsky, 1988; Bagdikian, 2004; Castells, 2009). Now these organisations, as the central engines of news, are key sites of the disruptions driven by digitisation and convergence.

The news media are among the creative industries – those that turn ideas into intellectual property that can be marketed (Department for Culture, Media and Sport [UK], 2001; Hartley, 2005). But paradoxically, they have not all shown evidence of having effective marketable ideas, creative or otherwise, about how to adapt their businesses to the digital environment. The Pew Project for Excellence in Journalism opened its 2009 annual report on US journalism with the words:

Some of the numbers are chilling. Newspaper ad revenues have fallen 23% in the last two years. Some papers are in bankruptcy, and others have lost three-quarters of their value. By our calculations, nearly one out of every five journalists working for newspapers in 2001 is now gone, and 2009 may be the worst year yet.

The problems go beyond a recession-driven fall in advertising income. Freedman (2010) points to a complex of additional factors, including fragmenting audiences, increased competition and, crucially, under-investment in journalism by news organisations (on which see also the chapters in this volume by McChesney, Fenton and Witschge, and Deuze and Fortunati). However, the digital challenge is real. Unlike their analogue and broadcast predecessors, digital media allow a wide range of actors to produce and distribute texts at very low cost, meaning those who have almost anything to say can exercise their right to say it, and can often afford to offer it to others over networks free of charge. In such an environment, organisations that have been used to defining what counts as news, and to controlling a limited set of commercially viable channels for its distribution, are challenged by the advent of a mass plurality of information available on the Internet.

Rupert Murdoch's announcement in August 2009 that his News Corporation's newspapers would all be charging their online users by the middle of 2010, and his public baiting of Google for their 'theft' of his content, have been perhaps the boldest interventions in this area to date. Yet although there are commentators who are optimistic about the prospects for this (see Brian McNair's chapter in this volume), working models for making money out of online news remain thin on the ground. Specialist business publications such as the *Financial Times*, which are routinely invoked as the model for paid content, are in an elite niche market, dealing with a very specialised readership who demand up-to-date information and analysis, and who, moreover, can charge their subscriptions as a legitimate business expense; the *Sun* is in a rather different market. Business models for online news have to address the problem of requiring hundreds of millions of people to change their attitudes, behaviour and expectations that Internet content will be free to access, and may also involve trying to create an artificial scarcity in an environment in which information is abundant.

A further problem for newspapers in particular is that their actual news content has only been one part of a package bought by readers – a package which has also included entertainment listings and reviews, crosswords and cartoons, comment, announcements and advertising, all of which can now be found elsewhere. Moreover, a crucial element of buying that package was participation in a moment of community (Carey, 1989; Anderson, 1991; Bird,

2010), a shared daily cultural habit which many are replacing with other forms of community, other forms of daily sharing, such as those offered by social network sites. Perhaps Clay Shirky (2009) is right when he writes 'Society doesn't need newspapers. What we need is journalism.'

Peter Horrocks, Director of the BBC World Service, has described current transformations as 'the end of fortress journalism' (2009). He was referring not just to the economic pressures on the news media, but to the erosion of the news as a discrete product:

> In the fortress world the consumption of journalism was through clearly defined products and platforms – a TV or radio programme, a magazine or a newspaper. But in the blended world of internet journalism all those products are available within a single platform and mental space. The user can now click and flit between each set of news. Or they can use an aggregator to pull together all the information they require. The reader may never be aware from which fortress (or brand) the information has come. (Horrocks 2009)

In this analysis, the challenge for journalists and news organisations is to better network their work, both internally and externally, to respond to audience demand – even if this cuts against decades of accumulated experience built around competition and differentiation.

More creative institutional responses to the new conditions harness the burgeoning of popular expression online and acknowledge shifting patterns of consumption. A leading force here has been that 1920s institution the BBC. As a public service broadcaster, with a guaranteed income from the licence fee and no shareholders to answer to, the BBC has been able to undertake experiments and make investments that many of its commercial rivals could not. In our first chapter, Stuart Allan and Einar Thorsen offer a richly detailed account of the development of BBC News Online, one of the world's most successful websites. They argue that it has been shaped by the public service ethos that has always been at the core of the BBC's approach, an ethos which can be summarised as having three central components: 'serving democracy, generating content that has cultural value and promoting social inclusion' (Curran and Seaton, 2010, p. 380).

Allan and Thorsen explore the rise of user-generated content (UGC), and the ways in which this has been incorporated into the BBC's news work, from its at first uncertain response to eyewitness and other non-professional material reporting on the Indian Ocean tsunami of 2004, to its incorporation of images and video of winter snow-scenes in the UK sent in by more than 35,000 people in February 2009. Matthew Eltringham, who runs the BBC's dedicated unit known as the 'UGC Hub', has explained how the BBC uses user-generated content in several key ways: it draws upon the users' opinions and experiences; it relies upon audiences to share their discoveries with the BBC; and it taps their collective knowledge. This UGC Hub, a 24-hour operation staffed by more than twenty journalists, can deal with up to 12,000 e-mails and hundreds of videos and images submitted by users on a typical day (Eltringham, 2009; for a complementary study of UGC at the *Guardian*, see Singer and Ashman, 2009). As Jeff Jarvis (2008) has it, 'the witnesses are taking over the news'.

In his chapter, Brian McNair examines the dissolution of traditional boundaries, such as those between information and entertainment, or between fact and opinion, that has followed the development of online journalism. He notes that the Internet leads to the enfranchisement of new voices due to low participation costs. However, in asking questions about how British professional journalism responds to the influx of the *vox populi*, amid some inevitable chaos he does not see the death of journalism as an automatic consequence. Rather than newly unleashed forces taking over from established news organisations, he argues that the latter will adapt to the changes, reconstructing their unique position to create high-quality content, and recasting editorial functions to include the management of popular expression.

McNair cautions against any simplistic view that the noticeably new aspects of communication culture that are allowed by new media will take over from all that people have previously valued. However, in his chapter Robert McChesney considers online news from a different premise: that it is emerging at a time when the virtues of professional news at its best are already thin on the ground. He posits a general crisis in American journalism. Investigative, political and international reporting have all declined in scope and quality, while celebrity and scandal make an inexorable rise. McChesney argues that the decline of conventional journalism is largely attributable to commercial factors, and that the technology of the Internet is itself neither the principal cause nor a guarantee of a better alternative. In this view, there is still a need for full-time, well-resourced, expert journalists, whose organisation protects them from political or corporate interference. And, in terms of its potential contribution to a democratic public sphere, citizen journalism can succeed only alongside such well-supported professional journalism – it will not replace it. The point is that enabling successful journalism, even in the digital era, requires institutional support and policy interventions. An open Internet is necessary for a recovery of journalism – although other factors are crucial as well. And yet media corporations increasingly attempt to reshape the net as a delivery mechanism for commercial content: 'in an extension of the logic that caused the crisis', as McChesney argues in his chapter.

While the political economy in which news emerges is key to understanding aspects of its form, just as the affordances of technology are, it is also important to consider how institutional news practices are shaped by social factors that might be contingent to territories and communities. Not every national news culture is led (some may say unfairly dominated) by an innovative public corporation such as the BBC. And not every national news culture manifests the confluence of commercial, professional and regulatory conditions that make possible the elided distinction between news and opinion on the Fox News network in the USA. The case studies from different territories presented in this volume provide between them an element of comparison that highlights how global digital networks are locally shaped in practice.

In their chapter, Jairo Lugo-Ocando and Andrés Cañizález examine the emergence of online news in Latin America in relation to the social forces that cut across the continent, particularly the political movements and tensions that impact on public life in distinctive ways. Socio-economic factors ensure that uptake of online news is comparatively low across the continent, and the media tend to view their online editions as supplementary to print editions. Internet newsrooms are dominated by republication of old stories, and despite the existence of a regional *lingua franca*, few media outlets are appealing to readerships across national boundaries (as, say, Al Jazeera does for Arabic speakers across the world). At the same time, established news organisations are being circumvented by online alternative media. The continent-wide trend towards democratically elected left-wing governments has created tensions between them and private media that were supportive of previous dictatorships. As the authors illustrate with reference to the Venezuelan case, this has led to popular citizen use of self-publishing sites to support the new governments in the face of perceived mainstream media bias against them.

Convergence and forms of news

News is not just an organisational product. It's also a cultural one. Our expectations of the news – and the news itself – are structured around story-telling (Carey, 1989; Schudson, 2003; Bird and Dardenne, 2009). News has, in the past, privileged narrative – 'tonight's top stories, not tonight's top facts', as Robert Stam (2000, p. 368) points out. But the convergent media environment offers new possibilities. While the term 'convergence' is often used to refer to the repurposing of content across multiple platforms (Quinn, 2004; Singer, 2008; Quandt and Singer, 2009), it can also describe the coming together of media forms that were previously completely separate – a striking example, the subject of our next chapter, is the increasing convergence between news and videogames.

At first glance, it's hard to think of two media forms that seem further apart. The news is a textual system built around public authority, social debate and cultural negotiation. For many people – although not necessarily younger people – the news is high-status and is taken seriously. News is the main forum for public discussion of matters of social concern. It's where decisions about how we organise our lives and communities are taken, presented and justified – and it's where we work out how we feel about those. News attempts to define reality through the industrial production of non-fiction drama about shared events.

Videogames, on the other hand, while enormously popular, enjoy a very different cultural status from the news. For many people, games still connote adolescence, even as the average age of gamers climbs into the thirties, and even as family-oriented consoles such as the Nintendo Wii and casual gaming platforms such as Apple's iPhone draw in new demographic groups. Much of the attention given to games still comes from a protective perspective, in which games are seen as a threat, a malign influence on impressionable younger players.

Yet these two cultural poles are converging. For example, game engines – the software that generates the onscreen environment through which players navigate – are being adapted to provide simulations that can extend the user's interaction with news content (Trippenbach, 2009). Indeed, new uses for games are developing rapidly as their increasing sophistication makes them viable as marketing, educational and political tools that transcend entertainment possibilities (Bogost, 2007). The chapter by Bogost, Ferrari and Schweizer offers a detailed overview of key categories in the emerging genre of 'newsgames', and points towards fascinating possibilities for both established news organisations and newer voices alike. It provides a striking response to Herbert Gans's suggestion that journalists 'will have to learn how complicated events can be described and explained in a more easily understandable fashion; and how connections between events and their contexts can be made intelligibly' (2009, p. 23). The news is a representation of social authority – a videogame simulation (Frasca, 2004) invites the user to identify how an environment works and what its rules are. The potential, when the two are brought together, is for new possibilities for users of both games and the news to engage with these representations of rules and of authority, the better to understand them – and the better to challenge them.

Personal communication and public media

News has traditionally had a *public* quality (Thompson, 1995, p. 31). Unlike a phone call or an e-mail or a letter, the news is addressed to nobody in particular. This public quality underwrites its perceived democratic importance and persuasive power, and is at the root of key debates around such issues as objectivity (Tuchman, 1972; Hallin, 1986; Lichtenberg, 2000; McChesney, 2002), infotainment (Postman, 1985) or the public sphere (Habermas, 1974, 1989). Above all, news, as Ericson et al. (1989, p. 3) have it, is 'a representation of authority ... news represents *who* are the authorized knowers and *what* are their authoritative versions of reality' (original emphasis). Michael Schudson (1995, p. 9), synthesising the literature on news professionals, finds that news can best be characterised as 'negative, detached, technical, and official' – characteristics which have been shaped by institutional demands and expectations of news.

Negative. Detached. Technical. Official. Yet increasingly the news is none of these things, as public communication and personal communication blur and intertwine. The explosive growth of social network sites has made what Castells (2009) terms 'mass self-communication' into a mainstream phenomenon. Blogs have been key here (Rettberg, 2008) in enabling more personal forms of publishing, including personalised commentaries on current affairs where your subjective point of view is on display next to photos of your cats. Social network tools such as Twitter or Facebook allow users to construct a profile of themselves, to develop a list of other users with whom they have some form of relationship or connection (called 'friends' on Facebook, although this may be best seen as a metaphor) and to maintain these relationships through the site (boyd and Ellison 2007). They provide a platform through which users can share personal, often intimate, responses to all kinds of public media, from a new music video to a new healthcare policy.

Our next two chapters explore some of the ways in which the private and the public blur in an increasingly *mobile* news environment. In his chapter, Gerard Goggin explores how the mobile is contributing to the development of a distinctive news terrain, one that has strategic importance in the workings of contemporary media. He also examines how far mobile news can be understood as part of what he has elsewhere described as the 'intimate turn' in online news:

> The locus and matrix of news appears to move from the professionalised routines and forms of circulation and production of newsrooms to the micro-arenas of personal life with their rules of relevance and tiny audiences defined by the indi-

vidual, and their immediate friends, colleagues, family, and networks. (Goggin, 2006, p. 148)

In her chapter, Kate Crawford also looks at the emerging methods of news dispersal by social networks – specifically Twitter – and how these reframe the news by blurring the distinction between personal communication (to be shared one-to-one) and public media (to be broadcast to no one in particular). Crawford interrogates the roles played by Twitter in the broader news environment, discussing how it is used both by established news networks to deliver breaking news and by other users to report on the news that happens around them – in some cases, committing 'random acts of journalism' as J. D. Lasica (2003) has it. She explores not only how its users customise and reorder the flows of public communication they receive, but also how they find opportunities for shared feeling and listening that are far removed from the 'negative, detached, technical, and official' approach of so much established journalism.

Creative audiences: the professional meets the non-professional

Journalists are licensed agents of symbolic power – authorised by their status as employees of news organisations to tell the stories through which we make sense of our society. They have claimed for themselves the role of the Fourth Estate, the unelected guarantors of democracy (Boyce, 1978; Schultz, 1998; Curran and Seaton, 2010), a role which sets them apart from their readers, viewers and listeners. But this dynamic is shifting in a dramatic way. Journalists no longer have a monopoly on writing the news (Hartley, 2000; Glaser, 2010; Singer, 2010). For many people, the news is no longer just something they read, listen to or watch – the news is now something they *do*.

Cheap hardware and software allow anyone to blog or comment, calling into question the distinction between news and views. Ubiquitous mobiles with inbuilt cameras make everyone a potential on-site correspondent. Higher-quality software and bandwidth bring near-broadcast quality to video blogs and citizen journalism. Aggregators such as Google News challenge audiences' long-established habit of choosing the source first and the content second. Video-sharing websites such as YouTube allow creative remixes of news broadcasts or political party campaign ads, and host new kinds of channel. Social network sites such as Facebook offer news applications as just one of an ever-expanding menu of convergent possibilities.

Platforms such as Twitter offer a stream of tiny headlines not only from news organisations, but also from (and about) celebrities, politicians and your next-door neighbour.

These transformations in audience roles take a number of different but complementary forms. News users can now quite simply access more news than ever – they can read, watch and listen to a greatly expanded set of resources. Anyone with a net connection or a smartphone can now read the *New York Times* over breakfast, no matter how far away from Manhattan they may be. Users can now create new content easily (text, image, audio, video, games, animation). They can register their reaction to an item on the CNN, *Daily Mail* or news.com.au websites, along a spectrum ranging from sophisticated insights to howling-mad graffiti (a thought-provoking blog that collects examples of the latter from BBC forums is *speak You're bRanes* at http://ifyoulikeitsomuchwhydontyougolivethere.com). They can contribute, not only to dedicated participatory journalism projects such as OhmyNews, Indymedia or Wikinews, but also to forums hosted by established news organisations (notably the *Daily Telegraph* in the UK). They can start their own platforms and write their own content, as tens of millions of blogs demonstrate. And, more and more, users can send out a stream of tiny updates of every thought, action or cup of coffee in their day, through Twitter or through their Facebook status updates, mixing these in with headlines from CNN or Al Jazeera, with the latest thoughts of their favourite TV quiz show host or of that guy they went out with when they were seventeen, in a personalised flow of intimate, ambient news for a self-selected audience of friends or followers.

Which of these activities constitute a 'citizen journalism' that might fundamentally alter news production, and which are better thought of as simply spicing up traditional news consumption? One challenge for scholars and journalists is exactly how to conceptualise the changing relations of production and consumption thrown up by technology and its emergent uses. But however we answer that challenge (and several approaches are represented in this volume), the interactions between transformations and continuities are more complex than a simple succession from the old to the new, or, in some cases, the former surviving the threat of the latter. Users can now manipulate news content in a new range of ways (Lessig, 2008). Digital information is so mobile and easily manipulated that it can become hard to separate contexts of production from those of consumption. Because of the input of multiple interactive users, news texts produced are not always self-enclosed. They can gain layers and shed skins, becoming moments in larger narratives that circulate and iterate around the net, rather than the neat, linear sender-to-audience flows traditionally associated with mass media.

Along these lines John Hartley (2000, p. 44) has suggested that we are moving from a culture that privileges writing to one that privileges editing. Editing, rearranging, recontextualising existing media material – these are the hallmarks of an increasingly participatory online culture. More and more of many people's daily media use can be thought of as processes of preparation, arrangement, editing, revision, shaping. Users can customise their news schedules (via web, RSS, iPlayer, podcasts or news apps on phones). They can personalise their intake of news (via Google Reader or Google News, customising their diet in a version of what Negroponte (1995) dubbed *The Daily Me*). They can save stories, building up their own custom archives. They can forward stories to others or post them on their social network site profiles, using them to trigger conversations – as Cory Doctorow of popular blog *Boing Boing* puts it: 'Conversation is king. Content is just something to talk about' (Doctorow, 2006; see also Rushkoff, 2002). They can rate or 'like' or 'favourite' stories on sites such as Digg or Slashdot or StumbleUpon or Delicious. And they can organise this content, often in collaboration with others, for people to access in new ways, through, for example, tagging (Bruns, 2008; Shirky, 2008; Horrocks, 2009; Liu et al., 2009).

Axel Bruns's chapter discusses the relationships between emerging forms of participatory journalism and the established practices of mainstream media organisations (which he calls 'industrial journalism'). It's common to claim that citizen journalists or bloggers only comment or offer opinions, whereas industrial journalists report. But a crucial argument in Bruns's chapter is that we can't maintain this distinction – both types of journalist analyse, discuss and comment upon material provided by others, perhaps more often than industrial journalists would like to admit; content analysis of leading UK newspaper and broadcasters, for example, shows the extent of their reliance upon media releases and agency copy (Lewis et al., 2008a, b). Moreover, as Couldry (2010) argues, specialist bloggers – whom he terms 'writer-gatherers' – increasingly add to the range of sources upon which the established media rely.

For Bruns, citizen journalism doesn't replace but rather displaces industrial journalism. How does it do this? Bruns suggests three key ways. Citizen journalism can extend the *breadth* of coverage, through covering areas that industrial journalists lack the flexibility or resources to tackle. It can extend the *depth* of coverage, through opening up debate to more and different voices. And it can extend the *duration* of coverage, through expanding the news cycle beyond the constraints of the print or broadcast media. Bruns concludes that industrial and citizen journalists have much to offer each other – the former may bring training, skills and contacts, while the latter bring sheer numbers and freedom from commercial imperatives. Each side of this divide, he argues, needs to develop greater respect for the other.

This last point is borne out by Natalie Fenton and Tamara Witschge, whose chapter explores the ways in which online media affect the roles of established journalists. Their research draws upon interviews and ethnographic observation, and asks reporters for their perceptions of bloggers and citizen journalists. The interviewees' at times dismissive reactions to non-professional journalists highlight the reporters' self-images and reveal what they believe to be their distinctive professional values, including objectivity, balance and rigorous fact-checking. Fenton and Witschge argue that journalism needs to reassert such basic professional ethics and values to complement the rise of online commentary and opinion. But they emphasise how much these values are the very ones put under pressure as news organisations respond to market pressures to cut costs and increase output. In this analysis, news organisations are undermining the very elements of their business that could most sustain it in the face of new kinds of competition.

In news, the dichotomy between professional journalist and amateur blogger gets harder to sustain each year. Anyone can now set themselves up as a publisher, although finding an audience is harder – something that the established media are finding too, with newspaper closures continuing to accelerate. This new freedom to contribute is often celebrated by media scholars and commentators as a democratisation of the public sphere, a redistribution of symbolic power, a sharing around of the licence to speak. It is all of those things. Yet it's also a crisis for those who work in the news industry – it's a financial crisis, of course, but it's also an existential crisis, as journalists, accustomed to thinking of themselves as the Fourth Estate, the unelected bulwark of democracy, have to adjust to finding their continued existence questioned every day (Terranova, 2004; Deuze, 2007; Lovink, 2007; Bird, 2009; Mosco, 2009).

Mark Deuze and Leopoldina Fortunati intervene in debates about the popular production of news by its online consumers. Their chapter proposes that the growth in unpaid journalism raises questions about shifting power relations between audiences, professional journalists and their employers. They examine what the apparent trend towards 'journalism without journalists' (professional ones) might mean for economies of news production. The celebratory rhetoric surrounding UGC can mask its status as unpaid labour. In their view, media organisations' use of content created by unpaid journalists is linked to shifts already taking place within their organisational cultures. The new supply of free news facilitated by the Internet may contribute to the disempowerment of professional journalists, whose power over their vocation is already diminishing as their employers demand flexible responses to market conditions. 'Contingency', as Deuze has written elsewhere, 'defines the lived experience of many if not most media professionals today' (Deuze, 2009, p. 83). In this context, amateurs represent a new element in organisations' outsourcing of news production, and are both 'co-creators' and 'competitor-colleagues' of professional journalists. But these unsettling effects may also constitute a shake-up of production hierarchies that has democratic potential, as the involvement of the 'long tail' of Internet users may fill gaps left by the professional production of news.

At the same time, such democratic potential is not evenly distributed, and political contexts are crucial. In her chapter, Xin Xin explores the uses and limitations of citizen journalism in China, where the possibilities of many-to-many communication on matters of public significance are clearly enormous. However, Xin cautions against overstating the progressive potential of online journalism by new kinds of actor. She shows instead, through a sequence of case studies, how citizen journalism can complement the established media or act as an alternative means of delivery for official information (for related case studies see also Nip, 2009; Reese and Dai, 2009). And she also shows how citizen journalism can be just as constrained by state censorship as its more established counterparts. Moreover, those who see citizen journalism as inherently progressive need to consider the extent to which, in China, it has been embraced by neo-nationalist forces.

In his chapter, An Nguyen broaches the tricky question of how to integrate user-generated content into news sites with mainstream appeal without jeopardising the long-held professional standards of journalists. Some kind of balance between the two is an ideal to strive for in many news organisations. Nguyen approaches the issue through a study of one international success story of citizen journalism: South Korea's OhmyNews website (Kim and Hamilton, 2006; Young, 2009). His interest is not only to recount the ingredients of the site's success, but to examine in some detail how popular and professional news production intersects in newsroom operations. A single editorial management mechanism manages this intersection: thousands of citizen reporters provide their first-hand accounts to the site, where professional journalists check and edit facts before publishing them.

However, Nguyen finds that the marriage between professional and amateur at OhmyNews is more than a matter of combining the best of both. In fact the whole is greater than the sum of the parts in that the professional and the popular exist in dynamic balance in the organisation. The professionals and amateurs modify each other's practices through a series of checks and balances that characterise OhmyNews operations. The mere fact of coopera-tion between the two groups through digital media is in itself no guarantee of success. The news culture of OhmyNews arises out of deliberative community structures and imperatives: ones that are informed by contextual factors such as Korean traditions of cultural participation and popular responses to the country's conservative mainstream media. Thus one of the lessons for observers wishing to learn about 'pro-am' cooperation (Leadbeater and Miller, 2004) from the case of OhmyNews is that success arises when partic-ular conditions interact. This also suggests that the sustainability of such proj-ects may depend on the sustainability of multiple underlying processes of adaptation amid change.

Conclusion

These twelve essays range over a very broad terrain – from the BBC to exper-imental videogames, from Latin American newsrooms to North-east Asian blogs, from the crisis in US newspapers to Twitter users in Iran. This serves to emphasise how digital convergence operates across multiple interrelated dimensions and in diverse socio-cultural contexts. Indeed, in choosing convergence as a key introductory concept we hope to have opened up a range of horizons for thinking through transformation and continuity, ones that are developed throughout the book and revisited in our concluding chapter. If there is an area of media practice that illustrates that convergence is much more than a matter of media corporations designing content that can be distributed on different platforms, it is news. News functions are merging with a range of other media forms, genres and modes previously unrelated or even seen as inimical to it. What had seemed to be settled distinctions between professional and amateur journalists, between producers and audiences, between public and private, are now all in question, as is the very language which associates news with a public democratic sphere and civil society, set in contrast with other aspects of social life and our private selves and concerns. In addressing moments in these complex processes, the chapters cohere into something more than the sum of their parts, sketching the coordinates of the news environment all of us now inhabit.

REFERENCES

Allan, Stuart (2009) 'Histories of citizen journalism', in Stuart Allan and Einar Thorsen (eds), *Citizen Journalism: Global Perspectives* (New York: Peter Lang), pp. 17–31.

Anderson, Benedict (1991) *Imagined Communities*, rev. edn. (London: Verso).

Bagdikian, Ben H. (2004) *The New Media Monopoly* (Boston: Beacon Press).

Bird, S. Elizabeth (2009) 'The future of journalism in the digital environment', *Journalism: Theory, Practice and Criticism*, 10: 3, 293–5.

Bird, S. Elizabeth (2010) 'News practices in everyday life: beyond audience response', in Stuart Allan (ed.), *The Routledge Companion to News and Journalism* (London: Routledge), pp. 417–27.

Bird, S. Elizabeth and Dardenne, Robert W. (2009) 'Rethinking news and myth as storytelling', in Karin Wahl-Jorgensen and Thomas Hanitzsch (eds), *The Handbook of Journalism Studies* (London: Routledge), pp. 205–17.

Bogost, Ian (2007) *Persuasive Games: The Expressive Power of Videogames* (Cambridge, MA: MIT Press).

Boyce, George (1978) 'The Fourth Estate: the reappraisal of a concept', in George Boyce, James Curran and Pauline Wingate (eds), *Newspaper History: From the Seventeenth Century to the Present Day* (London: Constable), pp. 19–40.

boyd, danah and Ellison, Nicole B. (2007) 'Social network sites: definition, history and scholarship', *Journal of Computer-Mediated Communication*, 13: 11, http://jcmc.indiana.edu/vol13/issue1/boyd.ellison.html, accessed 17 December 2007.

Bruns, Axel (2005) *Gatewatching: Collaborative Online News Production* (New York: Peter Lang).

Bruns, Axel (2008) *Blogs, Wikipedia, Second Life and Beyond: From Production to Produsage* (New York: Peter Lang).

Carey, James (1989) *Communication as Culture* (New York: Routledge).

Castells, Manuel (2009) *Communication Power* (Oxford: Oxford University Press).

Cohen, Bernard (1963) *The Press and Foreign Policy* (Princeton, NJ: Princeton University Press).

Couldry, Nick (2010) 'New online news sources and writer-gatherers', in Natalie Fenton (ed.), *New Media, Old News: Journalism and Democracy in the Digital Age* (London: Sage), pp. 138–52.

Curran, James and Seaton, Jean (2010) *Power without Responsibility: The Press, Broadcasting, and New Media in Britain*, 7th edn (London: Routledge).

Department for Culture, Media and Sport (2001) *Creative Industries: Mapping Document 2001* (London: Department for Culture, Media and Sport).

Deuze, Mark (2007) *Media Work* (Cambridge: Polity Press).

Deuze, Mark (2009) 'Technology and the individual journalist: agency beyond imitation and change', in Barbie Zelizer (ed.), *The Changing Faces of Journalism: Tabloidization, Technology and Truthiness* (New York: Routledge), pp. 82–97.

Deuze, Mark (2010) 'Journalism and convergence culture', in Stuart Allan (ed.), *The Routledge Companion to News and Journalism* (London: Routledge), pp. 267–76.

Doctorow, Cory (2006) 'Disney exec: piracy is just a business model', *Boing Boing*, 10 October, http://www.boingboing.net/2006/10/10/disney-exec-piracy-i.html, accessed 8 December 2009.

Eltringham, Matthew (2009) 'The audience and the news', in Charles Miller (ed.), *The Future of Journalism: Papers from a Conference Organised by the BBC College of Journalism,* http://www.bbc.co.uk/blogs/theeditors/future_of_journalism.pdf, accessed 6 August 2009.

Ericson, Richard V., Baranek, Patricia M. and Chan, Janet B. L. (1989) *Negotiating Control: A Study of News Sources* (Milton Keynes: Open University Press).

Frasca, Gonzalo (2004) 'Videogames of the Oppressed: Critical Thinking, Education, Tolerance, and Other Trivial Issues', in Pat Harrigan and Noah Wardrip-Fruin (eds), *First Person: New Media as Story, Performance, and Game* (Cambridge, MA: MIT Press), pp. 85–94.

Freedman, Des (2010) 'The political economy of the "new" news environment', in Natalie Fenton (ed.), *New Media, Old News: Journalism and Democracy in the Digital Age* (London: Sage), pp. 35–50.

Galtung, Johan and Ruge, Mari Holmboe (1965) 'The structure of foreign news', *Journal of Peace Research,* 2: 1, 64–91.

Gans, Herbert J. (1979) *Deciding What's News* (New York: Pantheon).

Gans, Herbert J. (2009) 'Can popularization help the news media?' in Barbie Zelizer (ed.), *The Changing Faces of Journalism: Tabloidization, Technology and Truthiness* (New York: Routledge), pp. 17–28.

Glaser, Mark (2010) 'Citizen journalism: widening world views, extending democracy', in Stuart Allan (ed.), *The Routledge Companion to News and Journalism* (London: Routledge), pp. 578–90.

Goggin, Gerard (2006) *Cell Phone Culture* (London: Routledge).

Habermas, Jürgen (1974) 'The public sphere: an encyclopedia article', *New German Critique,* 1: 3, 49–55.

Habermas, Jürgen (1989) *The Structural Transformation of the Public Sphere* (Cambridge, MA: MIT Press).

Hall, Stuart (1981) 'The determinations of news photographs', in Stanley Cohen and Jock Young (eds), *The Manufacture of News,* rev. edn (London: Constable), pp. 226–43.

Hallin, Daniel C. (1986) *The 'Uncensored War': The Media and Vietnam* (Berkeley: University of California Press).

Harcup, Tony and O'Neill, Deirdre (2001) 'What is news? Galtung and Ruge revisited', *Journalism Studies,* 2: 2, 261–80.

Hartley, John (2000) 'Communicative democracy in a redactional society: the future of journalism studies', *Journalism: Theory, Practice and Criticism,* 1: 1, 39–48.

Hartley, John (ed.) (2005) *Creative Industries* (Malden, MA: Blackwell).

Herman, Edward S. and Chomsky, Noam (1988) *Manufacturing Consent* (New York: Pantheon).

Horrocks, Peter (2009) 'The end of fortress journalism', in Charles Miller (ed.), *The Future of Journalism: Papers from a Conference Organised by the BBC College of Journalism,* http://www.bbc.co.uk/blogs/theeditors/future_of_journalism.pdf, accessed 6 August 2009.

Jarvis, Jeff (2008) 'In Mumbai, witnesses are writing the news', 1 December *Guardian,* http://www.guardian.co.uk/media/2008/dec/01/mumbai-terror-digital-media, accessed 13 October 2009.

Jenkins, Henry (2006) *Convergence Culture* (New York: New York University Press).

Kim, Eun-Gyoo and Hamilton, James W. (2006) 'Capitulation to capital? OhmyNews as alternative media', *Media, Culture & Society*, 28: 4, 541–60.

Lasica, J. D. (2003) 'Random acts of journalism', 12 March, http://www.jdlasica. com/blog/archives/2003_03_12.html, accessed 6 August 2009.

Leadbeater, Charles and Miller, Paul (2004) *The Pro-Am Revolution: How Enthusiasts Are Changing Our Economy and Society* (London: Demos).

Lessig, Lawrence (2008) *Remix* (London: Bloomsbury).

Lewis, Justin, Williams, Andrew and Franklin, Bob (2008a) 'A compromised Fourth Estate?' *Journalism Studies*, 9: 1, 1–20.

Lewis, Justin, Williams, Andrew and Franklin, Bob (2008b) 'Four rumours and an explanation' *Journalism Practice*, 2: 1, 27–45.

Lichtenberg, Judith (2000) 'In defence of objectivity revisited', in James Curran and Michael Gurevitch (eds), *Mass Media and Society*, 3rd edn (London: Arnold), pp. 238–54.

Liu, Sophia B., Palen, Leysia, Sutton, Jeanette, Hughes, Amanda L. and Vieweg, Sarah (2009) 'Citizen photojournalism during crisis events', in Stuart Allan and Einar Thorsen (eds), *Citizen Journalism: Global Perspectives* (New York: Peter Lang), pp. 43–63.

Lovink, Geert (2007) *Zero Comments* (London: Routledge).

McChesney, Robert W. (2002) 'September 11 and the structural limitations of US journalism', in Barbie Zelizer and Stuart Allan (eds), *Journalism After September 11* (London: Routledge), pp. 91–100.

McCombs, Maxwell (2004) *Setting The Agenda: The Mass Media and Public Opinion* (Cambridge: Polity Press).

McCombs, Maxwell and Shaw, Donald L. (1999) [1972] 'The agenda-setting function of mass media', in Howard Tumber (ed.), *News: A Reader* (Oxford: Oxford University Press), pp. 320–8.

Mosco, Vincent (2009) 'The future of journalism', *Journalism: Theory, Practice and Criticism*, 10: 3, 350–2.

Negroponte, Nicholas (1995) *Being Digital* (London: Hodder and Stoughton).

Nip, Joyce Y. M. (2009) 'Citizen journalism in China: the case of the Wenchuan earthquake', in Stuart Allan and Einar Thorsen (eds), *Citizen Journalism: Global Perspectives* (New York: Peter Lang), pp. 95–105.

Pew Project for Excellence in Journalism (2009) 'The state of the news media', http://www.stateofthemedia.org/2009/index.htm, accessed 13 October 2009.

Pool, Ithiel de Sola (1983) *Technologies of Freedom* (Cambridge, MA: Belknap Press of Harvard University Press).

Postman, Neil (1985) *Amusing Ourselves to Death* (London: Methuen).

Quandt, Thorsten and Singer, Jane B. (2009) 'Convergence and cross-platform content production', in Karin Wahl-Jorgensen and Thomas Hanitzsch (eds), *The Handbook of Journalism Studies* (London: Routledge), pp. 130–44.

Quinn, Stephen (2004) 'An intersection of ideals: journalism, profits, technology and convergence', *Convergence*, 10: 4, 109–23.

Reese, Stephen D. and Dai, Jia (2009) 'Citizen journalism in the global news arena: China's new media critics', in Stuart Allan and Einar Thorsen (eds), *Citizen Journalism: Global Perspectives* (Peter Lang: New York), pp. 221–31.

Rettberg, Jill Walker (2008) *Blogging* (Cambridge: Polity Press).

Rice, Ronald E. (1999) 'Artifacts and paradoxes in new media', *New Media & Society*, 1: 1, 24–32.

Rosen, Jay (2006) 'The people formerly known as the audience', *Press Think: Ghost of Democracy*, 27 June, http://journalism.nyu.edu/pubzone/weblogs/press-think/2006/06/27/ppl_frmr.html, accessed 6 August 2009.

Rushkoff, Douglas (2002) 'The Internet is not killing off conversation but actively encouraging it', in Rebecca Blood (ed.), *We've Got Blog: How Weblogs Are Changing Our Culture* (Cambridge, MA: Perseus), pp. 116–18.

Schudson, Michael (1995) *The Power of News* (Cambridge, MA: Harvard University Press).

Schudson, Michael (2003) *The Sociology of News* (New York: W. W. Norton & Co.).

Schultz, Julianne (1998) *Reviving the Fourth Estate* (Cambridge: Cambridge University Press).

Shirky, Clay (2008) *Here Comes Everybody* (London: Allen Lane).

Shirky, Clay (2009) 'Newspapers and thinking the unthinkable', 13 March, http://www.shirky.com/weblog/2009/03/newspapers-and-thinking-the-unthink-able, accessed 13 October 2009.

Shoemaker, Pamela J. (1991) *Gatekeeping* (Newbury Park, CA: Sage).

Singer, Jane B. (2008) 'Ethnography of newsroom convergence', in Chris Paterson and David Domingo (eds), *Making Online News: The Ethnography of New Media Production* (New York: Peter Lang), pp. 157–70.

Singer, Jane B. (2010) 'Journalism in the network', in Stuart Allan (ed.), *The Routledge Companion to News and Journalism* (London: Routledge), pp. 277–86.

Singer, Jane B. and Ashman, Ian (2009) 'User-generated content and journalistic values', in Stuart Allan and Einar Thorsen (eds), *Citizen Journalism: Global Perspectives* (New York: Peter Lang), pp. 233–42.

Stam, Robert, 2000 [1983] 'Television news and its spectator', in Robert Stam and Toby Miller (eds), *Film and Theory: An Anthology* (Malden, MA: Blackwell), pp. 361–80.

Terranova, Tiziana (2004) *Network Culture* (London: Pluto).

Thompson, John B. (1995) *The Media and Modernity* (Cambridge: Polity Press).

Trippenbach, Philip (2009) 'Video games: a new medium for journalism', in Charles Miller (ed.), *The Future of Journalism: Papers from a Conference Organised by the BBC College of Journalism*, http://www.bbc.co.uk/blogs/theeditors/future_of_journalism.pdf, accessed 6 August 2009.

Tuchman, Gaye (1972) 'Objectivity as strategic ritual: an examination of newsmen's notions of objectivity', *American Journal of Sociology*, 77: 4, 660–79.

White, David Manning (1950) '"The gatekeeper": a case study in the selection of news', *Journalism Quarterly*, 27, 383–90.

Young, Chang Woo (2009) 'OhmyNews: citizen journalism in South Korea', in Stuart Allan and Einar Thorsen (eds), *Citizen Journalism: Global Perspectives* (New York: Peter Lang), pp. 143–52.

CHAPTER 1

Journalism, public service and BBC News Online

STUART ALLAN AND EINAR THORSEN

In the months leading up to the launch of BBC News Online in the autumn of 1997, warning bells were sounding in journalistic circles – not least within the BBC itself – with respect to the impact of the Internet on news reporting. For every voice of optimism highlighting its transformative potential, it seemed, there were several others expressing their grave misgivings. Firmly aligned with the latter end of the continuum was the respected BBC foreign correspondent Fergal Keane. Delivering the prestigious Huw Weldon Memorial Lecture to the Royal Television Society in September that year, he argued that journalism's integrity was in danger of being compromised, if not irrevocably harmed, by the arrival of new challenges to its defining principles (broadcast on BBC1, 20 October 1997). Pointing to the 'hundreds of conspiracy theories floating around about the death of Diana' in cyberspace, he expressed his concern that 'calm and considered reportage' was at serious risk of losing out to 'the sensational and the spectacular', especially where 'the generation growing up on a diet of *The X-Files*' was concerned. At issue, he maintained, was a 'dangerous retreat from rationality', whereby 'truth-telling' that is 'artful, fearless and intelligent' all but disappears into the swirl of 'trivia, gossip and celebration of the banal'. Growing technological pressures – compounded by those from the market – must be resisted, he reasoned, in order to better protect the interests of truth. 'I am worried about the potential of the Internet to devalue the role of the reporter,' Keane revealed, before wondering aloud about what the future might portend. 'What a pity,' he mused, 'if technology, far from pushing us into another age of enlightenment, was to return us to the rumour-ridden gloom of the Middle Ages.'

Uncertainties about the promise and peril of change, where principles such as 'forensic accuracy' and 'intellectual rigour' – to use Keane's words – long associated with the best of BBC journalism were being recast anew, underline the tensions this chapter seeks to explore. It takes as its principal focus the emergent journalistic ecology of BBC News Online, from its inception in November 1997 to the tenth anniversary of the site in 2007 (see also Allan, 2006, 2009; Thorsen, 2009a). Specifically, it traces how BBC News Online has gradually evolved in reportorial terms – its forms, practices and epistemologies – in the course of becoming one of the most popular news websites globally. The discussion draws on the experiences of individuals directly responsible for the project so as to elucidate key tenets of the strategy informing the practical implementation of the BBC's move online. It shows that the website represented a significant initiative within the Corporation's attempt to reaffirm its public service ethos in a fledgling web environment, and thereby to better secure its place to ward off competition from commercial rivals in an increasingly converged media landscape.

In the course of highlighting a range of formative developments, special attention will be devoted to the ways in which the conventions underpinning an emergent ecology of online news reporting gradually began to consolidate. Here it is important to acknowledge from the outset that a number of ad hoc initiatives – including a Budget website in March 1995, one for the Olympics in 1996, an election site in the spring of 1997 (with some content syndicated from the BBC's Ceefax service) and a Death-of-Diana site in August 1997 – helped to set down precedents of form, but also reportorial craft, in ways which are more apparent in retrospect than they were at the time. Indeed, to this day, recollections by those involved in the launch of BBC News Online even differ over the precise time the site went live. 'We've talked to the original editor and the original product manager and nobody can put a finger on when exactly we switched to the new content system and started producing pages in the way that we have done ever since,' Pete Clifton, current head of BBC News Interactive, recently stated. 'We know that it was some time [during the first week of November 1997], but as for which moment of which day – we were probably just knackered at the time so nobody looked up to see what time it was' (cited in *Press Gazette*, 1 November 2007). Moreover, precisely what should count as 'online news' – as we discuss below – proved to be a controversial subject of considerable debate, inviting searching questions about how best to realise the potential of the Internet to deliver alternative types of coverage.

In seeking to contribute to efforts to trace this history, this chapter adopts a twofold strategy. First, we examine the actual launch of BBC News Online, devoting particular attention to the ways in ways in which the Corporation's public service commitments shaped its remit, in general, as well as its conception of online journalism, in particular. Second, we proceed to discern a number of the interactive features associated with this rapidly growing news provision over the first ten years of the site's operation. In offering an appraisal of the guiding imperatives of interactivity – not least with regard to user-generated content – we aim to identify for purposes of elaboration several issues warranting further investigation.

Rewriting the rules

The BBC News Online service officially launched on 4 November 1997. The design of its webpages at the time might have looked 'bleak and amateurish from the vantage point of today', admitted Bob Eggington (2007), but the 'site got off to a cracking start'. Eggington, first head of the service, recalled that staff were facing a 'nightmare' of a challenge from the outset. 'The price of building the content production system at such speed was six months of technical instability,' he stated. 'The bloody thing kept crashing.' It took a dedicated team, willing to experiment with new ideas, to ensure that logistical problems were soon resolved. While the question of which news stories featured on the front page on Day One lacks a ready answer (evidently no one thought to preserve them at the time), memories of technical challenges remain vivid:

> A distinguishing feature of the launch site was three clocks on the front page banner, indicating different world times, with the UK in the middle. 'Good evening, San Francisco,' the left clock would say. 'Good morning, Tokyo,' the right. It was a charming illustration of the instantaneous global reach of the web. Unfortunately, in a world with Netscape Navigator and 14.4k dial-up modems, it was also the single biggest reason the website would not load. The clocks quickly found their way into the Trash. (BBC News Online, 13 December 2007)

Similar recollections invite further consideration. 'What we didn't have was an abundance of text skills,' Eggington (2007) remembers. 'Broadcast scripts were not suitable for repurposing as text news stories. It became clear everything had to be written specifically for the web. The team quickly developed a style for the new service.' The team itself – with twenty editorial and six technical members – had been put together in a hurry, and was effectively made to revolve around a shared commitment to 'making it up as we went along' in a spirit of innovation. 'The only thing that mattered was momentum,' Eggington stated. 'We felt that if we didn't do it quick, someone would stop us' (cited in Connor, 2007).

The new website represented a significant initiative within the Corporation's strategy to reaffirm its public service ethos in a multichannel universe, and thereby be better placed to challenge commercial rivals such as CNN, MSNBC, EuroNews and News Corp. 'We are this autumn only at the starting block,' stated Tony Hall, chief executive of BBC News, the day before the launch. 'My ambition is, first, to ensure that we preserve and build a public service in news for the next generation. And, second, to ensure that BBC News develops as a global player' (cited in the *Guardian*, 3 November 1997). Widely perceived to be late on to the scene, arriving long after both British and international competitors had established their online presence, the initiative nevertheless represented a bold move. 'Our basic aim is to extend our public service remit on to the Web,' Eggington said at the time. 'The design is simple and it is easy to use.' The decision to proceed was justified, in his view, 'because that's where young people are going[.] We have to be there because the Web audience is increasing by 10 per cent every month' (cited in *The Times*, 5 November 1997). Much of the press commentary was focused elsewhere, however, namely on the other initiatives being unveiled around the same time. Easily the most significant of these was the Corporation's 24-hour rolling news channel, BBC News 24, which went to air with considerable fanfare the following week. Where the online commitment was generally regarded as being overdue, this venture invited a far more sceptical response. In the words of Damian Whitworth writing in *The Times*, 'dear old Auntie, always regarded as a little dotty, appears to have gone completely bats. As she celebrates her 75th birthday, she has suddenly decided to embark on some new adventures. The question is: is she up to it?' (*The Times*, 7 November 1997).

Not surprisingly, this question was answered rather emphatically in the affirmative by senior managers in the Corporation. 'This has been the most significant month in the history of BBC News,' Hall declared at the BBC News Online launch (cited in *European Media Business and Finance*, 17 November 1997). 'BBC News Online will, for the first time, put the entire wealth of BBC journalism at your fingertips,' he maintained. 'You will get the news you want and the news you need 24 hours a day' (cited in *Electronic Media*, 17 November 1997). The BBC, then as now, is one of the largest news gathering organisations in the world. Where rival sites – both television and newspaper-based – typically relied on copy from the wire services to provide breaking news, BBC News Online could draw on the expertise of over 2,000 members of staff and 250 correspondents across the globe. The online news team was composed of some forty journalists in addition to technical staff and graphic designers preparing news stories on the basis of reports provided by these correspondents. Staff members joined the site from other divisions within the BBC, as well as from other news sites outside the Corporation. 'It is easier to teach old media journalists new tools than to teach techies journalism', observed one of the site's reporters (cited in Perrone, 1998). A range of experiments was conducted to determine how best to present and package stories, a sense of standard practice being the subject of daily renegotiation. Journalists – in contrast with those at some of the major US sites – were expected to be multiskilled; that is, to package their stories up to and including the post-production stage, in addition to writing copy in the first place. As conventions gradually evolved through the trialling of ideas – new and borrowed ones alike – efforts were similarly made to incorporate feedback from users via devices such as online questionnaires to help shape form and practice. 'We don't have a set of rules because we're learning as we go along,' Smartt commented. 'I don't think anybody in the business knows precisely how to do this' (cited in Perrone, 1998).

By early 1998, BBC Online had been confirmed as the leading British Internet content site, with BBC News Online recording 8.17 million page impressions in March according to the Audit Bureau of Circulations (BBC Online overall recorded some 21 million page impressions from direct requests by over 900,000 users that month). Considered to be a 'strong driver of traffic', the news site was fast gaining a reputation for its immediacy – where the deadline is 'always now' – and the depth of its coverage. By June that year, BBC Online offered over 140,000 pages of content, some 61,000 of which consisted of news. Considered a great achievement by most commentators – and begrudgingly acknowledged as the leader in the field by rivals – its growing provision steadily improved, albeit not without the occasional instance of technical teething problems. 'We have found that [producing online content] is not as simple as we thought,' Dave Brewer, managing editor for the site, observed. 'The Web audience is sophisticated and will not stand for a simple reversioning of what was put on the TV or radio. We needed to learn to write for the Web and that meant starting from scratch' (cited in *The Australian*, 1 September 1998). This commitment to thinking afresh clearly played a significant role in defining the site's distinctive approach to public service, as well as the cultural authority of the journalism it sought to embody.

Breaking news

A number of instances emerged over the following months that helped to cast this distinctiveness in sharper relief. In August 1999, for example, BBC News

Online was relaying eyewitness reports from an earthquake in the town of Izmit in western Turkey before television news crews had arrived at the scene. Evidently the decision to post a message requesting information from anyone near the scene had been rewarded with four e-mails within the first ten minutes, followed by hundreds more over the following 24 hours. Jane Robins, citing this example of interactivity – and how it gives news on the site 'an immediacy which traditional media would find hard to match' – suggests it helps to explain why 'The industry is talking about BBC News Online as a working example of the journalism of the future.' Her description of the production process is revealing:

> Being the BBC, the News Online journalists are equipped with sophisticated desktop equipment that allows them to monitor a host of feeds from BBC correspondents and radio stations. They identify a story, write it into an established template, and write their own headlines.
>
> Unlike a newspaper reporter, the Online journalist then selects his [or her] own still photograph, crops it onscreen and adds it into the story. The self-editing process continues into audio and video material. Both can be selected and edited at the desk – the individual journalist becomes a writer, editor, picture editor, radio producer and video producer – his [or her] final product is checked by one of nine desk editors before going live on the site. (Robins, 1999)

She then proceeds to quote Alf Hermida (formerly a BBC foreign correspondent, and the output editor for the site at the time) to further discern the medium's qualities. 'In my experience it's more exciting than other sorts of journalism,' he states. 'In radio you might be restricted to sending a three-minute package – here you cover every aspect of a story, take a story and it [sic] explore it from a number of angles – and the deadline is always now' (Hermida, cited in Robins, 1999).

This heightened sense of immediacy afforded by online news recurrently figured in press commentary concerned with the relative advantages and limitations of the BBC's initiative (a watchful eye being kept on the Corporation's growing presence on the web, with concerns about the financial support derived from licence fee payers being a simmering matter of debate). Reinforcing perceptions that the BBC was leading the way in journalistic innovations in this regard was the glittering array of prizes the site was earning, including two Baftas, the British Press Award and the Prix Italia, by early 2000. In February of that year, BBC News Online was heralded as 'the world's best news site' at The Net Awards. The citation for the award praised its success, stating that in 'blending the many facets of multimedia with the old-fashioned simplicity of a strong layout and exclusive online features, the site has quickly become an essential bookmark'. Expressing his gratitude to the judges for the award, then-Project Director Bob Eggington stated: 'Maintaining this huge news site is a tremendous task and it's wonderful when the staff get some recognition for their efforts.' The hard work of maintaining the quality of the service would continue, he promised. Matthew Bingham, editor of *The Net* magazine, believed the award duly recognised the site's role in 'giving us a glimpse of the future' where headlines were being posted within minutes of news happening. 'It is the best for breaking news, unlike newspaper sites which might only have a few updates during the day,' he remarked. 'BBC News Online is a genuinely interactive Internet experience, managed as an Internet enterprise, not just some offshoot of a print or other media company' (cited in BBC News Online, 8 February 2000).

This commitment to breaking news was the subject of considerable discussion within the BBC in the months leading up to the general election in June 2001. In formulating its online strategy, careful consideration was given to the possible impact of the Internet on campaigning. 'This will be the first full Online election', the *Guidance for All BBC Programme Makers during the General Election Campaign* announced. A key feature of the strategy was the BBC's *Vote 2001* site, intended to provide several animated interactive features, and two key sections for civic engagement in the form of *Talking Point* and *Online 1,000* (see also Thorsen, 2009b). The site promptly proved to be a success, registering about 500,000 page views every day throughout the campaign, with a significant surge to 10.76 million on polling day, 7 June, and results day, 8 June (Coleman, 2001). Events later in the year see these figures overshadowed in comparison, with the attacks on 11 September proving to be a 'tipping point' of sorts – figuratively and almost literally – with regard to the sheer volume of traffic to the site. BBC technologist Brendan Butterworth (2007) described how the surge in traffic initially appeared to be the work of a malicious hacker:

> I was sat in an operations meeting when the pager went off and didn't stop: something big was happening. There was a massive influx of traffic to the site – a DoS [denial of service] attack, it seemed. Damion called us back: *'there was this plane . . .'* We turned on a TV and saw a burning World Trade Center Tower. Then another plane. Ops worked on keeping the servers happy, raising the webmaster and News to agree sheddable load. This was the first time, so it took a while to get a new light home page in place. Our New York server farm was two blocks from the WTC site; it survived but suffered as power failed. The dust eventually clogged the generators and there were problems getting in fuel. The only outage

was in the days after; we covered that by moving all traffic to London. The sites were designed to operate as hot spares for each other. We had planned around London suffering at some point, but it was the opposite. (Butterworth, 2007)

The template for the BBC homepage was not designed to cope with a breaking news story of this magnitude, and 'all that could be done was to edit the three promotional slots on the page to carry news of the unfolding events' (Belam, 2007). Eventually, the technical team bypassed the content management system altogether and uploaded small HTML updates via FTP. Content was reshaped to focus on the single story, as Mike Smartt, BBC's new media editor-in-chief at the time, recalled:

> We decided to clear everything off the front page, which we've never done before and concentrate all our journalists on the story. We work hand in hand with the broadcast teams but don't wait for them to report the facts. It works both ways. . . . Most important to us were the audio and video elements. It was among the most dramatic news footage anyone has ever seen. The ability to put all that on the web for people to watch over again set us apart. (Cited in Allan, 2006, p. 64)

The BBC's servers experienced hits in the millions, far surpassing the record set during the election earlier that year. The efforts made by staff to maintain its presence online were truly remarkable.

Interestingly, with regard to the coverage of the crisis, the BBC elected not to capitalise on the array of material – firsthand accounts, photographs, video clips and so forth – being posted online by ordinary citizens using forums, weblogs and personal websites. That is, while the BBC later acknowledged that it had received thousands of e-mails from individuals to the events, only two of these e-mails led to live news interviews being held with people in New York (Wardle and Williams, 2008, p. 2).

Blurring boundaries

The importance of online news as a source of breaking news and ongoing story updates is particularly noticeable during times of crisis. A case in point was the invasion of Iraq in 2003, which came after ongoing negotiations for a peaceful resolution had, in the eyes of the US administration, broken down. On 17 March 2003, US President George W. Bush issued an ultimatum to Saddam Hussein and his sons: leave Iraq within 48 hours. 'Their refusal to do so will result in military conflict commenced at a time of our choosing,' Bush announced in a televised address to the nation (cited in BBC News Online, 18 March 2003). As the deadline for war grew ever closer, online news websites witnessed a surge in traffic from people wanting to keep up with the latest developments. In the case of the BBC this amounted to an increase of about 30–40 per cent, with servers struggling to cope with the unprecedented demand (see Timms, 2003). Evidently the BBC's news site received the greatest share of 'hits' – numbering into the millions – from US users looking abroad for alternative perspectives (see also Allan, 2006; Matheson and Allan, 2009).

In marked contrast to the challenges of reporting on the deliberate unfolding of a governmental resolution to wage war was the sudden, horrific crisis engendered by the Indian Ocean Tsunami on 26 December 2004. Generally considered to be one of the most powerful ever recorded, it left over 283,000 people dead or reported missing in its wake. Few Western news organisations had reporters nearby, and many of those scrambling to the scenes of devastation found their access was restricted by the same logistical problems facing aid workers. Significantly, however, ordinary citizens – many of them tourists, who had the presence of mind to record what was happening with still and video cameras – provided the most visually compelling imagery used in the mainstream media (see Allan, 2006, 2009). While the BBC cleared its broadcasting schedules to make room for extended bulletins and special programmes, BBC News Online provided extensive contextual information, including graphics explaining why earthquakes occur and a seven-page animated guide to the tsunami. The BBC received thousands of e-mails containing eyewitness accounts, some including digital photographs and even video shot using mobile phones. Audiovisual material was used to illustrate news packages, while e-mails sent to the news website were read out on BBC News 24. The BBC News website also used its *Talking Point* section, now rebranded as *Have your say*, to help people establish contact with missing friends or relatives. The message board was incredibly popular, receiving more than 250,000 hits on the first day alone. Using the website in this way was new territory for the BBC. 'This has grown out of nothing – but we've managed to reunite six sets of people so far,' Matthew Eltringham, then an assistant editor on the site, explained. 'One Dutch man found his brother via a Vietnamese woman living in Stockholm' (cited in Price, 2005).

As the concept of 'citizen journalism' entered the journalistic lexicon in the aftermath of the tsunami, important lessons were being learned about audience interactivity. Once again, it was in preparation for covering a UK general election campaign that several important issues came to the fore. Following BBC News Online's tentative steps in 1997, and its more robust execution in 2001, the dedicated election provision was this time entitled *Election 2005* (see also Thorsen, 2009b). Several sections were introduced to complement its reporting by offering users a more in-depth treatment of election issues. New to the site was the BBC's election blog, entitled *Election Monitor*, which announced on the main page that it was 'bringing you first-hand reports from around the country from our team of correspondents, as well as the best of the newspapers, choice morsels from the web, and your e-mails'. By the end of the campaign, the blog had presented 276 posts (in addition to the main holding page), of which 189 received one or more comments from members of the public, totalling 783 comments across all blog posts. However, the election blog was surpassed in popularity by the *UK voters' panel*. Created in collaboration with breakfast television, it consisted of twenty voters who had been asked in advance to contribute their views 'in text and in video, using 3G mobile phones', throughout the election. There were nine different debate topics with an average of six panellists publishing a response on each occasion. Users could discuss each of these entries – the section attracted some 524 comments in total. The election site was also supported by the *Have your say* section, which covered fifty-three topics across sixty-eight pages. Some 7,684 comments appeared, with a small minority of news and feature articles also containing comments posted by citizens. All in all, this level of interactivity on the *Election 2005* site was widely regarded as firm evidence that the BBC was facilitating spaces for public dialogue. Vicky Taylor (2007), the Editor of BBC Interactivity at the time, justified these features in terms of public service. She argued that it is 'much better if you're getting your audience telling you what they think than just the officials or people in power'. Moreover, she added, 'it's a form of democracy – more people get their chance to have their say about something'.

Echoing the sequence of events in 2001, the general election was followed a few months later by another terror attack, this time in London. At approximately 8:50 a.m. on 7 July 2005, three bombs exploded within a minute of one another on the London Underground. Initially it was not clear what was happening, with early news agency reports suggesting it could be a power-surge. At 9:47 a.m., a fourth bomb detonated on a double-decker bus in Tavistock Square; an hour later the police formally announced that there had been a coordinated terror attack. For many Londoners, the principal source of breaking news, especially for those in the workplace, was the Internet. Ordinary citizens' firsthand reports, together with mobile telephone images and video clips (some of the more iconic of which were shot underground in tragic circumstances), were rapidly dispersing across the web. The BBC News website was among the first to break the story online. In contrast to 11 September 2001, the Corporation had put in place 'an established process of handing control of the main picture promotional area of the homepage directly over to BBC News in the event of a major story breaking' (Belam, 2007). With the website receiving on average 40,000 page requests per second, it soon became clear that the technical team would have to reduce the content on the page 'in order to minimise the download footprint for each page view' (Belam, 2007). The solution was to deploy an experimental 'proof of concept' XHTML/CSS table-free version, which eased the bandwidth usage, thus allowing a greater number of connections.

Putting into motion a strategy derived, in part, from previous experience with the tsunami reporting, the BBC quickly began soliciting eyewitness accounts and imagery from members of the public. Richard Sambrook (2005), Director of Global News for the Corporation, recalls the incredible response:

> Within six hours we received more than 1,000 photographs, 20 pieces of amateur video, 4,000 text messages, and 20,000 e-mails. People were participating in our coverage in a way we had never seen before. By the next day, our main evening TV newscast began with a package edited entirely from video sent in by viewers.

The four people responsible for managing 'user-generated content' (then as now the BBC's preferred term for 'citizen journalism'), whose team had only been set up as a temporary measure for the 2005 election and then made permanent, were struggling to cope with the wealth of material arriving at such considerable speed. Audiences, as Sambrook explained, 'had become involved in telling this story as they never had before', providing contributions that were extraordinarily rich in quality. 'Our reporting on this story was a genuine collaboration,' he added, 'enabled by consumer technology – the camera phone in particular – and supported by trust between broadcaster and audience.' This impromptu collaboration signalled, in his view, that 'the BBC's news-gathering had crossed a Rubicon'.

Crossing the Rubicon

In recognition of this important shift, the BBC formalised the management of user-generated content through its 'UGC Hub'. Launched soon after the London bombings, it was designed to harness the power of the new, two-way relationship between the Corporation and its audiences. It was not long before events conspired to test its viability, of course, the first major one engendered by the explosions at the Buncefield fuel depot near Hemel

Hempstead in Hertfordshire on 11 December 2005. An oil tank had exploded at 6:01 in the morning and several others followed, causing a fire that was described by the Chief Fire Officer, Roy Wilsher, as potentially one of the largest in peacetime Europe. The BBC was quickly inundated by eyewitness accounts and amateur video footage, receiving its first photograph at 6:16, only minutes after the initial explosion (Eltringham, cited in BBC News Online, 11 April 2006). More than 6,500 photographs were reportedly sent to yourpics@bbc.co.uk on the first day, which was a new record for the site (Taylor, cited in BBC News Online, 13 December 2005). One of the photographs was taken by David Otway, who was on a flight to Ireland at the time and so able to shoot images from above the scene. 'I just happened to be in the right place at the right time with the right equipment,' he recalled. 'My first thought was that it was a really big news event and I wanted to share the experience and pictures with people' (cited in BBC News Online, 13 December 2005). The BBC collated the best of these contributions into image galleries on its website, which received 657,367 page impressions on the day of the blast – thereby reaffirming, as if any proof was needed, the remarkable popularity of such material with the audiences.

The speed at which the BBC UGC Hub was able to react to user-generated content was highlighted again on 30 June 2007 – three days after Gordon Brown was sworn in as British Prime Minister – when the UK was subject to an attempted suicide attack at Glasgow airport. Pictures taken by ordinary citizens quickly found their way into the public domain. Online editor Vicky Taylor explained that 'the pictures from bystanders arrived in the BBC central UGC Hub area 30 minutes after it first happened and were on air or on BBC sites shortly afterwards' (cited in Beckett, 2008, p. 81). Two hours after the incident, the BBC website was already featuring a gallery of such images, entitled 'Your pictures: Glasgow alert', together with a news report made up entirely of eyewitness reports and images. The relative ease with which this material was handled signalled the extent to which its use had been rendered almost routine in times of intense pressure. Further examples to emerge in the months ahead included 'amateur video' (taken by mobile telephone) of the execution of Iraqi President Saddam Hussein on 30 December 2006. 'That video completely subverted the official version that the execution was dignified and that Saddam was treated humanely,' Peter Horrocks, head of television news at the BBC, argued. 'The most significant thing,' he maintained, was 'that the footage was shot in the first place' (cited in the *Independent*, 7 January 2007). The unofficial video also caused an extraordinary ethical dilemma for the Corporation. That is, how much of it should be broadcast, considering the video was already widely available to its audience on other websites? The BBC 'decided to show the noose around the neck on News 24 but not on BBC1 at a time when children might be watching,' Horrocks explained, and it 'would not show the moment of death' – an ad hoc policy decision that was extended to the website as well.

Another relevant example surfaced during the uprising by monks in Myanmar (formerly Burma, which is still the recognised name in the UK) in September–October 2007, also known as the 'Saffron Revolution'. The BBC and other news organisations were forced to rely on reports, photographs and videos posted by bloggers from within the conflict zone to illustrate their stories. 'With the Burmese authorities clamping down on information getting out of the country, we [the BBC] – like other news organisations – have been relying more than ever on what people caught up in the events are telling us,' Steve Herrmann (2007) noted at the time. The BBC was able to publish daily reports and images, and occasionally audio and video, from eyewitnesses inside Myanmar, e-mailed directly to its website. 'The pictures are sometimes grainy and the video footage shaky – captured at great personal risk on mobile phones,' BBC News Online correspondent, Stephanie Holmes, commented, 'but each represents a powerful statement of political dissent' (BBC News Online, 26 September 2007). Vicky Taylor explained how social media networks, such as Facebook, also facilitated the Corporation's efforts in actively seeking out relevant sources. As she later recalled:

> When the Burma [Myanmar] uprising was happening, a colleague found the Friends of Burma [Facebook] group and through them got in touch with many who had recently left the country and had amazing tales to tell.
>
> Journalists now have to know how to seek out information and contact from all sorts of sources and social network sites are key to this (Taylor, cited in Journalism.co.uk, 29 February 2008).

Social networking sites, it seemed, were rapidly coming into the frame as potential sources of news and information.

The level of audience material submitted to the BBC is such that the UGC Hub – a 24/7 operation – is staffed by twenty-three people to handle what on an average day typically amounts to 12,000 e-mails and about 200 photographs and videos. This commitment is intended, in part, to enhance the experience for users engaging in moderated debates in the *Have your say* section, although primarily it is intended to ensure that the Corporation is able to react immediately to news events as they unfold. These moves have resonated in positive ways, with BBC News Online routinely serving more than one billion pages per month (with some fourteen million unique users per week). This success has been used by managers to justify their decision to restructure the BBC's news operations, merging radio, television and online news into a single, converged multimedia newsroom. Originally announced in late 2007, the move was said to be a pragmatic response to the licence-fee settlement, which required the BBC to cut costs in its news operations by some £155 million a year by the end of the Charter period. However, it also forced the Corporation to rethink and reform its approach to journalism in the light of the realities of a new media landscape. The first phase of the plans was executed in April 2008 and finalised when the online news teams merged with the rest in June 2008. Signalling the importance of audience material, the so-called UGC Hub was placed at the heart of the new multimedia news operations.

Conclusion

Speaking at an e-Democracy conference on 11 November 2008, the BBC's director of news Helen Boaden (2008) outlined what she perceived to be the main challenges at stake for its online provision. 'Our journalism is now fully embracing the experiences of our audiences, sharing their stories, using their knowledge and hosting their opinions,' she declared; 'we're acting as a conduit between different parts of our audience; and we're being more open and transparent than we have ever been.' The 'accidental journalism' performed by ordinary citizens during the London bombing attacks in July 2005 was a watershed, in her view, 'the point at which the BBC knew that newsgathering had changed forever'. Since then, the BBC has become much more proactive in soliciting this type of content from its audiences. In Boaden's words:

> It's not just a 'nice to have' – it can really enrich our journalism and provide our audiences with a wider diversity of voices than we could otherwise deliver. As well as voices we might not otherwise hear from, there are stories about which we would never have known. ... For many of our audiences, this has opened their eyes to something very simple: that their lives can be newsworthy – that news organisations don't have a monopoly on what stories are covered. Indeed, that news organisations have an appetite for stories they simply couldn't get to themselves and they value information and eye witness accounts from the public – as they always have done. (Boaden, 2008)

In learning to accept the tenet that 'someone out there will always know more about a story than we do', the BBC has embraced citizen newsgathering as a vital resource. This newly forged relationship, Boaden is convinced, represents a positive opportunity for journalism to improve in a way that reinforces informed citizenship. 'Smart news organisations are engaging audiences and opening themselves up to the conversation our audiences clearly want', she contends. In addition to helping to preserve the BBC's core journalistic values of accuracy, fairness and diversity of opinion, she adds, this type of interactivity reaffirms a commitment to reporting in the public interest. 'In order to survive,' Boaden concludes, 'journalism must be trusted.'

Public trust can never be taken for granted, of course; instead, it must be earned each and every day, often under circumstances that defy easy comprehension. A case in point revolved around BBC News Online's reporting of the Mumbai attacks in November 2008, when the sudden and dramatic influx of material from social networking sites – not least Twitter – provided material that posed unique challenges to process. Even before news of the attacks had begun to appear in the electronic media, Twitter was providing eyewitness accounts from users describing what was happening as well as they could manage under the circumstances. In the hours to follow, the BBC drew upon 'tweets' (messages limited to 140 characters) to supplement the information being provided by the Corporation's correspondents, news agencies, Indian media reports, official statements, blog posts and e-mails. Steve Herrmann (2008), editor of BBC News Interactive, explained:

> As for the Twitter messages we were monitoring, most did not add a great amount of detail to what we knew of events, but among other things they did give a strong sense of what people connected in some way with the story were thinking and seeing. 'Appalled at the foolishness of the curious onlookers who are disrupting the NSG operations,' wrote one. 'Our soldiers are brave but I feel we could have done better,' said another. There was assessment, reaction and comment there and in blogs. One blogger's stream of photos on photosharing site Flickr was widely linked to, including by us. All this helped to build up a rapidly evolving picture of a confusing situation. (Herrmann, 2008)

Despite these advantages, however, Herrmann and others were aware of the risks associated with using material when its veracity could not be independently verified. One instance of false reporting, repeatedly circulated on Twitter, claimed that the Indian government was alarmed by what was happening on the social network. Fearful that the information being shared from eyewitnesses on the scene was proving to be useful to the attackers, government officials – it was alleged – were urging Twitter users to cease their efforts, while also looking to block Twitter's access to the country itself. On the BBC's Mumbai live event page, it was reported:

1108 Indian government asks for live Twitter updates from Mumbai to cease immediately. 'ALL LIVE UPDATES – PLEASE STOP TWEETING about #Mumbai police and military operations,' a tweet says.

The BBC was criticised by some commentators for reporting a claim that was later revealed to be untrue. Speaking with the benefit of hindsight, Herrmann responded to questions regarding the decision to post it:

> Should we have checked this before reporting it? Made it clearer that we hadn't? We certainly would have done if we'd wanted to include it in our news stories (we didn't) or to carry it without attribution. In one sense, the very fact that this report was circulating online was one small detail of the story that day. But should we have tried to check it and then reported back later, if only to say that we hadn't found any confirmation? I think in this case we should have, and we've learned a lesson. The truth is, we're still finding out how best to process and relay such information in a fast-moving account like this. (Herrmann, 2008)

to explain the mess online

Bearing these constraints in mind, he believed it was justifiable for the BBC to be sharing what it knew as quickly as possible, even before facts had been fully checked, as a general principle. In this way, users gain an insight into how a major story is being put together, even when it entails having to accept some responsibility for assessing the quality – and reliability – of the information being processed.

Notwithstanding examples such as the news reporting of the Mumbai attacks, the everyday challenge engendered by the sheer volume of audience material received by the BBC is formidable in its own right. In February 2009, when the UK experienced its heaviest snowfall in eighteen years, the widespread disruption experienced across the country was newsworthy enough to generate a record amount of UGC material. According to Peter Horrocks (2009), head of the BBC Newsroom, more than 35,000 people submitted pictures and video of the heavy snow. 'This was a record both for the sheer number of pictures,' he argued, 'and almost certainly for the size of the audience response to a news event in the UK.' This popularity was also reflected in visitor statistics, with the BBC News website attracting some 8.2 million unique visitors (5.1 million from the UK) on Monday 2 February – which was also a new record. Meanwhile, the BBC News channel had a peak audience of 557,000 viewers, 'no doubt boosted by huge numbers of people taking an enforced day off work', as Horrocks points out. In a significant demonstration of convergence between the online and broadcast platforms, there were also 195,000 plays of the BBC News channel live on the website.

This example would suggest that convergence, long a buzzword within BBC circles, is rapidly becoming a reality, often in ways that underscore the contributions of 'the people formerly known as the audience', to use Jay Rosen's (2006) phrase. In any case, there can be little doubt that this type of ordinary news story highlights the dramatic journey of BBC News Online as effectively as the more extraordinary examples that tend to be celebrated in journalistic and academic accounts alike.

REFERENCES

Allan, S. (2006) *Online News: Journalism and the Internet* (Maidenhead and New York: Open University Press).

Allan, S. (2009) 'Histories of citizen journalism', in S. Allan and E. Thorsen (eds), *Citizen Journalism: Global Perspectives* (New York: Peter Lang).

Beckett, C. (2008) *Supermedia: Saving Journalism so It Can Save the World* (Malden, MA: Wiley-Blackwell).

Belam, M. (2007) 'The BBC's homepage on July 7th 2005', BBC Internet Blog, 3 December.

Boaden, H. (2008) 'The role of citizen journalism in modern democracy', Keynote speech at the e-Democracy conference, RIBA, London, 13 November.

Butterworth, B. (2007) 'Brandon's history of online BBC', BBC Internet Blog, 18 December.

Connor, A. (2007) 'Revolution not evolution', BBC Internet Blog, 4 December.

Eggington, B. (2007) 'In the front line, online', *Press Gazette*, 13 November.

Herrmann, S. (2007) 'Information from Burma', BBC News, The Editor's Blog, 28 September.

Herrmann, S. (2008) 'Mumbai, Twitter and live updates', BBC News Online, 4 December.

Horrocks, P. (2009) 'Thanks from BBC News', BBC News, The Editor's Blog, 3 February.

Matheson, D. and Allan, S. (2009) *Digital War Reporting* (Cambridge: Polity Press).

Perrone, J. L. (1998) 'Spotlight on the Beeb', *Online Journalism Review*, 22 July.

Price, J. (2005) 'Tsunami test for news teams', BBC NewsWatch (online), 4 January.

Robins, J. (1999) 'The global correspondent', *Independent*, 24 August.

Rosen, J. (2006) 'The people formerly known as the audience,' *Pressthink*, 27 June.

Sambrook, R. (2005) Citizen journalism and the BBC. *Nieman Reports*, 59: 4, 13–16.

Taylor, V. (2007) Interview conducted by E. Thorsen, 27 March.

Thorsen, E. (2009a) 'BBC News Online: a brief history of past and present', in N. Brügger (ed.), *Web History* (New York: Peter Lang).

Thorsen, E. (2009b) 'News, citizenship and the Internet: BBC News Online's reporting of the 2005 general election', unpublished PhD thesis, Bournemouth University.

Timms, D. (2003) 'News websites see traffic soar', *Guardian*, 20 March, http://www.guardian.co.uk/media.2003/mar/20/digitalmedia.iraq.

Wardle, C. and Williams, A. (2008) 'UGC@THEBBC', Research Report, Cardiff School of Journalism, Media and Cultural Studies, Cardiff University, 16 September.

CHAPTER 2

Managing the online news revolution: the UK experience

BRIAN McNAIR

'Revolution' is an over-used word, applied as much to superficial trends in fashion and style as to radical, qualitative shifts in socio-economic or political organisation. If, however, we intend it to mean, as Wikipedia (2009) defines the term, 'a fundamental change in power or organizational structures that takes place in a relatively short space of time', then it is appropriate to describe the past fifteen years or so in the development of British journalism as a revolution – an online revolution, to be precise, in which the long-established and until recently stable structures of print and broadcast news in the UK have been seriously weakened, in some sectors to the point of collapse.

Newspapers and, if to a lesser extent as yet, linear broadcast news providers on TV and radio are in the process of being replaced as the dominant carrier media of journalism by an emerging network of online outlets. Some of these are vast digitised hubs operated by the established providers of news and journalism in the UK – the BBC, the *Guardian*, the *Telegraph*, Sky News. Many other online providers of news-based content – the great majority – are independent of, and often perceived to be in competition with, the journalistic 'establishment'. They do things in very different ways, play by different rules, subverting hitherto sacrosanct notions such as copyright on content, or objectivity and the various professional practices associated with it, or traditional (if already fragile) notions of journalistic civility and ethics. They include the celebrity news site TMZ.com, which broke the story of Michael Jackson's death; blogger Guido Fawkes, who broke the 'dirty tricks' story which led to the resignation of a key Downing Street media adviser, Damian McBride; news aggregators big (Google News) and small (the Huffington Post), which make journalism produced by a multitude of providers available at one easily searchable online location. They include the social networking sites such as

Facebook and Twitter, which enable news and other types of information to circulate faster and more freely, to more people in more places, than ever before in the history of human communication.

The online revolution has profound implications for all aspects of communication and culture across the world (McNair, 2006; Castells, 2009). This chapter explores its impact on news media in the UK, and how the challenges that it poses have been managed by British journalistic organisations.

The online revolution and the crisis of journalism

The term 'crisis', like 'revolution', has lost much of its impact through excessive application. But once again it is justified in the context of online journalism and its implications for organisations rooted in the pre-Internet era.

There is in British journalism, first, a real and widespread crisis of confidence, of professional identity; an existential crisis, one might say, triggered by the realisation, after a period of collective denial, that the age of unidirectional, top-down, elite-mass, print and linear broadcast journalism is coming to an end. Or more precisely, that its monopoly of a public sphere that is increasingly networked, interactive, participatory, globalised, has been broken.

Journalists and their organisations are challenged by new digital platforms for the delivery of journalistic content, associated changes in patterns of cultural consumption and production and, as a consequence, the collapse of business models that have supported journalism for centuries. In addition to a deep professional crisis, therefore, the online revolution has generated a financial crisis.

Newspapers all over the world are closing, or shrinking their staff, as audiences migrate to the Internet, taking with them advertising and circulation revenues. The process has been apparent for some years, but reached a tipping point in 2008–9 when the credit crunch and global recession pushed many titles and groups into financial deficit. In July 2009 the *Observer* newspaper announced yearly losses of £37 million on sales of 400,000 per issue. Closure of the 218-year-old title was widely predicted. After years of industry and academic debate on the future of print the newspaper, as a delivery vehicle for journalistic content, was recognised to be bust, at least on the traditional model of dependence on advertising and circulation revenue. In all advanced capitalist societies newspaper circulations are in decline (around 3 per cent per year in the UK for the past ten years – see McNair, 2009a). Advertising revenue in the UK print sector fell by between 20 and 40 per cent in 2008–9. As the World Association of Newspapers notes, the position is different in

India, China and other developing markets, where newspaper circulations continue to expand. In these countries, still lagging the developed world in online connectivity and Internet literacy, print remains an efficient and affordable vehicle for delivering journalism. As economic growth and digitalisation proceeds in Asia, however, so newspapers will go into decline there too.

Traditional linear journalism on terrestrial TV and radio (the fixed-time bulletin format) is also losing audience share, to the point in Britain where, post-analogue switch-off in 2012, commercial TV news in the regions and nations will no longer be financially viable in the advertising-funded, free-to-air model of the past half century. The UK government's June 2009 *Digital Britain* report acknowledged these concerns, and included proposals to replace the estimated £43 million shortfall required to enable ITV's regional affiliates such as STV in Scotland to continue broadcasting local news after full digitalisation (http://www.culture.gov.uk/what_we_do/broadcasting/5631. aspx, accessed 13 October 2009).

The news about journalism's current health and future prospects is not all bad, however. As journalism organisations founded in the pre-Internet age struggle to cope with change, there has never been more news and journalism available to the audience, on free-to-air broadcasting, cable and satellite real-time news channels, and online platforms. Over five editions of *News & Journalism in the UK* I have noted the exponential, quantitative expansion of journalism in the British public sphere, and globally, since the early 1990s. News was once, and not so long ago, a scarce resource, amounting in the UK to a few hours per day on free-to-air analogue TV and radio channels, some two dozen national newspapers and local outlets. Today there is much more UK-produced news available than any individual could conceivably access and assimilate. Online, an entire planet of networked news sites, bloggers and aggregators is accessible to audiences in the UK, 99 per cent of whom will have broadband Internet in the home by 2012. We have become used as a culture to a media environment in which output by CNN and Al Jazeera as well as the BBC and Sky can be viewed on laptops and mobile phones, where any newspaper, anywhere in the world, with an online presence, can be read at leisure, over a cup of coffee in a wi-fi hotspot; where news updates and summaries are fed automatically by RSS to our desktops. We are hungry for news and journalism, and we have never had more of it.

Nonetheless, many professional journalists feel themselves part of an endangered species, their authority and status challenged as never before, their jobs at risk. They are at the sharp end of what I described in *Cultural Chaos* (McNair, 2006) as the age of dissolutions – a period characterised by the technology-driven erosion of boundaries that have hitherto structured the production, distribution and consumption of journalism, and that threatens so much that was familiar in the professional lives of those schooled in the pre-Internet era.

For some observers, this 'online revolution' is just another phase in the ongoing process of cultural globalisation that has been unfolding for centuries, if not millennia. The world has been shrinking, barriers coming down, ever since human beings began to venture out of their caves and into the territories of other tribes. From this perspective the revolutionary nature of the digital transformation is overhyped, its potential for progressive social change exaggerated. Armand Mattelart's *Information Society* (2003) describes the rhetoric of online revolution as a 'redemptive discourse', masking business as usual in capitalist societies.

I disagree. Not since the invention of print have we seen a technological leap that so radically transforms the economics and social relations of cultural production, and journalism in particular; that reduces the marginal cost of entry to public discourse – entry as a writer, a speaker, a voice – to near zero. This *is* a revolution, in the structures and practices governing journalism since the seventeenth century. It is, also, a crisis for those whom the revolution threatens to depose.

Cultural dissolution and online revolution: the production–consumption axis

The technologically driven erosion of boundaries between once-distinct and separate media platforms, which began in the 1990s with 'bi-media' and related concepts, has now led to multimedia news production as the norm. Journalists today work not for TV, or radio, but for both, and probably for online too, in the form of blogs, podcasts and videocasts. Print journalists have online versions of their newspapers to supply, and add-ons such as online commentary sections. The notion of 'print journalist' or 'radio correspondent' is all but redundant, replaced by that of the journalist as information architect, someone who can work across multiple platforms with equal facility, adapting content to the needs of different media and consumption patterns.

This process predates the Internet, and is not in itself the cause of the current crisis in journalistic identity. More threatening to the professional journalist than the dissolution of boundaries between platforms – what communication scholars call convergence – is the erosion of the professional boundary itself, the line that says over here is journalism, over there is something else, something that isn't journalism and that does not have the same value, and does not therefore deserve the same cultural status or respect. Since the late 1990s, and accelerating after 9/11, we have seen the rise of the *content-generating user* – the blogger, the citizen journalist, the accidental eyewitness in possession of a digital camera and access to the Internet. ('Citizen journalism' is not a term I like, because not all suppliers of the material often associated with it – Burmese and Chinese pro-democracy campaigners, for example – are citizens in democratic states, and very few are journalists.)

Many of the pioneers of online journalism were professional journalists who had the foresight to see the communicative potential of personal web pages and blogs. Nearly all of them – Andrew Sullivan of the *Daily Dish*, for example – built their reputations in print. To this extent online journalism merely extends the research, writing and rhetorical skills long associated with print and broadcast journalism into new, digital channels of distribution. The more troubling dissolution here, for journalists, is in the capacity of people completely untrained in professional journalistic practice to produce content that can become part of the globalised public sphere, to cross the professional barrier that has policed entry to the practice of liberal journalism for a century and more.

This is particularly true in the category of commentary, or opinion. The rise of the blogosphere includes not just the professionals of the online commentariat (see Burkeman, 2005), such as Andrew Sullivan, Guido Fawkes and others, but the hundreds of thousands, if not millions, of bloggers all over the world who use their online access to post opinions and views about the news of the day. Even in relation to established platforms – newspaper commentary columns, for example – audiences are much more active than ever before. Every newspaper has its online comment section, where members of the public place their opinions on what they have read.

All good, one might assume, from the perspective of cultural democratisation. The dissolution of the production–consumption boundary, the increased merging and overlapping of hitherto separate communicative spheres, is accompanied by a decentralisation and diversification of public discourse. Media power, so often criticised by scholars as monopolistic and over-concentrated, is diluted and disrupted. What's not to like?

But the dissolution of the production–consumption boundary has provoked anxiety, anger, rejection from those journalists, and some academic observers, who perceive that the privileged but essential role of the Fourth Estate is being undermined by amateurs, the quality of the public sphere degraded. Oliver Kamm (2007), for example, concedes that blogging is 'a democratic medium, allowing anyone to participate in political debate without an intermediary, at little or no cost'. There is a downside, however: 'It is a direct and not deliberative form of democracy. You need no competence to join in.' Blogs, therefore, are frequently inaccurate, opinionated without being authoritative, and add little to the stock of knowledge in the public sphere.

On the other hand, as Martin Conboy (2004) and others have shown in their histories of the form, journalism has been about comment and opinion, as well as reportage and fact, since the English civil war. The professional pundits of print and broadcast journalism, whose numbers have increased hugely since Jeremy Tunstall's *Newspaper Power* (1996), routinely express opinions that do not stand up to scrutiny a month or a year after their publication and, as the unexpectedness of the credit crunch and global recession showed, have no special access to predictive power. They are at their best skilled narrators of ongoing events and processes, entertainers, read and listened to for their innovative use of language, their wit and artistry as much as their knowledge of their subject. The blogosphere simply makes it easier for more people to participate in this narrative, not only as readers and spectators – forming their opinions second-hand by virtue of what elite, professional journalists tell them – but as writers and authors, engaging directly with the process of agenda-setting and public opinion formation, and not only within national boundaries, but globally.

User-generated content is also criticised for its alleged flaws as information – it is said to be unreliable and inaccurate, often based on rumour and gossip rather than research and investigation. All of this may be true, at least some of the time, but the same criticisms can be applied to established journalism, even that produced by the most prestigious outlets. Plagiarism and fabrication scandals such as those involving Jayson Blair at the *New York Times*, Stephen Glass at the *New Republic* (McNair 2010) and many one could mention in the UK media have required what we used to call the 'old media' to abandon their complacency in the face of the digital upstarts, and to engage with the content-generating users of the new media. These stories remind us of what critical media scholars have always argued – that professional journalism is highly vulnerable to human error, editorial manipulation, ideological bias and downright lying. In recent times it has often been digital outlets that have exposed those lies and biases.

Some critics have argued that the rise of online journalism threatens the principle of objectivity itself. Eric Alterman warns that:

we are about to enter a fractured, chaotic world of news, characterised by superior community conversation but a decidedly diminished level of first-rate journalists. The transformation of newspapers from enterprises devoted to objective reporting to a cluster of communities, each engaged in its own kind of 'news' – and each with its own set of 'truths' upon which to base debate and discussion – will mean the loss of a single national narrative and agreed-upon set of 'facts' by which to conduct our politics. (Alterman, 2008)

But after the scandals of Blair and Glass, the general crisis of trust in journalism to which they contributed and the long history of journalistic bias so thoroughly documented in the media studies literature, would that be such a bad thing?

Generic dissolution

A second axis of dissolution relates to the content category distinctions that have traditionally structured public and professional understanding of journalism's functions, its status as knowledge, its value as democratic resource. The boundary, for example, between information and entertainment in journalism has traditionally corresponded to normative definitions of 'serious' and 'not serious', the former referring to the traditionally patriarchal worlds of politics, economics and foreign affairs, the latter to the feminine fluff of human interest, lifestyle, celebrity. These divisions have broken down. So the death of Michael Jackson – broken by an LA-based online outlet, TMZ.com – headlined not only in the UK red tops, but also in the *Guardian* and *Times*. And if one can justify the headline status of the death of such an iconic and notorious celebrity in normative terms, less inevitable is the fact that all news media covered the story in broadly the same, 'soft' way – rumour, gossip, speculation, souvenir pull-outs. Dan Berkowitz (2009, p. 290) observes:

> When electronic media were in their infancies, the boundary lines were clearer. Journalism was journalism. Popular culture was popular culture. And we could easily tell which was which. In an era when journalism consisted of something that you could hold in your hand, distinctions between news, analysis, opinion and entertainment were clearly labelled.

No longer. Although this formal or generic dissolution, and critical anxiety about the rise of infotainment, long predates the Internet, much of the rhetoric of crisis that accompanies the online revolution is founded on concern about the continued viability of categories and boundaries that for decades have allowed journalists and news organisations to locate themselves within democratic society as important, nay essential, watchdogs, scrutineers, educators.

The death of journalism?

The way journalism is made is changing, then, and by whom, as is the way it is consumed. The increasing involvement of the non-professional newsmaker and commentator – call her the citizen journalist, the blogger, the content-generating user – means that millions of ordinary people, all over the world, linked by the Internet to the established, professional news outlets, have become a visible presence in the globalised public sphere, with the potential to make a significant input to the news production process.

During the post-election protests of June 2009 in Iran, while professional correspondents were holed up in hotels, confined to quarters, words and pictures produced by ordinary people on the ground in Tehran provided much of the raw material for the unfolding news story across the world. This was a positive benefit for the BBC, as the director of its global news division stated in a speech to a Reuters seminar on 16 June. Richard Sambrook noted that the BBC, like other news organisations, had experienced disruption to its coverage due to Iranian government restrictions and censorship, but that 'a wealth of multimedia reports and information directly from citizens [had] helped counter this limited access' (Oliver, 2009). He added that:

> UGC has been 'an extremely valuable supplement' to the work of the BBC's journalists and has illustrated why news organisations need to embrace new technologies. International newsgathering is going through a profound period of transition at the moment and I don't think it's going to be a smooth transition. The big model of the foreign bureau is not economically viable and increasingly in the new world it lacks an authenticity that we're starting to see emerge from the means of gathering news from the internet.

As in previous global stories, such as the 7 July 2005 bombings in London, the 2007 Glasgow airport attack and the 2008 terror attacks in Mumbai, much of what was shown on TV news and in other media around the world was derived from accounts and pictures provided by people involved in the story: eyewitnesses, participants, victims, survivors. In Iran, the difference was that the authorities did not wish this material to get out, but were unable to prevent it.

Elsewhere I have observed that 'the authority of the trained professional is under challenge from amateurs' (McNair, 2009b, p. 348). This is of course the cause of the crisis of journalistic identity mentioned above. On 30 June 2009, observing events in Iran and the role of non-professional sources in their communication to the outside world, the BBC's *Newsnight* current affairs magazine ran an item asking if this meant that what it called 'citizen journalists', using social networking sites and other online tools, would eventually replace professional journalists altogether.

The answer to that question is, I believe, no. The dissolution of the production–consumption boundary, and the associated decentralisation of journalistic production, is welcome, for all kinds of reasons. But if it is to help global news audiences to understand complex events decentralisation has to be managed, given structure and meaning. This is where the professional journalist retains her use-value and cultural role.

Veracity, reliability, accuracy – these are just as important for content-generating users, bloggers and social networkers as for BBC correspondents. They are the prerequisite of journalism having any social impact, whether it is produced by amateur or professional. The on-the-ground authenticity of user-generated content, central though that is to its appeal, is not enough in itself – there must also be a perception of honesty and accuracy, and of intelligibility. Professional editors, correspondents and producers have the time and the resources to reflect on and analyse the meaning of events, rather than merely report them, or pass on what others are reporting about them. They add value to user-generated content, screening, packaging and refining it.

People on the ground tweeted, e-mailed and mobile-phoned the news out of Mumbai when Islamist terrorists attacked that city. They provided powerful images and eyewitness accounts of what was happening, hour to hour, in multiple locations; images and accounts that no news organisation could hope to match in their instantaneity and intensity. Digital technology made this possible. But it took time, and the work of trained journalists and editors in newsrooms all over the world, to establish an authoritative account of the event in its totality, and then to analyse its meaning, as reflected, for example, in the Channel 4 *Dispatches* documentary of July 2009, *Terror in Mumbai*. User-generated content provided much of the visual material that gave the documentary its power. Professional journalists shaped that material into a coherent and credible narrative of complex, chaotic events.

If the age of dissolutions is also the age of cultural chaos, of communicative turbulence and discursive democratisation, the professional standards of journalism, and properly resourced outlets, are the anchor in a sea of potential confusion. People tweet out of Iran, but it's the BBC and CNN that give that information global visibility and significance (by selecting it and taking it seriously) and then context. The social networker on the ground is no more privy to the totality of an event and its manifold aspects than is the institutionalised primary definer of old. He or she needs the expertise of the professional to communicate effectively.

Managing the online revolution

The online news revolution began slowly, and it took a long time for the established providers of journalism to respond. Three years after the launch of the user-friendly Netscape Mosaic browser in 1994, which allowed the Internet to make the leap from specialist tool to mass communication medium, there were still only some 700 Internet news sites operating in the USA (McNair, 1998). Some of these were net-only publications such as *Slate*, *Salon* and the *Drudge Report*. A few were early online versions of print and broadcast news outlets.

In the UK, early adopters of the Internet platform included the BBC, the *Guardian*, the *Financial Times* and the *Telegraph*. Those early sites seem crude and rudimentary today, but they were pioneering at the time, with their capacity to allow the reader to leap from one page to another on a different but related subject with the click of a mouse, or to follow a story back to a reference or source.

These are among the organisations that saw at an early stage that the Internet was going to change fundamentally how journalism would be delivered and consumed. They remain ahead of the game in online news, their sites exemplars of innovation and user friendliness. According to ABCe, which measures unique monthly users of all UK-based news sites, in May 2008 the BBC's site was the most used in the UK, and probably the world, with more than 50,000,000 unique monthly users. The *Guardian* and *Telegraph* both had more than 18,000,000 users in that same month.

Being first is not the only path to online success, of course. The print and broadcast news organisations that have proven to be the most successful in the first decade of the online revolution have not simply been the early adopters, but those that have invested substantially in the infrastructure required not just for multiplatform journalism, but for genuine interactivity with and participation by users and audiences, sometimes against the protests of staff and unions reluctant to make the change. At the end of 2006, for example, the *Telegraph* group invested more than £100 million in creating a 'digital hub' within its London operations. Staff were made redundant in the process, generating much criticism in the trade press, but a few years on, the wisdom and farsightedness of that investment is beyond dispute.

In 2007 the BBC faced opposition from staff as it announced plans to invest in multimedia news and journalism production through facilities such as the £180 million centre at Pacific Quay in Glasgow. At a conference in Leeds in 2008 Peter Horrocks, head of the BBC's converged newsroom, gave a picture of what this investment meant in practice: the abolition of separate output departments (TV, radio, interactive), replaced by a simpler multimedia operation:

> Within the multimedia newsroom department we are now preparing a major physical re-organisation to accompany the structural changes. All of the key daily news teams in radio, TV and the web will be seated alongside each other next to the people who run the newsgathering. And close to the middle of that operation will be our User Generated Content unit. It will be right alongside the news-gathering teams that deploy our conventional journalistic resources. And the UGC team will be deploying and receiving our unconventional journalistic resources – information and opinion from the audience.
>
> When that information is received and assessed it will be passed immediately to our journalists on any platform and will be on air on News 24, Radio 5 Live or on the site as soon as possible. (Horrocks, 2008)

Horrocks acknowledged that online public participation in news production had augmented the BBC's output, but cautioned that forms of gatekeeping and editing were required to manage the process. 'Citizen journalism' – and he provided examples – was often angry, abusive, racist, and had to be handled in ways that did not cause undue offence.

The head of Sky News, Simon Bucks, also gave a presentation at this conference, in which he described how his organisation was incorporating You Tube, Twitter and other forms of 'citizen journalism' into the channel's online service, enabling ordinary people throughout the UK to have a much greater role in news output than ever before, embedding their video and texts at the heart of the channel's coverage and thus, he argued, enhancing its local reach and relevance. In an April 2005 speech Bucks's boss, Rupert Murdoch, noted that, on the one hand, the integration of blogging and other forms of user-generated content into journalism represented 'a huge opportunity to improve our journalism and expand our reach'. On the other:

> There are inherent risks in this strategy – chief among them maintaining our standards for accuracy and reliability. Plainly, we can't vouch for the quality of people who aren't regularly employed by us – and bloggers could only add to the work done by our reporters, not replace them. But they may still serve a valuable purpose; broadening our coverage of the news; giving us new and fresh perspectives to issues; deepening our relationship to the communities we serve. So long as our readers understand the distinction between bloggers and our journalists. (Murdoch, 2005)

At the level of the regional press, big providers such as Johnston Press and Newsquest have spent recent years restructuring their operations for the Internet era, merging titles, sharing back-room resources and shedding posts, often with what seems like brutal insensitivity. The Glasgow managers of the Herald group, for example, chose the 2008 pre-Christmas period to announce that all editorial staff were being made redundant, and that all would have to reapply for posts in a newly configured newsroom. As a senior manager defended the announcement on BBC's *Newsnight Scotland* his argument that the online revolution required major change of Newsquest employees was beyond dispute; but the style and timing of the management response provoked widespread revulsion. Johnston's *Scotsman* titles announced the merger of their newsroom operations in early 2009, following the appointment of John McLellan as editor-in-chief of the Edinburgh-based group. Again, journalists were made redundant.

Faced with the short-term economic pressures of the credit crunch in 2008–9, between 1,000 and 2,000 journalistic posts were lost in the UK's regional journalism sector, much of this justified by management in terms of the cost-cutting potential of the Internet. Whether this would restore the financial fortunes and secure the long-term futures of once highly profitable regional titles remained to be seen as of this writing.

On 29 July 2009 the *Herald* newspaper reported a deal by the BBC to share some of its online video content with a number of newspaper groups (Williams, 2009). Notwithstanding complaints from commercial companies that this would distort the market for the supply of video news, few doubted that such pooling arrangements would become more commonplace in the UK news industry, and would indeed be the key to survival for some organisations.

Making online pay

Generating revenue streams from online that compensate for the loss of print circulation and advertising revenue remains the greatest challenge for media managers in the UK, as in other countries. In an environment where Internet users, be they accessing music, movies, TV programmes or journalism, increasingly expect content to be free, how can online content be monetised sufficiently to support quality journalism of the kind most observers (and publics) agree to be important?

Murdoch and News Corp believe that content of a certain kind – premium – is something for which users will continue to pay, a strategy being applied to the *Wall Street Journal* and the *Times/Sunday Times*. In Britain the owners of the *Financial Times*, Pearson, announced in July 2009 that paid-for digital services now accounted for 67 per cent of FT Group revenues, as compared with just 20 per cent from advertising. While FT profits were down that year, amidst an unprecedented global recession, CEO Marjorie Scardino stated her confidence that the newspaper and its online operation would survive the crisis by supplying paying customers with valuable, specialist information (Tryhorn, 2009).

There are forms and types of journalistic information, then, for which people will pay, even in the online era. The challenge for media managers is to identify these, and resource them, be they the writings of a particularly witty columnist, in-depth foreign coverage or exclusive access to discounted holidays and restaurant meals. The subscription model of journalism is not bust, but determining what consumers will pay for requires expensive market research, experimentation and the acceptance of risk by media organisations. Inevitably, organisations with deep pockets are better placed in this regard.

Advertising is still an important source of income, if a declining one, and in relation to journalism much depends, as it always has, on the perceived quality of the news brand. Audiences are attracted to some news brands more than others, for a variety of reasons, and advertisers follow audiences. If TMZ.com leads the global news market in speed of disclosure, or in its readiness to reveal all about a celebrity scandal, *Guardian* readers know that they are more likely to find in the title considered cultural analysis of the story in question, its context and meaning. The *Guardian* covers Michael Jackson and *Big Brother*, yes, as much as if not more than the red tops, but its approach is different, and as the success of both print and online editions shows, there is a demand for it.

Whether journalistic content is free or not, there remains the issue of intellectual property, and the Internet's capacity to overthrow traditional copyright conventions. In July 2009 *Guardian* commentator Roy Greenslade reported on a growing campaign by European news publishers for stronger copyright protection of their content: 'The publishers claim that widespread use of their work by online news aggregators is undermining their efforts to develop online business models at a time when readers and advertisers are defecting from print' (Greenslade 2009). Rupert Murdoch's News Corporation has been particularly critical of Google News' 'parasitism' and has called for reform of copyright law. Media managers are not the only ones challenged by the online revolution, then. Regulators too must adapt their principles and practices for the digital era. Mathias Döpfner, CEO of the German Axel Springer publishing group, argues that 'the internet is not our enemy but rather the future of journalism, if intellectual property is respected in the digital world' (Greenslade 2009).

[handwritten marginalia: there's no solution for newspapers]

Conclusion

The online news revolution does not mean the death of journalism, then. Newspapers and linear broadcast bulletins will continue to see their audience share decline, and their place in the information market place will change, but journalism will survive as a cultural form, and in an environment where more people than ever before can both produce and consume it, it may even prosper. As S. Elisabeth Bird (2009, p. 295) observes:

> The new digital environment has jolted traditional journalism out of its conservative complacency; news operations are much more responsive to their empowered and engaged audiences. Yet surely effective democracy requires the existence of news organisations that employ professional journalists who know how to report new information, not merely recirculate it. The challenge will be whether the current economic and cultural climate will permit the survival of an informed and independent journalism, along with both the imperative for profit and the clamor for every voice to express itself.

It will, I believe, not least for economic reasons. In a news market of many providers, consumers, users, audiences will prefer those they perceive to be of the highest quality, the greatest value in terms of satisfying their information needs. Advertisers will follow those audiences.

The BBC, News Corp, indeed most newspaper groups, have invested substantially and reformed their operations to enable more productive interaction with content-generating users. They encourage users of their websites to post footage, to comment on stories; and they maintain professional editorial teams to manage the process. They recognise that management of the online revolution isn't either/or – professional or amateur – but both, integrated within a news brand to provide the speediest, most authentic and yet most authoritative accounts of events.

Notwithstanding the brutality of some managements in their handling of the crisis, the notion of professional journalism will survive, as embodied in adherence to learned practices of information gathering, processing and presentation that mobilise trust and confidence among audiences. It will coexist with the millions of online voices, who will feed it with raw material, keep it on its toes, challenge it. Professional journalism will be refreshed and revitalised, not abolished.

REFERENCES

Alterman, E. (2008) 'Out of print', *New Yorker*, 31 March, http://www.newyorker. com/reporting/2008/03/31/080331fa_fact_alterman, accessed 13 October 2009.

Berkowitz, D. (2009) 'Journalism in the broader cultural mediascape', *Journalism: Theory, Practice and Criticism*, 10: 3, 290–2.

Bird, S. E. (2009) 'The future of journalism in the digital environment', *Journalism: Theory, Practice and Criticism*, 10: 3, 293–5.

Burkeman, O. (2005) 'The new commentariat', *Guardian*, 17 November.

Castells, M. (2009) *Communication Power* (Oxford: Oxford University Press).

Conboy, M. (2004) *Journalism: A Critical History* (London: Sage).

Greenslade, R. (2009) 'Publishers claiming copyright theft by aggregators aim to protect content', http://www.guardian.co.uk/media/greenslade/2009/jul/13/digital-media-downturn, accessed 13 October 2009.

Horrocks, Peter (2008) 'Value of citizen journalism', 7 January, http://www.bbc. co.uk/blogs/theeditors/2008/01/value_of_citizen_journalism.html, accessed 13 October 2009.

Kamm, O. (2007) 'A parody of democracy', *Guardian*, 9 April.

McNair, B. (1998) *The Sociology of Journalism* (London: Arnold).

McNair, B. (2006) *Cultural Chaos: News, Journalism and Power in a Globalised World* (London: Routledge).

McNair, B. (2009a) *News and Journalism in the UK*, 5th edn (London: Routledge).

McNair, B. (2009b) 'Journalism in the 21st century – evolution, not extinction', *Journalism: Theory, Practice and Criticism*, 10: 3, 347–9.

McNair, B. (2010) *Journalists in Film: Heroes and Villains* (Edinburgh: Edinburgh University Press).

Mattelart, A. (2003) *The Information Society* (London: Sage).

Murdoch, Rupert (2005) 'Speech to the American Society of Newspaper Editors', 13 April, http://www.newscorp.com/news/news_247.html, accessed 13 October 2009.

Oliver, Laura (2009) 'UGC offering authenticity despite restrictions in Iran, says BBC's Richard Sambrook', *Journalism.co.uk*, 17 June, http://www.journalism.co. uk/2/articles/534793.php, accessed 13 October 2009.

Tryhorn, C. (2009) 'Pearson "delighted" despite pink paper's deluge of red ink', *Guardian*, 28 July.

Tunstall, J. (1996) *Newspaper Power* (Oxford: Clarendon Press).

Wikipedia (2009) 'Revolution', http://en.wikipedia.org/wiki/Revolution, accessed 13 October 2009.

Williams, M. (2009) 'BBC and UK newspapers to share video', *Herald*, 29 July, http://www.heraldscotland.com/bbc-and-uk-newspapers-to-share-video-1.915632, accessed 13 October 2009.

CHAPTER 3

The crisis of journalism and the Internet

ROBERT W. MCCHESNEY

'The condition of American journalism in the first decade of the twenty-first century can be expressed in a single unhappy word: crisis' (Powers, 2007, p. 1). So began a report made by a scholar ensconced in the heart of mainstream academia. Such a comment would have been far less plausible in the political mainstream only a decade earlier, and its rapid evolution to becoming the new conventional wisdom among both academics and much of the news media is little short of breathtaking. For the past quarter-century this argument was made primarily by critical analysts of the US news media, especially those from the political economy of media tradition. In the 1980s and well into the 1990s it was subject to categorical dismissal by many journalists and journalism professors, if not outright ridicule. No longer do critical scholars need to present piles of evidence to make even mild criticism of the status quo. Today it is those who wish to defend the commercial system as doing a superior job at generating quality journalism that must provide the hard evidence. Only a handful of true believers, often those wed materially to the system, make much of an effort to do so.

In this chapter I address the contours of the now-roundly accepted crisis in journalism, and suggest how we may most fruitfully consider it, and prospective solutions, including online news. I argue herein that the political economy of media is uniquely positioned to provide the insights necessary for constructive action.

The place to start is by understanding what we mean by viable journalism for a democracy, what the crisis of journalism entails and what caused it. What exactly does a democratic journalism entail? I believe it must provide a rigorous accounting of people who are in power and people who wish to be in power, in both the government and corporate sectors. It must have a plausible method to separate truth from lies, or at least prevent liars from getting away scot-free. And it must provide a wide range of informed opinions on the most important issues of our times; not only the issues of the day, but the major issues that loom on the horizon. These issues cannot be determined primarily by what people in power are talking about. Journalism must provide our early warning system. It is not necessary that all news media provide all these services; that would be impractical. It is necessary that the media system as a whole make such journalism a realistic expectation for the citizenry. Indeed, the measure of a free press is how well a system meets these criteria. Understood in this manner, journalism requires resources, institutions, legal protection and people who work at it full time to be successful. It may benefit from more than that, but these conditions are indispensable. And understood this way, our current news media earn a low grade, even using a curve.

What does the crisis of journalism entail? The corruption of journalism, the decline of investigative reporting, the degeneration of political reporting and international journalism, the absurd horserace coverage of campaigns, the collapse of local journalism, the increasing prevalence of celebrity and scandal are now roundly acknowledged by all but the owners of large media firms and their hired guns. *Washington Post* editors Len Downie and Robert Kaiser wrote a critique of journalism in 2002 that was nothing short of devastating in its evaluation of how commercial pressures are destroying the profession (Downie and Kaiser, 2002). The 2006 Report from the Project for Excellence in Journalism observes, 'At many old-media companies, though not all, the decades-long battle at the top between idealists and accountants is now over. The idealists have lost.' The accountants have been left to cut reporter numbers, replace specialist reporters with generalists, shut down foreign bureaus and cut news while narrowing its scope to topics like crime, sport, traffic and weather. The same report suggests, however, that the Internet is not a straight alternative to this world: 'On the Web, the Internet-only sites that have tried to produce original content (among them Slate and Salon) have struggled financially, while those thriving financially rely almost entirely on the work of others. Among blogs, there is little of what journalists would call reporting (our study this year finds reporting in just 5% of postings).'

So thorough is the recognition that the existing corporate system is destroying journalism that the acclaimed scholar Michael Schudson – who has been a singular critic of political economists who made structural criticism of US news media, and who for years has argued that things are not so bad with the press – is concerned about Wall Street's negative impact on journalism. He wrote in 2007:

While all media matter, some matter more than others, and for the sake of democracy, print still counts most, especially print that devotes resources to gathering news. Network TV matters, cable TV matters, but when it comes to original investigation and reporting, newspapers are overwhelmingly the most important media. Wall Street, whose collective devotion to an informed citizenry is nil, seems determined to eviscerate newspapers. (Schudson, 2007, p. 58)

The real concern is what accounts for the present crisis. In much of conventional parlance, the crisis is due primarily to the Internet providing competition to the dominant commercial news media and draining resources from the traditional journalism. This has led to an economic downturn for broadcast news and, especially, for daily newspapers, the guts of news procurement in the United States. As the Internet takes away advertisers and readers, daily newspapers lay off journalists, board up newsrooms and prepare to join the horse-and-buggy in the annals of US history. And the market place has provided no economic alternative to generate the resources for journalism as we know it online, so society loses. The market has spoken, for now at least. Technology killed the goose that laid the golden egg. To add insult to injury, in the minds of some professional journalists, for all the blather about 'new media' and their empowering effect, on balance the Internet has hastened the degradation and commercialisation of news values across the board (Henry, 2007).

The solution, to listen to the media corporations, is to permit existing media companies to merge and combine and become effective monopolies at the local level. Governments should, in effect, ratchet up their inducements, privileges and direct and indirect subsidies to the media giants so they will have the resources to provide us with the journalism we need (see the defence of allowing greater media concentration by FCC Chair Kevin Martin, 2007). And we need not worry about monopoly because the Internet is providing a forum for everyone else.

The strength of this argument is that it has an element of evidence to support it. Newspaper revenues and profits are falling as their readership has flattened and is skewing older, much older. Moreover, at present, it is nowhere near profitable to transition from ink and paper to digital production and online distribution for newspapers. One study concluded 'that a newspaper needs to attract two or three dozen online readers to make up for – in terms of advertising revenue – the loss of a single hard-copy reader' (Patterson, 2007, p. 13). But to stop the analysis here is misleading. Newspapers remain profitable on their operating expenses. They may not be raking in the monopolistic profits that made the balance of the business community envious for much of the twentieth century, but very few are shuttering their doors. And newspapers may well find a way to remain viable in the digital era (Saba, 2008, pp. 22–4). The matter is less clear with regard to broadcast news media, which have gone even further in abandoning journalism. But the merger of broadcast news with Internet operations is advancing as well.

The weakness of the 'Internet has killed the economic basis for journalism' argument is that the crisis in journalism emerged long before the Internet. In the 1980s and certainly by the 1990s news media were cutting back on reporters and resources. They were doing so when they were flush with money, because it was the profitable thing to do in the short term, and in the long run we will all be dead. News media were discouraging hard-hitting and expensive investigative reporting and softening their standards on trivial but commercially friendly news stories about celebrities and the like. By the early 1990s, in fact, a small but vocal group of prominent journalists were already declaring the 'death of journalism' (Underwood 1993; Kimball 1994; McManus 1994; Squires 1995). The corporate mindset had little respect for the autonomy of professional journalism and was inclined to seeing the news converted into an immediately profitable undertaking first and foremost.

There is an even larger problem with the conventional wisdom that the crisis in journalism is due to the Internet: it rests on the assumption that all was fine with the world of US news media in the not-to-distant past. Such an assumption is bogus. The conventional explanation for the emergence of professional journalism had relied upon technology – for example, the telegraph and Associated Press making it necessary to have neutral content acceptable to a broad range of papers – or how it was in the economic interest of monopolistic publishers eager to serve the public-at-large to publish non-partisan journalism so as not to alienate part of the market. Although these were important factors, what tended to be missing was a crucial component: the immense public dissatisfaction with the sensationalistic and decidedly conservative journalism of the times. In addition, there was a concurrent intense struggle between newspaper publishers and journalists to define professional journalism and gain control over the newsroom. This struggle boiled over in the 1930s and 1940s with the organisation of the Newspaper Guild. I will not keep you in suspense: the journalists lost.

Understood this way, professional journalism, which emerged over the course of the first half of the twentieth century, was far from perfect. The type of professional journalism that emerged was one more conducive to the needs of media owners than to journalists or citizens. Professional journalism's capacity to keep implicit commercial values out of the news was always nebulous, as the power to hire and fire and set budgets always resided with the owners. It allowed a certain measure of autonomy and independence for journalists from commercial and political pressures – and it certainly looked to be an improvement over what it replaced – and it has a commitment to factual accuracy that is admirable and perhaps its greatest legacy. Professional journalism's core problem, and by no means its only problem, is that it devolved to rely heavily upon 'official sources' as the basis of legitimate news. Official sources determined what professional journalists could be factually accurate about in the first place. It gets worse. When elites were in general agreement, as was often the case concerning fundamental economic and foreign policies, professional journalism spoon-fed the conventional wisdom, which was often dead wrong, and offered little protection for the citizenry. But from the Gulf of Tonkin to Operation Iraqi Freedom our finest professional journalists did spoon-feed the misleading propaganda accurately.

This reliance upon official sources has always made professional journalism especially susceptible to well funded corporate public relations, which could mask its self-interest behind a billion dollar fig leaf of credentialled expertise. This problem only increases as newsrooms have fewer and fewer journalists to interrogate the PR claims. So it was that between 1995 and 2005 nary a single one of the nearly 1,000 refereed academic research journal articles on climate change disputed the notion that something fundamental, dangerous and influenced by humans was taking place. Yet our news media sources representing the interests of oil companies and other major polluters provided a significant official opposition to the notion that global warming was a problem or that pollution had anything to do with it. How significant? Over one-half of the 3,543 news articles in the popular press between 1991 and 2005 expressed doubt as to the existence and/or cause of global warming. The public would rationally assume that this was an issue very much under debate by scientists and the best policy would be to do nothing until it was sorted out. This is often presented as prima facie evidence of the power of corporate public relations laid bare. It is that, but it is even more a statement on weaknesses built into professional journalism as it developed in the United States (see Gore, 2006, pp. 160–5, 2007, Chapter 7).

No better example of the consequences of this comes with the build-up to the US invasion of Iraq in 2003. In 2002 and 2003 the news media largely abrogated their duty by uncritically publishing administration lies and exaggerations that were instrumental in taking the USA to an unnecessary, illegal and disastrous war (see, for example, Nichols and McChesney, 2005). So indefensible was the press coverage that both the *New York Times* and the *Washington Post* issued apologies. In January 2008 a comprehensive study by the non-partisan Center for Public Integrity (CPI) determined that there were fully 935 lies – with several hundred coming from President Bush and

Vice President Cheney – told to the American people to generate popular support for a war in Iraq. These were not 'grey area' statements, as the CPI's detailed database makes clear (see www.publicintegrity.org; Cushman, 2008). Nor were they oversights or merely clumsy missteps. As the report concludes, the lies 'were part of an orchestrated campaign that effectively galvanized public opinion and, in the process, led the nation to war under decidedly false pretenses'. In mainstream professional journalism this has all been filed away in the dark memory hole, to the extent it is even acknowledged.

So if having viable journalism is mandatory for a self-governing society, the current crisis is at the very centre of what type of world we will be living in for the coming generations. And here, as with the disastrous invasion and occupation of Iraq, the place to look for answers is not with the people who created the problem or ignored the smoke signals and pooh-poohed the critics until the status quo was up in flames. Instead, the prudent course would be to look at the critics whose analysis best explains the current crisis of journalism and whose analysis has been on the mark the longest. In short, this is where we need to look to the political economy of media.

The starting point for a political economic analysis is that structure matters. Institutions matter. They matter a great deal. The importance of structures, of institutions, in shaping journalism and media content directly and indirectly is well understood when we look at other nations; it is only recently that American exceptionalism in this regard has begun to erode. It is not that owners and advertisers and managers need to directly interfere with or censor editors and journalists; it is more the case that organisational structures transmit values that are internalised by those who successfully rise to the top.

US journalists have internalised the values of their profession and those values have biases built into them. The professional code has eroded, but values – political and commercial – are still communicated to journalists. And those that rise to the top of the corporate news media in the United States today tend to be those who internalise them and regard them as appropriate. When they see an iconic editor of the stature of Bill Kovach leave the *Atlanta Constitution* and *Atlanta News* because, in part, he had the temerity to suggest that great journalism is willing to critically investigate the most powerful businesses in Georgia against the wishes of the papers' owners, smart journalists accept that there are some stones best left unturned. When they see an accomplished investigative journalist like Gary Webb driven from the profession for having the audacity to investigate the CIA, smart journalists learn that this is a topic best left to others, unless they are clearly encouraged or supported by someone inside the intelligence establishment. I could go on and on and I have in my earlier work (McChesney, 1997).

Those journalists whose antennae fail, or who do not internalise the dominant institutional values, end up working beats other than politics, or they end up at the bottom of the journalism food chain, maybe as freelancers, or they look for work teaching journalism at a college or university, or they go into some other line of work. But the starting point everywhere is to understand that the institutional and structural context is the main determinant. It does not answer all questions surrounding journalism, but for even those it cannot answer it can provide necessary and useful context. This is where political economy of media has proven to be so valuable during this crisis. It explains how we get the institutions that produce the crisis in journalism. Accordingly, it points the way forward: structural change, through policy reform. We have to create a system that makes it rational to produce great journalism, and the clear lesson we have is that the really existing market place will not do the job. It has failed. As our friends in public relations like to say, we have to go in a different direction.

The prospect of engaging in policy reform and structural change is a difficult pill to swallow for many journalists and citizens, weaned on the notion that we have a press system entirely independent of the government, and that any government involvement puts us dangerously close to a slippery slope to tyranny. Even recognising the failures of the market place and the cornerstone role of government policies and subsidies in building our press system, for many observers the notion of recognising the state's role remains anathema, and there is an almost palpable desperation to find an alternative that avoids politics. This is understandable, but a frank recognition of the government role should also make possible a careful consideration of enlightened government policies. What political economy recognises is that the policies, and the structures they foster, implicitly encourage certain values and discourage others, encourage certain types of content, and discourage alternatives. Enlightened policy-making recognises that and seeks to create a range of structures that can provide for the information needs of the people, and that allow for as much openness, freedom and diversity as possible. That is freedom of the press.

This does not mean that reforms that do not directly challenge the commercial system are meaningless, merely that they are insufficient on their own to get the job done. Nearly all of the seemingly non-structural solutions to the crisis in journalism are worth pursuing and have some value.

It would be outstanding, for example, if our schools and universities did a better job of educating budding journalists. At the same time, this approach is of limited value. What good is it to educate journalists in public service values if there are few paying jobs for them or if they end up covering celebrity scandals or regurgitating press releases and providing stenography to power? It would also help if our schools and colleges educated students in general to appreciate the role and importance of news, and how media operate. This is often termed media literacy. This would create better content and market demand for that content. Likewise, it would be helpful if student media were expanded at universities and high schools across the nation, rather than being cut back. Research demonstrates the key role student media play in fostering an appreciation for journalism and freedom of the press. (The Knight Foundation produced research along these lines in 2006: http://firstamendmentfuture.org/.)

It would also be helpful if entrepreneurs could find ways to use the new communication technologies to find a lucrative market for quality popular journalism. But so far this has not happened, and even if it does, the effect of the Internet on commercial journalism, as noted earlier, has been to accentuate the flaws in contemporary journalism as much as to erase them (Strupp, 2008). We need to have a sector producing journalism walled off from corporate and commercial pressures. It would help matters if philanthropists and foundations began to devote significant portions of their portfolios to increasing the amount and quality of news and public information. But that has not happened yet, and if it did there would remain knotty problems about where these funds would go and how these news media would be managed.

Note, too, that while these approaches may not be especially 'structural', *all* of these approaches in fact are determined by public policies, by politics, to varying degrees. Journalism education and media literacy require resources, often public resources. Indeed, media literacy probably necessitates a public campaign to win over school boards. Getting viable student media in high schools and colleges is very much a public policy issue, and a crucial one for media reform at that. Making it possible for new entrepreneurs to enter the journalism field is greatly aided by government anti-monopoly regulation, and by tax and credit rules that lower barriers to entry. Government advertising and postal rates can also play a significant role in easing the way for new media players to enter markets. Likewise, it will need policy assistance to make it possible for philanthropies or non-profit organisations to play a larger role. These organisations exist and have their range of operations determined by public policy. In fact, all of these seemingly 'inside the system' efforts to rejuvenate journalism depend upon an aroused citizenry and public policy activism. They are elements of the media reform movement.

Nowhere is the importance of policy more striking than with the Internet and the digital revolution, and it is here that people often regard the Internet as some sort of magical technology unaffected by policy. As noted before, media chieftains argue that ownership restrictions are irrelevant today because the Internet has blasted open the system, generating millions of new media. They are not the only ones. Critics of corporate media and capitalism sometimes join the chorus, stating that citizens can do whatever they want online, as long as they get their act together. Technology has slain the corporate media system, and the future is very much up for grabs. The blogosphere is democracy's tidal wave to overwhelm the commercial news media status quo. The King is Dead. Long Live the King.

Wouldn't our lives be easy if this were true? The argument is fatally flawed: the openness of the Internet is due to policy as well as technology. Telecommunication companies and cable companies have the power to censor the Internet, and work hand-in-hand with the governments that grant them monopoly licence to do exactly that. We see that in nations like China, where major US firms work with the Chinese authorities to create a tightly controlled web and digital communication world (*The Economist*, 2008). But it is also true in the United States, where the largest telecommunication companies worked closely with the Bush administration to illegally spy on US citizens. In 2008, as these words were written, the Senate was enmeshed in an intense fight between Democrats and the Bush administration, which was obsessed with getting 'retroactive immunity' for the telecommunication companies for their illegal spying written into the extension of the Foreign Intelligence Surveillance Act (*New York Times*, 2007).

This matter deserves more treatment, because for all the understandable hype about how the Internet and digital communication liberate people and revolutionise our lives, they also come at a price: the elimination of privacy as we have known it, and allowing the government and corporate interests to know a great deal more about us, generally surreptitiously. The threat of state harassment is greater today than at any time in our history. For many Americans this may seem like an abstract threat, or a concern only to those engaged in crime or terrorism. Far more apparent is how marketers and commercial interests are extending and deepening their penetration of our lives through cyberspace. Back in the early 1930s, James Rorty called advertising 'our master's voice', referring to corporations and the power they held in US society (Rorty, 1934). In his view advertising provided a pervasive propaganda for capitalism and corporate domination of society. To the extent that this is true, Rorty lived in a non-commercial socialist republic in the 1930s compared to what Americans experience today. These intrusions can be limited, but technology will not do the job for us. To protect privacy and freedom requires explicit policies, and a government committed to the rule of law. Unless we take proactive steps, we may come to regret the day the computer was invented.

There are additional policy issues that must be resolved successfully for the Internet to even begin to fulfil its promise for society, and for journalism. For starters, if the Internet is to provide the foundation for free speech and a free press, it has to be ubiquitous, high-speed and inexpensive.

Our goal should be to have broadband access as a civil right for all Americans, at a nominal direct fee, much like access to water. This is not simply for political and cultural reasons, but for economic reasons as well. Already the decline of broadband speeds and the broadband penetration rate in the United States compared to European and Asian rivals is a factor under-mining economic innovation and growth. A 2007 article in *Information Week* put the US situation in context:

> The United States currently ranks 12th in broadband adoption rates, significantly down from its ranking of fourth in 2001, according to the Organization for Economic Co-operation and Development, a 30 member-nation group commit-ted to the development of democratic governments and market economies. The International Telecommunications Union lists the US as 21st worldwide for broadband penetration rate in 2005. Point Topic shows the United States is in 20th place by number of households with broadband access and in 19th by indi-vidual broadband access. Those ranks have been falling, not rising, in recent quarters. (Hoffman 2007; see also Turner 2006)

What accounts for the US decline? The first place to look is the stranglehold of the telephone and cable giants over broadband, due to their government-granted monopoly franchises granted in the pre-Internet era. These firms have no great desire to offer a service to poor people or difficult-to-reach rural areas, and they certainly have no interest in a ubiquitous service. It is far better to have a dirt lane to scare consumers into paying more to get faster service. And because broadband is an effective duopoly in the United States there is little market pressure to generate the speeds and lower costs that other nations are achieving. That would require enlightened regulation and plan-ning in the public interest, something the battalions of lobbyists these firms employ are commissioned to prevent.

The relationship of the telecommunication and cable giants to the progres-sive development of the Internet is not in doubt: it is almost non-existent. As Representative Edward Markey, Democrat of Massachusetts and chair of the subcommittee that oversees the Internet and telecommunication matters, put it in a 2007 speech,

> AT&T was offered, in 1966, the opportunity to build the Internet. They were offered the contract to build it. But they turned it down. Now let me ask you this:

what has AT&T done since then to develop the Internet? The answer is: nothing. What has Verizon done to help invent the World Wide Web? Nothing. What did they do in order to invent the browser? Nothing. These companies did virtually nothing to develop anything that has to do with what we now know as the Internet today. (Markey, 2007)

What the telephone and cable companies are singularly distinguished in is lobbying; their entire business models have been built on wooing politicians and regulators for monopoly licences and sweetheart regulations much more than serving consumers. It is the basis of their existence (see Lipartito, 1989, for a discussion of AT&T). They hope to parlay their world-class lobbying muscle into carving out a digital gold mine in this critical juncture. The boldest effort, and where the most important fight lays, is over their efforts to effectively privatise the Internet. The telephone and cable companies want the right to control which websites and services you can have access to, and which you cannot. If the AT&Ts and Verizons and Comcasts of the world are able to pull this off, all bets are off for the revolutionary potential of the digital revolution.

This struggle to keep the Internet open, to prevent the telephone and cable giants from controlling which websites get favoured treatment, is the battle to preserve Network Neutrality. The huge cable and phone companies are champing at the bit to set up a 'fast track' on the Internet for their favoured sites or those sites that gave them a cut of the action. Websites that refused to pay a premium would get the slow lane, and probably oblivion. The cable and telephone companies claim they need to have this monopoly power to generate sufficient profits to build out the broadband network, but the evidence for this claim is non-existent. Jeff Chester states that 'Cable and telephone subscribers have paid for a super-fast broadband network several times over. Network Neutrality will do absolutely nothing in terms of denting returns or slowing down deployment. Look, the reason that the cable and phone companies oppose Network Neutrality is they're desperate to extend their monopoly business model from multichannel video to the broadband world' (Gibbons, 2007). As an appalled Markey put it in 2007, 'And now they say they have a right to put up the toll roads, showing up as though they should own it all.' The stakes are so high that much of the balance of the business community, not to mention everyone else in society, is in favour of Network Neutrality, to the extent they know it is an issue at all.

The future of a free press is dependent upon ubiquitous, inexpensive and super-fast Internet access as well as Network Neutrality. In 2008, for example, the *Capital Times* of Madison, Wisconsin, became the first US daily newspaper to convert its operations to primarily digital production and distribution

– it went from ink and paper to bits. It could do so because of an agreement with the other daily newspaper in Madison that allowed the *Capital Times* a revenue base to cover what would be obvious losses for the immediate future as it entered the digital world (Rosenthal, 2008). It did this despite concerns that many of its older and poorer readers would lose access to the paper, and recognising the uncertainty that Net Neutrality would be maintained so the phone and cable companies wouldn't demand a ransom for the newspaper to have access to the public. For the Internet to develop as the viable basis for a free press, ending the digital divide and stopping corporate privatisation of the Internet (and the broader realm of digital communication) are mandatory.

That being said, although necessary, protecting online privacy, establishing a ubiquitous and high-speed Internet and maintaining, Net Neutrality will not solve the crisis of journalism. Among the most important lessons we have learned in the past decade has been that doing good media, even in the digital era, requires resources and institutional support. The Internet does many things, but it does not wave a magic wand over media bank accounts. I recall a conversation I had with a prominent retired television journalist in 2004. He told me with great enthusiasm that with the Internet all his journalistic needs were met: he could find all the reporting he needed from around the world on his computer. He went on and on about how he now read the great newspapers of the world online every morning. He compared his blissful situation with the Dark Ages BI (Before Internet), when access to such a range of news media would have been pretty much impossible, even for world leaders and corporate CEOs. I asked this retired journalist what the Internet informed him on doings in Schenectady, New York. He looked at me quizzically, thinking I must be from Schenectady and probably feeling some measure of sympathy for me. But, as I explained, my point was that the Internet made existing journalism available, but it was not creating lots of new journalism, and by that I mean research and reporting, not just commenting on someone else's research and reporting. And, I told him, it was not clear how existing journalism would segue to the Internet and maintain its revenue base while commercial pressures were lowering the resources going to journalism overall. In community after community, like Schenectady, there was precious little journalism, and *Le Monde* was assigning no correspondents to cover the Schenectady School Board meeting. He conceded the point.

This is not to deny the potential of the blogoshere, social networks and citizen journalists. No matter what happens, their emergence is radically changing journalism, and often for the better (Gant, 2007). Even beyond the notion of citizen journalists, the digital revolution is opening up the potential of access to information that still boggles the mind, even as we approach the end of the second decade of the world wide web. The ability of people to collaborate and work together to share and expand knowledge – exemplified by wikis – is revolutionary, in the literal meaning of the word (Sunstein, 2006). But the need for paid journalists who work full time, have resources, generate expertise and have institutional support to protect them from governmental or corporate harassment remains as strong as ever. And having competing newsrooms of such journalists is just as important. Citizen journalism and social information networks will flower in a marriage with enhanced professional journalism, not as a replacement for it.

So we cannot sit by and expect the Internet or the market place to solve the crisis. In fact, the crisis is so severe, and the stakes are so high, that even if we could win the policy fights for more journalism education, more media literacy, more student media, more local commercial media, more foundation support, digital privacy and ubiquitous, inexpensive, super-fast Internet access with Net Neutrality, that would be helpful but insufficient to accomplish the task at hand. There is no magic policy bullet to solve the problem, no single policy to pursue to correct the situation, and any possible solutions might only come about as part of a broader movement for social reform.

Another layer of policies are those that more aggressively shape the news media system and that are legitimate within the range of policy debates in the United States. These include anti-trust and communication laws to promote diverse media ownership, as well as using postal subsidies to encourage a broad range of publications. The single most valuable of these may be the tradition of establishing non-profit and non-commercial broadcast media, specifically public and community broadcasting, and public access television channels. In other nations public and community broadcasters have been a stalwart of quality independent journalism, and buffers against commercial degeneration.

We can now see that the obituary for public broadcasting was premature. In the 1990s it was widely assumed that the plethora of digital channels rendered publicly subsidised media moot, because there would be an array of commercial options for every conceivable need. Now it is clear that this is not the case, and in fact there are core media needs that commercialism can never fulfil. Accordingly, we have to rethink public media in a revolutionary manner, and with digital technologies we have the tools to do so. It can be a pluralistic and heterogeneous sector with a variety of structures and missions. Non-commercial and non-profit public media remain strikingly popular in those nations where the institutions have been well established, and even in the United States, where public broadcasting has been at most a marginal institution, it has shown surprising resiliency. (Britain spends more than fifty times more per capita in public funds on the BBC than the United States does on

NPR and PBS.) It is true that the *broadcasting* in 'public broadcasting' may soon be obsolete, but the *public* will not.

There are two areas where public and community broadcasters cum media can play a central role: first, in the provision of local journalism. The commercial broadcasting system has degraded, if not abandoned, this aspect of its operations. If US public and community broadcasters had BBC-type funding, which would translate into some $20 billion annually, there could be multiple competing public newsrooms, with different organisation structures, in scores of communities. That might provide a competitive spur to the commercial news media to get back in the game, especially as they see there is an interest in the material. Yes, I know, people will say $20 billion is a lot of money, and will require massive tax hikes to be justified, and nobody will be willing to go for that. But spending that sort of money is small potatoes and hardly subject to debate when Wall Street howls about a crisis or when there is a Third World country to invade on the other side of the globe. It is all a matter of priorities. And even with far less than $20 billion, public and community media could do wonders for the currently decimated local news media landscape.

Second, one concern generally under-discussed is how the Internet allows Americans to construct a personalised media world where they share common experiences with fewer and fewer of the fellow citizens. As Cass Sunstein argues, this 'Daily Me' that people construct on their web makes them share far less with each other than in the past, especially with people they might disagree with on matters of politics or culture. This may be a form of 'freedom' for the individual, but it exacts what may be a very high social cost. What follows is a 'group polarisation', as people grow less informed, less respectful and more distrustful of people outside their own group. There is a withering of the experiences that provide the bonds that make us understand that we are all in this together. Sunstein concludes that this produces a 'real problem for democracy' (Sunstein, 2008). In addition, this 'group polarisation' is strongly egged on by the desire or need of marketers to split Americans up into bite-sized demographic groups so that it is easier to sell them things. As Sunstein's analysis implies, journalism is at the centre of what Americans need to share if they are going to have a viable republic.

The evidence is in: commercial journalism is comfortable serving the demographic groups that are most profitable for the owners and desirable to advertisers, and disregarding less lucrative parts of the population (Fairness & Accuracy in Reporting, 2007). It is these and other supply-side factors – far lower costs and lack of controversy with powerful political and commercial interests – that pushed the news to celebrity and scandals and natural disasters and regurgitating political spin, not public demand.

The political economy of media has always been about the task of enhancing participatory democracy; media and communication systems are a means to an end, with the end being social justice and human happiness. We need satisfactory journalism and media systems to have a just and sustainable society. We study media so closely, because in a democratic society journalism is the primary means through which the mass of people may effectively equip themselves to effectively participate. The assumption that new media technology, such as the Internet, provides grounds for such participation regardless of political economy is incorrect and misleading. It would certainly aid a recovery from the crisis of journalism to ensure universal access to an open Internet at a time when corporate interests would have it become primarily a conduit for commercialised content, in an extension of the logic that caused the crisis. However, whether digital or not, it is public broadcasting cum media that is in the best position to provide the basis for a common shared journalism to which all Americans can relate. Public and community media cannot do this by themselves, nor should they, but they can provide a necessary and valuable foundation.

REFERENCES

Cushman, John H. Jr (2008) 'Web site assembles US prewar claims', *New York Times*, 23 January, A12.

Downie, Leonard Jr and Kaiser, Robert G. (2002) *The News About the News: American Journalism in Peril* (New York: Alfred A. Knopf).

Economist (2008) 'Alternative reality', *The Economist*, 2 February, 69–70.

Fairness & Accuracy in Reporting (2007) *Extra!* September–October.

Gant, Scott (2007) *We're All Journalists Now: The Transformation of the Press and Reshaping of the Law in the Internet Age* (New York: Free Press).

Gibbons, Kent (2007) 'Five questions for Jeff Chester', *MultiChannel News*, 5 February, http://www.multichannel.com/article/CA6413144.html?display=Opinion, accessed 7 October 2009.

Gore, Al (2006) *An Inconvenient Truth: The Crisis of Global Warming* (New York: Viking).

Gore, Al (2007) *The Assault on Reason* (New York: Penguin).

Henry, Neil (2007) *American Carnival: Journalism under Siege in an Age of New Media* (Berkeley: University of California Press).

Hoffman, Richard (2007) 'When it comes to broadband, US plays follow the leader', *Information Week*, 15 February, http://www.informationweek.com/story/show Article.jhtml?articleID=197006038, accessed 7 October 2009.

Kimball, Penn (1994) *Downsizing the News: Network Cutbacks in the Nation's Capital* (Washington, DC: Woodrow Wilson Center).

Lipartito, Kenneth (1989) *The Bell System and Regional Business: The Telephone in the South, 1877–1920* (Baltimore: Johns Hopkins University Press).

McChesney, Robert (1997) *Corporate Media and the Threat to Democracy* (New York: Seven Stories).

McManus, John H. (1994) *Market-Driven Journalism: Let the Citizen Beware?* (Thousand Oaks, CA: Sage).

Markey, Edward (2007) Comments made at National Conference on Media Reform, Memphis, TN, 13 January.

Martin, Kevin J. (2007) 'The daily show', *The New York Times*, 13 November.

New York Times (2007) 'Spies, lies and FISA', *New York Times*, 14 October.

Nichols, John and McChesney, Robert W. (2005) *Tragedy and Farce: How American Media Sell Wars, Spin Elections and Destroy Democracy* (New York: The New Press).

Patterson, Thomas E. (preparer) (2007) *Creative Destruction: An Exploratory Look at News on the Internet* (Cambridge, MA: Joan Shorenstein Center on the Press, Politics and Public Policy, Harvard University).

Powers, William (2007) 'Hamlet's blackberry: why paper is eternal', Discussion Paper Series, Joan Shorenstein Center on the Press, Politics and Public Policy, Harvard University.

Rorty, James (1934) *Our Master's Voice: Advertising* (New York: John Day).

Rosenthal, Phil (2008) 'Cap Times puts cap on print editions', *Chicago Tribune*, 10 February.

Saba, Jennifer (2008) 'The new math: putting numbers to work for you', *Editor and Publisher*, January, 22–4.

Schechter, Danny (2008) 'New study claims mistruths shaped rush to war', 27 January, http://www.commondream.org, accessed 7 October 2009.

Schudson, Michael (2007) 'Owning up: a new book stops short of deepening the discourse on media concentration', *Columbia Journalism Review*, January–February, 58.

Scott, Ben (2007) 'Labor's new deal for journalism: the Newspaper Guild in the 1930s', PhD thesis, University of Illinois.

Squires, James D. (1995) *Read All About It! The Corporate Takeover of America's Newspapers* (New York: Random House).

Strupp, Joe (2008) 'Another chip in the wall', *Editor and Publisher*, January, 30–6.

Sunstein, Cass R. (2006) *Infotopia: How Many Minds Produce Knowledge* (New York: Oxford University Press).

Sunstein, Cass R. (2008) 'How the rise of the Daily Me threatens democracy', *Financial Times*, 11 January, 9.

Turner, S. Derek (2006) *Broadband Reality Check II: The Truth Behind America's Digital Decline*, Free Press, http://www.freepress.net/docs/bbrc2-final.pdf, accessed 7 October 2009.

Underwood, Doug (1993) *When MBAs Rule the Newsroom: How Marketers and Managers are Reshaping Today's Media* (New York: Columbia University Press).

CHAPTER 4

When magical realism confronted virtual reality: online news and journalism in Latin America

JAIRO LUGO-OCANDO AND ANDRÉS CAÑIZÁLEZ

Very few regions in the world have raised, and crushed, as many hopes as Latin America. If the United States is often referred to in the folk imagination as the land of opportunities, Latin America instead figures as the land of wasted opportunities. As in the recurrent myth of *El Dorado*, the region has constantly searched in vain for quasi-miraculous new discoveries to wrench it free from poverty and unfulfilled potential. However, for the region, modernity in the face of technology has a very different meaning: one of imposed expectations. One could almost say that Latin Americans have come to see the arrival of the Internet in the same way that the town of Macondo came to see the ice brought by the gypsy Melquíades in Gabriel García Márquez's novel *One Hundred Years of Solitude*. In no place in Latin America is this more true than in the newsrooms across the region. In a continent that still stumbles through democracy, the arrival of the Internet has meant that news media are expected to be better, more open and far more accurate. But, as with the ice in the story of Gabriel Garcia Márquez, these expectations can rapidly melt in the daylight.

This chapter discusses the arrival of the Internet in Latin America and asks what it means for newsgathering and news dissemination in the context of the region's politics and development. In so doing, it aims to provide a comprehensive and critical understanding of the significance of online news in the construction of media politics. The aim is to explore issues relating to the news agenda, social mobilisation and political power in the light of the emergence of interactive and digital media. We address how online news is affecting the way journalists gather news, the manner in which media outlets disseminate news content and how Latin Americans are consuming online news in the context of the different social dynamics happening in the continent.

We argue for a distinction between mainstream online provision and alternative news media. In the first case, we examine the online outlets created by traditional mainstream media and how they have developed over the years. In the second case, we study the role of civil society in using the Internet as a way of breaking the monopoly of traditional mainstream media over the news agenda: when, for example, the Internet is used by third party sectors to disseminate information that otherwise would have little or no resonance in the mainstream media.

Latin America online

When it comes to the media, one should not adopt generalist approaches that assume a homogeneous Latin America (Lugo, 2008, p. 2). However, there are common trends regarding the media landscape that can provide a useful understanding of online news in the area. For example, it is noted that the region has embraced the Internet as quickly as its limited resources have allowed. By 2008, 154 million people – nearly one-quarter of the entire population of Latin America – connected to the Internet on a regular basis (Datanálisis, 2008). The same data suggest that, at the current growth rate, this usage will reach 40 per cent of the population in the next five years.

However, even though the media landscape is changing at an astonishing pace in this part of the world, the use of the Internet is still widely defined by income. The US Internet consultancy firm ComScore in its World Metrix Report of 2007 states that only 53 million people (less than 10 per cent of the whole population) have Internet access in their homes. Furthermore, the relationship between Internet usage and the position of the country in the Human Development Index is revealing:

> the further down a country goes on the HDI table, the less likely it is that its citizens use the Internet on a regular basis; all of which suggests that the Internet is a mirror that reflects 'the inequalities and injustices of the societies into which it is inserted'. (Gomez, 2004, p. 72)

Other studies suggest that the Internet is mainly accessed from public places such as cybercafés and libraries (Lugo and Sampson, 2008, p. 110). This is of particular significance in understanding online news consumption in the region. Previous research has shown that the same user at home or on a private computer tends to view different pages from those they view when accessing the Internet from a public library or cybercafé (Datanálisis, 2009, p. 8).

Despite the fact that access to and use of the Internet follows income and wealth distribution, there are other intervening variables in defining exceptional cases in terms of usage. For example, the expansion of particular technologies – such as mobile phones – needs additional research. Indeed, there are increasing numbers of people connecting to the Internet via their mobile phones in Latin America without the limitations imposed by income. Fifty-four per cent of the 523 million people living in Latin America in 2007 had a mobile phone (Uval, 2008). In some countries, such as Venezuela and Argentina, the penetration of the mobile phone is even higher: 80–90 per cent of people in these two countries have a registered mobile line.

It is possible to predict that the future of online news in Latin America will be via mobile phone, for both commercial and alternative news. This was clearly exemplified by the role played by mobile phones in allowing people to bypass traditional media agendas and organise protests from 2001 during 'The corralito' when the Argentinean government froze all bank accounts (René, 2002) and in 2002 in Venezuela during the attempted coup against President Hugo Chávez (Hernandez, 2007). In both cases mobile phones were instrumental in informing people of what was happening after the traditional news had blacked out the events.

However, a predominant characteristic of online news in Latin America is that it is still by far an activity carried out by white middle-class men who have in mind other white middle-class men as their main public. With few exceptions, the diversity of cultures and gender realities is often ignored by online news editors in the same way that they were also largely ignored by their broadcast and print predecessors. In Bolivia, where there are more than thirty-five officially recognised cultures and languages, and in Peru, where more than 45 per cent of the population are Native Americans who do not speak Spanish as their first language, there are only a few online provisions for the widely spoken languages Quechua and Aymara (Díaz Nosty, 2007, p. 55). For millions of Native Americans there is hardly any or no online provision from the mainstream outlets (Cely, 2006, p. 133). On top of this, mainstream online news outlets have continued with the old practices of ignoring indigenous issues in their agendas, where there is little or no presence of indigenous people's themes and problems (Convenio Minga, 2005, p. 165).

Nor has the Internet ended gender discrimination in the news. Women account for only 38 per cent of the total number of Internet users, even though they represent 51 per cent of the population in the region (Castellanos, 2002). Although the Internet has created a lifeline for some women activists (Friedman, 2007, p. 799), their socio-economic and political issues are nevertheless largely absent from the mainstream online news agenda, in which they are largely underrepresented (Gerber, 2003, p. 3); this in a continent where women still lag behind men in terms of income, education and civil rights. Mainstream online news outlets have continued with old practices of essentialising women in stereotypical representations, while excluding them from participating in the net; the proportion of women journalists in editorial and managerial positions in the online newsroom is still below their representation in society (WACC, 2005). It is not very different in the case of participation in publishing on the Internet, where overall women are still underrepresented (Erazo and Schmitt, 2006, p. 10). Indeed, research sponsored by Fundación Telefónica in twenty-three countries in Latin America showed that fewer than 30 per cent of all blogs were set up and updated by women (Díaz Nosty, 2007, p. 49).

What is it for?

This lack of representation and diversity in online news is complicated by the fact that the Internet in Latin America is not necessarily being used to gather hard news by the wider public. Instead, usage data suggest that the main sites visited by Latin Americans are those that offer general services (Datanálisis, 2009) or that can be used as a diasporic networking platform by those living abroad (Bailey, 2007). Because of this, the most visited sites in Latin America are those that offer e-mail services, chartrooms, information reference and electronic commerce. Website groups such as Microsoft (with 47,342,000 unique visitors), Google (46,496,000), Yahoo! (35,075,000), Terra Networks (27,421,000), MercadoLibre (23,739,000) and Wikipedia (20,984,000) ranked in 2008 as the most visited places by users in that region. Only sports news sites related to Fox Interactive Media (with 14,078,000 unique visitors) manage to position themselves among these groups (Lipsman, 2007).

Nowadays, online media in Latin America seem to be evolving in ways that can adapt to the patterns of consumption where service and entertainment are a priority, and not hard news (Cabrera Paz, 2005, pp. 12, 159), and where the predominance of infotainment demands that mainstream online news is accompanied or even preceded by lighter content and services (Ford, 2005, p. 32). Newspapers such as *El Universal* in Mexico, which in the past were very conservative in their approach towards journalism in general (Hughes,

2006, p. 132), have now created their own TV channel for the net (so people can see their news instead of reading it), while adding as prominent features of their menu services such as classified, a television guide, discussion blogs and even a guide to what to do in one's free time.

The problem for mainstream media ventures on the Internet is that they rushed to develop their websites following the promises of new markets. In most cases this translated into electronic versions of their print or broadcast counterparts, copying both style and content. The traditional media outlet did not always have a clear idea of where to go or what to do in the new digital age. During an interview with a news editor in Venezuela, he confessed that back in 2000 the company had decided to take the newspaper online because it was the general trend, but that in fact no one on the editorial board 'knew exactly what market niche they were suppose to target' (interview with the authors on 20 February 2009).

Commercial online news ventures are still struggling to develop into sustainable projects: 61 per cent of online news ventures in Latin America do not cover their costs and are 'subsidised' by their print newspapers, while 28 per cent of them do not generate any kind of income (ElTiempo.com, 2007). Fifty per cent of these sites do not sell advertising at all or report a very small income from it, while only 10 per cent sell some type of content. This has led to 83 per cent of all news online sites considering charging their users, and 61 per cent have managed to register users that access the site. Among the models considered for future operations is charging micro-payments in a similar way to Apple's iTunes Music Store. But as Eladio Muchacho, owner of *El Diario de Los Andes* in Venezuela, states: 'We are still a long way from seeing people paying for content' (interview with the authors on 20 February 2009). In other cases, mainstream online news media are developing business models that are less dependent on advertising revenue. For example, *El Nacional*, the second most read newspaper in Venezuela, is now charging its customers for access to its content, while *El Comercio* in Ecuador and *El Mercurio* in Chile have created a series of pay-as-you-go services for mobile phones. In so doing, they are trying to diversify their sources of funding.

Despite the fact that the market for the 'new media' has still not materialised in the anticipated form that many predicted (Mansell, 2002, p. 409), this has not affected subsequent waves of interest in participating in the Internet phenomenon. After the dotcom burst of the late 1990s the traditional media outlets in Latin America cut back on their initial investment in the net. The twenty-first century did see a renewed interest in online news ventures but with far less investment (Vialey et al. in Lugo, 2008, p. 18). This meant embracing convergence not only as a technological reality but also as a managerial strategy to reduce costs and rationalise operations (Mastrini and Becerra, 2007, p. 19).

One of the most emblematic cases appears to be Casa Editorial El Tiempo, publisher of daily newspaper *El Tiempo* in Colombia and one of Latin America's top online news content providers. After experimenting with an ambitious online project in the early 1990s, the daily newspaper *El Tiempo* moved in the mid-1990s to outsource its website to the ISP Terra (ElTiempo.com, 2000), a project that failed to fulfil the expectations of both partners. However, since 2001 Casa Editorial El Tiempo, which by then also owned the television channel CityTV and a series of bestselling magazines, has pursued a more convergent strategy by merging its different newsrooms and integrating content from all of its media outlets in its Internet sites. Bought in 2007 by the Spanish Group Planeta, one of the biggest media groups in the world, Casa Editorial El Tiempo has now announced further synergies in all its media outlets and the recycling of its news content to mobile phones used by Colombians in the country and abroad (Crisp Wireless, 2008).

A national issue

It is precisely these types of media conglomerates that have come to dominate online news in Latin America, which in itself is largely defined by national audiences. Indeed, the news sites that receive the highest number of visitors are those of the three top selling newspapers in the most populated countries: Brazil (*O Globo* and *Folha de São Paulo*), Argentina (*La Nación* and *Clarín*) and Mexico (*El Universal* and *Reforma*). The promise of a new world in which independent and alternative sites would overtake mainstream commercial media did not materialise in the region.

If it is true that some independent players stepped in, it is no less true that they had limited impact in terms of reaching mainstream audiences inside their own countries. Latin America does not have an equivalent to blogs such as Gizmodo or Perez Hilton that reach mass audiences. While hits to US bloggers reach the millions, Latin American bloggers hardly reach the thousands. Yoani Sanchez in her *Generación Y* blog manages to reach hundreds of thousands abroad, but fewer than 1 per cent of Cubans, for whom the Internet is a 'political luxury' (Kalathil and Boas, 2003, p. 49). Even well publicised sites such as Indymedia have struggled to reach out in such a difficult market where 'only a fraction of those that use the Internet read news online in Latin America' (Criterios, 2008) and where those who do so tend to go directly to mainstream sites.

One of the few areas where there seems to be a slightly different pattern emerging is in the use of news portals similar to the *Drudge Report* in the USA. In Venezuela, for example, the news portals *Noticierodigital.com*, *Aporrea.org* and *Noticias24.com*, both with hyperlinks to the news of the day from other media but with almost no original content, compete directly on the Internet with the mainstream news content providers. These portals not only provide a place to find most of the available news of the day, they also offer forums and blogs for each news item that receive dozens if not hundreds of responses. But these portals seem to be the exception, since it is the commercial mainstream media that are the dominating news sources on the Internet.

Another important aspect to mention is that neither commercial nor alternative news sites have been able to transcend national frontiers beyond their own diasporas. Not even across Latin America itself has it been possible to reach continental audiences. For example, despite several revamp efforts, CNN's Latin American news website (which took its content from the news channel CNN en Español) was unable to become economically viable or reach enough audiences and was finally turned into a static promotional site for the television channel, with no news updates. A more recent attempt by the governments of Argentina, Bolivia, Cuba, Ecuador and Venezuela to develop a Latin American news website (which takes its content from the news channel TeleSur) has not been very successful either (Cañizález and Lugo, 2007, p. 58). In this region, online news consumption still depends on the ability of the media to successfully engage with national and local markets rather than creating new transnational ones.

The 'new' newsroom

In such limited national markets, news media are merging their newsrooms to save costs. A survey carried out by the Inter American Press Association (IAPA) among the forty-three top-selling newspapers in Latin America showed that 74 per cent of them were planning to merge their print and online newsrooms into a single team, although so far only 4 per cent have done so (Espinosa, 2007). Online news is in fact a neglected area in terms of resources to carry out high-quality and investigative journalism. Only 24 per cent of the newspapers in Latin America have more than three journalists dedicated to their online version and most of the journalists (53 per cent) had no formal training in this area before being entrusted with developing the news site.

The study, which was co-sponsored by the Foundation for New Latin American Journalism, created by the Nobel Prize winning novelist Gabriel

García Márquez, indicated that online journalists receive lower pay than their counterparts and suffer 'discrimination' in the news organization. The same study underlines that almost 90 per cent of all online journalists are aged between twenty and thirty and that this is their first full-time job. According to Guillermo Franco, the director of Eltiempo.com who produced this report for IAPA, over 60 per cent of all news online content comes from the print and broadcast media. He also indicates that only 10 per cent of the online versions of newspapers are updated constantly, while 61 per cent are updated once every 15–20 hours.

This research confirms that on very few occasion do online news media themselves carry out investigative reporting. Instead, they limit themselves to writing and editing for the web what others produce. Furthermore, investigative work or in-depth reporting carried out by print and broadcast media is not posted on the net until it has exhausted its commercial cycle or is outdated. The majority of online journalists and editors are limited to performing basic sub-editing functions, while very few go out onto the streets to gather news:

> None of the Latin American papers' online operations consider reporting to be the focus of their journalists' activity; the vast majority believe their focus is text writing and editing. A small percentage think it is the generation of multimedia content. (Franco and Guzmán, 2004)

Nevertheless, the introduction of the Internet into the newsroom has had an important impact on journalistic practices in general and newsgathering techniques in particular. Although excessive dependence on the Internet in the process of newsgathering has been criticised in places such as the United Kingdom (Davies, 2008), it has nevertheless provided newsrooms in Latin America with additional tools for gathering information, with the potential to support more contextualized news reporting (Buitrón, 2005).

This is especially true in areas such as current affairs and foreign news, where access to sources is chronically limited and dependent on international news agencies: this has historically represented a huge financial burden for local and national newspapers (Díaz Rangel, 1976, p. 101). Ninety-one per cent of Latin American newsrooms now use the Internet to enrich their own coverage of international news and help them contextualise current affairs instead of relying only on the versions of events offered by the traditional news service such as Associated Press, EFE and Reuters (Espinosa, 2007).

Resistance and censorship

However, commercial online news ventures are just one part of the story in Latin America. The emergence of a blogosphere, in which alternative voices are able to break the information oligopoly of the mainstream media, is a story that deserves equal attention and that offers a slightly different perspective. The rise of 'participatory publishing' (Nguyen, 2008, p. 94) has coincided with important political transformations in Latin America, where there has been a shift to the left of the political spectrum in places such as Argentina, Bolivia, Brazil, Ecuador, Guatemala, Honduras, Nicaragua, Uruguay and Venezuela.

In the past ten years in all of these countries voters have elected left-wing leaders who, almost immediately after assuming power, have clashed with large sections of the mainstream private media. This is because many of the new governments have put social justice and wealth redistribution at the core of their political programmes, something that has encountered the stiff opposition of the mainstream media, which have traditionally been allied to the right and often defenders of neoliberal ideas. In places such as Bolivia, Ecuador and Venezuela, this has meant an open confrontation between the new left-wing governments and the mainstream media. In some cases, the media have promoted and supported protests and even military coups against democratically elected governments (Lugo and Romero, 2003).

Commercial mainstream media had an instrumental role in the 2002 coup in Venezuela (Díaz Rangel, 2003). In order to break the news fence imposed by the private commercial media, which saw the self-proclaimed socialist President Hugo Chávez as a threat to their own interests, some government supporters went online and started spreading messages through mobile phones. The objective was to explain to the world what was really happening, while trying to influence public opinion inside the country by deconstructing the news agenda (Hernández Montoya, 2002).

However, online news in Latin America has not escaped censorship, even at the start of the Internet revolution. On 12 April 1997 Jose Vicente Rangel – who would later become vice-president under Hugo Chávez – in an article in the newspaper *El Universal* registered the fact that Venezuela witnessed the first case of Internet censorship in Latin America. Indeed, *El Diario del Lago* was removed from the net by officials, who closed it down (Revista Producto, 1997) after the online site published a story about a coal company linked to one of the president's sons, which had obtained permission to install a coal port in the Gulf of Venezuela, in an area considered to be ecologically fragile.

A more recent case of censorship of online news services in Latin America involves the Cuban blogger Yoani Sánchez, who has been constantly harassed by the authorities. In addition to this, Sánchez, who has received the prestigious Ortega y Gasset prize for online journalism, was beaten up by security forces in August 2008 and since then her blog has been blocked on several occasions. Sánchez was subsequently accused by the Cuban authorities of undermining the revolution and denied the right to travel abroad (Israel, 2009).

Despite these cases, overall there are important new possibilities in the region thanks to the Internet. The IAPA study highlights the fact that 85 per cent of all newspapers would allow their journalists to start their own blogs, although news editors do consider that some type of filters and mediation to comments made by readers should be put in place beforehand. It also says that 92 per cent of online newspapers have 'more autonomy and freedom' to publish than their print counterparts.

However, it is in alternative websites such as aporrea.org in Venezuela that most expectations are now placed. Created in 2002 after the attempted coup and as a response to the general strike called by the opposition to overthrow the government, aporrea.org was from the beginning a site dedicated to counterbalancing the news agenda set by the private media in Venezuela. The site defines itself as a 'collective and voluntary effort' to provide an alternative view of the news (Aporrea.org, 2007). The website is part of a wider effort to influence the news agenda in Venezuela and an active source of political support for Hugo Chavez's government. It is now among the ten most visited news sites in Venezuela and has an active role in counterbalancing the news agenda of the mainstream commercial media.

These types of alternative news sites and the proliferation of blogs have opened up an important space for news items that would had been in the past censored or ignored. So even if some of these new alternative voices struggle to reach mass audiences they should nevertheless be welcome. Their very presence in a region that still exhibits one of the worst records in terms of journalists censored, imprisoned and killed is a beacon of hope in the darkness of Latin America's media history.

Beyond 'El Dorado'

As we discussed above, the arrival of the Internet in Latin America coincided with a time of profound political transformations. The Internet was hailed as a new medium that would allow the emergence of a new global public sphere that was not conditioned by the old national imperatives of the traditional media. The experiences of resistance groups such as the Zapatistas in Mexico were highlighted by some authors as the beginning of a new era (Castells,

1997, p. 80). For these authors, the new technologies permitted the Zapatistas to gain a presence on the world news agenda and gather global support (Knudson, 1998, p. 509), preventing the Mexican armed forces from crushing them militarily as they had done in 1968 with the students at Tlatelolco in a similar movement (Villasmil, 2002).

This was nevertheless part of the myth of the so-called digital era in Latin America, since the guerrilla group did not actually have access to the Internet, a laptop or even a fax (Ronfeldt et al., 1999, p. 23). These technological devices were in the hands of transnational actors represented in Mexico by NGOs, and it was their intervention that in part prevented a second massacre from happening (Hughes, 2006, p. 170).

Far from the original promise of being ground-breaking, irreverent or influential, online journalism practised in the Latin American mainstream media is still in its infancy; it is still by far a marginal activity restricted to the very few. Largely underresourced and disregarded by news editorial management, online news still struggles in the market and hardly makes it onto the news agenda. Not even the news sources themselves seem to take online news seriously, and they often ignore it all together and rarely invite online journalists to press conferences or media events. Even in places such as Argentina, Bolivia, Ecuador and Venezuela, where tensions have politically mobilised those societies, online news is still far from capturing the imagination of the collective.

In this context, online journalism in Latin America is no different from any other place in the world since it still has one unique imperative: to make news relevant again for the individual (Singer, 2008, p. 124). However, the difference in the case of online news is that it has the time, space and potential to achieve this. It can offer context and depth that neither radio nor television can offer. It does not have to deal with the distribution issues that print media have to confront. And thanks to the exponential growth in mobile phone use it can also potentially overcome socio-economic gaps.

Nevertheless, online journalism is not solely about technology but also about content. Therefore to succeed it needs equally to engage with a public that is increasingly detached from the political process. Its future achievements will depend on the quality of the news gathered and produced and its ethical relevance to national and regional development. As Gabriel García Márquez said in a 2008 interview, it will only be when 'those media spaces which have been marketised are able to assume the true dimension of their own value as vehicles for the transformation of society [that] the path of transition will be [made] easier for all' (interviewed by Rodríguez Leija, 2008).

However, to achieve this, online journalism needs to realise its potential to foster diversity and to create new spaces for dialogue and – why not? – also to facilitate confrontation when required. It needs to boldly go where very few traditional media have dared to go: that is, to embrace the new political realities and aspirations of social inclusion. After all, and despite all the techno-hype and hopes regarding Latin America and the Internet, the truth is that development, politics and journalism are as intertwined as ever in this part of the world.

REFERENCES

Aporrea.org (2007) Sobre Aporrea.org, http://www.aporrea.org/nosotros.php, accessed 12 February 2009.

Bailey, O. G. (ed.) (2007) *Transnational Lives and Media: Re-imagining Diasporas* (London: Palgrave).

Buitrón, R. D. (2005) 'Nuevos desafíos en las salas de redacción', *Revista Latinoamericana de Comunicación Chasqui*, 90, http://chasqui.comunica.org/content/view/57/55, accessed 22 January 2009).

Cabrera Paz, J (2005) *Náufragos y navegantes en territorios hipermediales. Experiencias psicosociales y prácticas culturales en la apropiación del Internet en jóvenes. Internet y Sociedad en América Latina y el Caribe* (Quito: FLACSO Ecuador/IDRC).

Cañizález, A. (2008) 'Capítulo venezolano', in C. Castro (ed.) *Industrias de Contenidos en Latinoamérica. Comisión Económica para América Latina y El Caribe (CEPAL)* (Santiago de Chile: Unión Europea y Alianza para la Sociedad de Información).

Cañizález, A. (coordinater) (2009) *Tiempos de cambio. Política y comunicación en América Latina* (Caracas: Universidad Católica Andrés Bello y Asociación Latinoamericana de Investigadores de la Comunicación).

Cañizález, A. and Lugo, J. (2007) 'Telesur: estrategia geopolítica con fines integracionistas', *Revista Confines*, 6, 53–64.

Castellanos, A. (2002) 'Women in action. ICT applications in Latin America: from information to knowledge-building, no. 2, http://www.isiswomen.org/wia/wia2202/ictlatam.htm, accessed 4 March 2009).

Castells, M. (1997) *The Information Age: Economy, Society and Culture Volume II: The Power of Identity* (Malden, MA: Blackwell).

Cely, A. (2006) 'Estructura editorial de los cybermedios en Venezuela', In M. Rojano (ed.), *Diez annos de periodismo digital en Venezuela 1996–2006* (Caracas: Publicaciones UCAB).

Convenio Minga (2005) *Monitoreo de Medios. La representación de lo indígena en lops medios de comunicación* (Santiago de Cali, Colombia: Universidad del Valle).

Crisp Wireless (2008) 'El Tiempo and Crisp Wireless create first Latin American mobile news website', *Crisp Wireless Press Release*, 23 June, http://www.crispwireless.com/about/news?content_id=1134, accessed 2 April 2009.

Criterios (2008) 'SIP: los diarios y el desafio de las audiencias on-line', *Criterios Periodismo Independiente*, http://www.criterios.com/modules.php?name=Noticias&file=article&sid=14073, accessed 10 February 2009.

Datanálisis (2005) 'Indicadores de penetración y uso de Internet en venezuela', http://www.tendenciasdigitales.com.ve/td/documentos/Penetracion_ In ternet_Diciembre_2004.pdf, accessed 18 March 2009.

Datanálisis (2008) 'Internet market penetration and usage indicators in Latin America', Tendencias Digitales, May, http://www.datanalisis.com/website/site/ p_contenido.asp?sec=11&det=21, accessed 12 June 2009.

Datanálisis (2009) *Estudio de Usos de Internet en Latinoamérica* (Caracas: Tendencias Digitales).

Davidziuk, A. (2007) 'Cannibalism, creolization and baroque mobile use', Regulateonline.org, http://ci-journal.net/index.php/ciej/article/view/455/344, accesssed 11 December 2008.

Davies, N. (2009) *Flat Earth News: An Award-winning Reporter Exposes Falsehood, Distortion and Propaganda in the Global Media* (London: Chatto & Windus).

Díaz Nosty, B. (2007) *Tendencias '07. Medios de Comunicación. El Escenario Iberoamericano* (Madrid: Editorial Ariel, SA).

Díaz Rangel, E. (1976) *Pueblos sub-informados* (Caracas: Monte Avila Editores).

Díaz Rangel, E. (2003) '¿Dónde está la sociedad civil?', *Ultimas Noticias*, 9 March, 4.

ElTiempo.com (2000) 'Alianza Terra-El Tiempo', *El Tiempo*, 17 July, http:// www.eltiempo.com/archivo/documento/MAM-1279727, accessed 29 March 2009.

ElTiempo.com (2007) *Periodistas digitales en America Latina discrimnados y con menores ingresos que sus colegas del papel* (Bogota: Sociedad Interamericana de Prensa).

Erazo, V. and Schmitt, O. (2006) *Panorama de la Observación Critica de los Medios de Comunicación en America Latina. Visión Global y Local – Perspectiva de Género – Participación Ciudadana* (Santiago de Chile: Observatorio de medios FUCATEL/OXFAM).

Espinosa, C. (2007) '¿Cómo le va al periodismo digital en América Latina? El 74% anuncia fusión de las redacciones', 16 March, http://www.coberturadigital.com/ 2007/03/16/¿como-le-va-al-periodismo-digital-en-america-latina-el-74-anuncia-fusion-de-las-redacciones, accessed 12 December 2008.

Ford, A. (2005) *Resto del mundo. Nuevas mediaciones en las agendas criticas interna-cionales* (Buenos Aires: Editorial Norma).

Franco, G. and Guzmán, J. C. (2004) 'The state of online journalism in Latin America', *PoynterOnline* 5 May, http://www.poynter.org/content/content_view. asp?id=64532, accessed 5 January 2009.

Friedman, E. J. (2007) 'Lesbians in (cyber)space: the politics of the internet in Latin American on- and off-line communities', *Media, Culture and Society*, 29: 5, 790–811.

Gerber, E. (2003) *Género y Comunicación. Las mujeres en los medios masivos y en la agenda política* (Bueno Aires: Fundación Friedrich Ebert).

Gomez, R. (2004) 'The hall of mirrors: the Internet in Latin America', http://web.idrc.ca/uploads/user-S/10370336440The_Hall_of_Mirrors.pdf, accessed 2 March 2009.

Guia.com.ve (2008) 'Noticias y titulares de Venezuela', http://www.guia.com.ve/ noticias/?id=20202, accessed 19 March 2009.

Hernandez, R. (2007) 'Chávez y los otros comunicadores', *Rebelión*, 1 December, http://www.rebelion.org/noticias/2007/12/59883.pdf, accessed 20 March 2009.

Hernández Montoya, R. (2002) 'Nuevos medios contra viejos golpes', *Analitica.com*, http://www.analitica.com/Bitblio/roberto/nuevos_medios.asp, accessed 11 January 2009.

Hughes, S. (2006) *Newsrooms in Conflict. Journalism and the Democratization of Mexico* (Pittsburgh, PA: University of Pittsburgh Press).

Israel, E. (2009) 'Cuba accuses blogger Yoani Sanchez of "provocation"', *Reuters*, 1 April, http://www.reuters.com/article/technologyNews/idUSTRE5306NP20090401, accessed 2 April 2009.

Kalathil, S. and Boas, T. (2003) *Open Networks, Closed Regimes. The Impact of the Internet on Authoritarian Rule* (Washington, DC: Carnegie Endowment for International Peace).

Knudson, J. W. (1998) 'Rebellion in Chiapas: insurrection by Internet and public relations', *Media, Culture and Society*, 20: 3, 507–18.

Lipsman, A. (2007) 'Average Latin American Internet user spent 29 hours online in June', comScore, Inc., 25 July, http://www.comscore.com/press/release.asp?press=1531, accessed 4 February 2009.

Lugo, J. (ed.) (2008) *The Media in Latin America* (Maidenhead: Open University Press).

Lugo, J. and Romero, J. (2003) 'From friends to foes: Venezuela's media goes from consensual space to confrontational actor', *Sincronía*, 4: 2, http://sincronia.cucsh.udg.mx/lugoromeroinv02.htm, accessed 20 June 2009.

Lugo, J. and Sampson, T. (2008) 'E-informality in Venezuela: the "other path" of technology', *Bulletin of Latin American Research*, 27: 1, 102–18.

Mansell, Robin (2002) 'From digital divides to digital entitlements in knowledge societies', *Current Sociology*, 50: 3, 407–26.

Mastrini, G. and Becerra, B. (2007) 'Presente y tendencias de la concentración de medios en América Latina', *Zer*, 22, 15–40.

Mattelart, A. (1999) 'La communication-monde', in *Histoire des idées et des stratégies* (Paris: La Découverte).

Meikle, G. (2002) *Future Active: Media Activism and the Internet* (London: Routledge).

Nguyen, A. (2008) *The Penetration of Online News: Past, Present and Future* (Saarbrücken: VDM Publishing House).

René, M. (2002) 'También hubo ruido en La Plata', *Diario Hoy*, 11 January, http://pdf.diariohoy.net/2002/01/11/pdf/02.pdf, accessed 20 March 2009.

Revista Producto (1997) 'Veraz o ya verás', *Grupo Editorial Producto*, August, http://www.producto.com.ve/167/veraz.html, accessed 10 March 2009.

Rodríguez Leija, M. (2008) 'García Márquez y el periodismo actual', *El Mañana*, 23 September, http://www.elmanana.com.mx/notas.asp?id=79908, accessed 12 January 2009.

Ronfeldt, D., Arquilla, J., Fuller, G. and Fuller, M. (1999) *The Zapatista 'Social Netwar' in Mexico* (Washington, DC: RAND Corporation).

Singer, J. B. (2008) 'Five Ws and an H: digital challenges in newspaper newsrooms and boardrooms', *International Journal on Media Management*, 10: 3, 122–9.

Thussu, D. (2008) *News as Entertainment: The Rise of Global Infotainment* (London: Sage).

Uval, N. (2008) 'Celulares y reducción de pobreza: ¿es viable este atajo en América Latina?', *Asociación para el Progreso de las Comunicaciones*, 26 March http://www.apc.org/es/news/lowcost/lac/celulares-y-reduccion-de-pobreza-es-viable-este-at, accessed 12 November 2008.

Villasmil, J. (2002) 'México 1968: Tlatelolco y medios', *Cuestiones de América*, http://www.cuestiones.ws/semanal/021003/sem-oct03-02-mex-jv.htm, accessed 2 March 2009.

WACC (2005) *¿Quién figura en las noticias? Proyecto Global de Monitoreo de Medios 2005* (Buenos Aires: Asociación Mundial para la Comunicación Cristiana).

CHAPTER 5

Newsgames: an introduction

IAN BOGOST, SIMON FERRARI AND BOBBY SCHWEIZER

Given the financial state of journalism today, everyone knows that a change is coming. Newspaper advertising revenue was down nearly 30 per cent in 2009 (Chittum, 2009). Some papers, especially smaller ones, have cut staff or shut down. Community bloggers and big city newspaper publishers may not agree on the best form for the news, but they do agree that digital media will play an important role in its future. Yet most discourse about the way news and computers go together has focused on translations of existing approaches to journalism for the web.

Despite the differences in popularity and accessibility afforded by web publication, much journalism practice remains the same online. Online news sites large and small still publish written stories similar to those inked onto newsprint. They upload video segments like those broadcast for television. They stream monologues and interviews like those sent over the radio airwaves. The tools that make the creation and dissemination of news possible have simplified and become more widespread, but the process remains almost identical: stories still have to be written and edited, films shot and cut, radio recorded and uplinked.

But there is something different about videogames. Unlike stories written for newsprint, or programmes edited for television, videogames are computer software rather than a digitised form of earlier media. Games may sometimes display text, images, sounds or video, but they also do much more than this: games simulate how things work by constructing models that people can interact with. This is a type of experience irreducible to another, earlier medium.

For this reason it is necessary to understand the uses of games in the news, both new and old, in different terms. In this chapter, we offer an introduction to the concept of newsgames, a term we understand broadly as work produced at the intersection of videogames and journalism. It provides a basic but deliberate understanding of how games have been used in news in the past, covering the different applications, methods, styles and genres of news-games. Within this context, we suggest seven key areas for understanding the present state of the field and its future potential: infographics, current events, documentaries, puzzles, literacy, community and platforms – each of which we describe here in brief.

Infographics

Visual matter has long done journalistic work by visually representing data and thus synthesising information. At the start of the twentieth century, larger newspapers began integrating visual representations of data into papers to help the reader draw connections between complex networks of information and events. The resulting 'information graphics' come in many formats, from the traditional forms of pie chart, line graph, data map and diagram to more experimental forms. Information designer Edward Tufte calls them 'instruments of reasoning about quantitative information' (Tufte, 1983, p. 9).

The amount of data that can be represented in print is limited to the space on the page; therefore, the adaptation of infographics in computational form has broadened their scope in addition to changing their methods of author-ship. Digital infographics can display data on multiple axes, allow the explo-ration and manipulation of the data in new dimensions, depict vast quantities of information and integrate multimedia into the experience. As digital info-graphics mature and become more interactive, they take on game-like quali-ties. Users can explore information to find surprising new revelations, engage with processes that depict how information arises or interacts, reconfigure information to replay possible scenarios or experiment with information for the simple enjoyment of play itself. Some infographics might take the form of proper games, while others might simply be 'game-like', adopting some of the conventions and sensations of games.

We identify three primary forms of playable infographics: explanatory, directed and exploratory.

Explanatory graphics display static information that has been rendered by a computer program rather than an illustrator's hand. They value overt conclu-sions over organically developed logic. For example, the *South Florida Sun Sentinel* published a 'Virtual Butterfly Ballot' that recreates the experience of the confused Palm Beach County voter punching in their choices for the 2000 presidential election (Wittekind and Horner, 2000). The player's goal is to vote correctly for a chosen candidate. Oddly aligned boxes and text make it easy to understand why a voter might have inadvertently cast a vote for an undesired candidate. If the intended and actual vote do not match, a message explains why the user might have been confused by the interface.

Directed infographics guide the viewer to a predetermined conclusion as synthesised by a journalist beforehand. Directed activity encourages constrained exploration. Direction can be created in non-linear graphics by prompting the user to explore information with their personal experience in mind. The *New York Times* 'rent–buy calculator' is an online tool that prompts user input by asking for data to be entered into an array of fields that would affect the cost of purchasing a home (Jackson and Tse, 2008). The user begins by inputting their own current financial information, but the tool allows for adjustments to explore the changes caused by different variables.

Exploratory graphics show information that is meant to be synthesised by the viewer. The journalist shapes possible approaches to, or paths through, information with tools that allow the viewer to arrange, filter, zoom or otherwise explore it. *USA Today*'s Presidential Primary Delegate Tracker offers a good example (Hatch and Thomassie, 2008). This infographic shows a map of the United States, with Democratic and Republican event timelines extending from January to June, and displays a bar graph with the total number of delegate votes cast for each presidential candidate. Mousing over different points on the map and timeline reveals specific information, which the user can then configure to develop a better sense of the unfolding drama of the primaries.

Despite infographics' potential to help readers refigure data in informative new ways, such visualisations must not become the fix-all solution of a lazy journalist. In recent years, Internet culture has speciously privileged the very idea of data access as a democratising force. Proponents of this movement claim that these graphical tools free data from the meddling hand of the author, allowing audiences to draw their own conclusions rather than relying solely on a journalist's interpretation. For example, the US government's Data.gov site claims to 'enable the public to participate in government by providing downloadable Federal datasets to build applications, conduct analyses, and perform research'. And the ManyEyes project at IBM hopes to '"democratize" visualization and to enable a new social kind of data analysis'. While this watchdog spirit is admirable, journalists should not relinquish their responsibility to synthesise news in favour of purely technical solutions like the ones just mentioned. Infographic games offer journalists the opportunity to lead citizens through synthesised information spaces and to make insightful commentary, rather than relying on an empty rhetoric of open data that leads to confusion just as often as it creates knowledge.

Current events

In 2003, Uruguayan game developer Powerful Robot released a game called *September 12th* about the war on terror. Gonzalo Frasca, the game's designer, dubbed it a 'newsgame', an artefact in which 'videogames meet political cartoons' (Frasca, 2006, p. 2). We adopt Frasca's umbrella term 'newsgame' in the title of our research, but generalise it to refer to all intersections of games and journalism. Frasca's goals are more specific: he envisioned short, quickly produced and widely distributed games about current events.

Over time, three distinct subgenres emerged: editorial games, tabloid games and reportage games. *Editorial* games like *September 12th* offer the videogame equivalent of columns and editorial cartoons, conveying an opinion with the goal of persuading players to agree with embedded bias – or at least to consider an issue in a different light. *Tabloid* games offer a cruder form of editorial, focusing primarily on scandals related to celebrities and politicians. For example, *So You Think You Can Drive, Mel?* (Game Show Network) offers a satirical recreation of Mel Gibson's drink driving arrest, in which he insulted both police officers and Jews. In the game the player must acquire alcohol while avoiding state troopers, Hasidic Jews and falling Stars of David. *Reportage* games are an emerging form, owing more to the goals and style of extended news coverage. *Wired* magazine's *Cutthroat Capitalism* (Conde Nast Digital and Smallbore Webworks, 2009) allows players to understand the social and economic models of Somali pirates by putting them at the helm of a fledgling crew. Through the same journalistic values of objectivity and transparency, reportage games attempt to present a comprehensive playable version of a news event without bias – or at least, they embrace the same values of truth that characterise traditional written or filmic journalism.

Several considerations arise when creating current event games: their timeliness, accessibility and editorial line. Creators of these games typically strive to release such a game while the story it covers is still relevant, a goal whose viability varies greatly depending on the depth of the simulation and whether the event or problem is simple or complex, singular or interconnected, cyclical or novel. Thus, Frasca's *September 12th* took three months to create, while his *Madrid* (Powerful Robot Games, 2004), about the 2004 terrorist bombing of the Madrid subway, took only a day. Miguel Sicart contends that such games must be 'as ephemeral as the news they illustrate – able to be thrown away after experienced' (Sicart, 2008, p. 27). Yet some seem to be more timeless than others, depending on the duration of the event they cover and how they do it, and just like the print news they now serve an archival or encyclopaedic function.

There are many ways to create a small-scale game today: as a downloadable PC program, within a web page or on a mobile device, for example. Current event games are most often created in web authoring programs like Flash for embedding in a web page, because the system requirements for such games are so low, because a website requires no special installation and because familiarity with Adobe's Flash rich media authoring environment is very high among web developers and the general public. The simplicity of game development in Flash also creates a low barrier to access for budding designers, as evidenced by the number of tabloid games made by non-professionals. Flash games also often embrace embedding or redistribution on any website, a feature that frequently results in numerous copies of a current event game on a multitude of web portals. Also adding to the accessibility of newsgames is the fact that their interaction models skew towards the simplistic, often relying on tried-and-true mechanics from arcade and casual games.

Editorial games are simple and small, so they serve as good examples for the theory of procedural rhetoric – the way that games persuade and express through their rules alone (Bogost, 28–9). A current event game models an experience with a real-world system. Editorial games and tabloid games tell their players about their opinions and biases not in on-screen text, but through their rules of behaviour. Their editorial lines are determined by the information they include and exclude from this model. For example, *September 12th* argues against US military action in the middle east by depicting how apparently 'surgical' airstrikes inevitably result in civilian casualties, inspiring rather than reducing terrorism. By contrast, reportage games seek to match their simulation to the most complete understanding of an event or problem as possible; they minimise their editorial line.

In all of these cases, some level of abstraction is required. Because of this, one can accept or reject either the editorial line or the representation of the event, or both. Sometimes the rejection of the game is so intense that it inflames the player, and sometimes this is exactly what the designer wants. Getting people to talk about them thus serves as a primary goal of current event games, an accomplishment that can expand discourse around an issue, thus embracing a core value of journalism.

For example, when *September 12th* was released, it inspired a flurry of conversation on websites that covered the game (Hall, 2003). Even though many of these sites were devoted to games and game culture, the ensuing discussions delved into the political implications of the game, not just its design or appeal. In some cases, debate dipped into the game's assumptions ('the authors believe terrorists to be peaceful civilians?'); in others, the discussion revealed how the game had helped some players to explore and clarify their own positions ('even a simple simulation gives me room to actively participate in creating meaning in a different way than static textual or visual presentations like editorials and cartoons. Which led me to think more deeply about these issues').

Documentary

While current event games cover isolated stories in a short and accessible way, 'docugames' engage larger historical and current events. Usually larger in scale and scope, these games offer experiences of newsworthy events, something impossible to capture in print or broadcast news. In the case of past events, they recreate times, spaces and systems that one can otherwise only understand from archival film footage or one's own imagination.

We identify two primary types of documentary games, spatial and procedural.

In *spatial* docugames, players experience the setting of a recreated event. Some simply offer a construction of the relevant space and let players do what they want with it; in the case of *9/11 Survivor* (C-Level, 2003), players can understand what it felt like to be trapped in the World Trade Center just before it collapsed. Others, such as *Kuma\War*'s 'John Kerry's Silver Star' mission, give the players objectives to guide them through the experience while enforcing a strict, often linear, representation of historical events (Kuma Reality Games, 2004). Mise-en-scène is important for the creation of a feeling of authenticity in spatial docugames. In *9/11 Survivor*, for example, the player finds himself inside a high story of the World Trade Center, looking from an ordinary office out of the fiery windows to the ground below. In *Kuma\War*'s John Kerry mission, the player pilots a swift boat through the meandering jungle of Vietnam, offering a perspective on the geographical setting for the infamous mission.

Because games are not particularly well suited to presenting evidence like interviews and testimony (the typical way documentaries establish actuality and present different sides of a story), some docugames interrogate these systems *procedurally*, by modelling the behaviour of a particular situation. These investigative journalism games seek to expose the occluded rationales that produce real-world problems. *Escape from Woomera* (selectparks, 2003) gives players an inside glance at life in an internment camp for asylum seekers in Australia, exposing the brutality of life, the difficulty of escaping and the varied life stories behind the people who found themselves captive there. Journalistic non-fiction or 'human interest' games attempt to share lived experiences by expressing personal feelings and ideas through the way the game world is coded and constructed. For example, Jason Rohrer's *Gravitation* (2008) abstractly captures the centripetal tug between creative work and spending time with one's family. In the game, the player must find inspiration in a fantastic world and then put it to use by creating work, but doing so requires taking time away from playing with the character's young child.

Can games serve as historical documents in the way that photographs and films can? The jury is still out, but factors at work in the debate include the objectivity of documentary reality, the issue of players altering the actual course of history and whether or not a game made partially or primarily for entertainment can do justice to the tragedy of real-world problems. The last case arose during the development of *Six Days in Fallujah* (Atomic Games), perhaps the first mainstream attempt at a docugame. The creators cast the game as a tactical shooter and 'survival horror' game about the most bloody battle of the war in Iraq. But its creation came under scrutiny when a press conference revealed that it seemed to diverge significantly from the realities of war. While the game's publisher eventually cancelled the title, the discourse that its development produced demonstrates an evolution from the wholesale rejection of the very notion of docugames to a sense of how they should be made properly in the future.

Puzzles

Games have been a part of the news for almost a century, since the first 'word-cross' puzzles appeared in the New York *Sunday World* in 1913 (Arnot, 1981, p. 28). By the 1920s, the crossword was a sensation, becoming so popular that it even incited a moral panic (*New York Times* 1924). When the *New York Times* finally revised the form and made it more 'literate' at the end of the Second World War, the public was sold. Since then, many newspaper readers have looked forward to the puzzles as one of the most joyous and intellectually engaging moments of their day. Puzzles have not always carried news content, but experiments such as editorial crosswords and news quizzes have tried to do so.

Some examples of such puzzles do exist. On 5 July 2003, in the Op-Ed page of the *New York Times*, a large puzzle took the place of the usual daily columns. The puzzle, entitled 'Patriot Games' (Puzzability, 2003), is one of ten so-called 'Op-Ed Puzzles' created by Puzzability, a firm made up of three veteran crossword and other puzzle constructors. The fastest turnaround time for creating a *New York Times* crossword is about ten days, making the form less than ideal for covering breaking news. These experiments have the potential to serve as public forums for discourse; however, this would require a very fundamental change in how puzzle constructors and editors view their roles within the larger context of both the newspaper in particular and journalism in general.

While the crossword hasn't frequently carried deliberately journalistic content, another familiar, traditional form of the puzzle has: the quiz. The earliest use of quizzes in an entertainment setting occurred in 1929, as a reference in the *Oakland Tribune*. Since then, the quiz format has taken on various forms. The *New York Times* News Quiz has a strictly pedagogical bent, aiming to instruct younger readers about techniques of reading and synthesising information from a newspaper article. The *New Yorker*'s quiz, by contrast, occasionally has a goal of sharing factual information. Usually, the themes of these news quizzes are political or focused on softer, pop-cultural news. Unlike the *New York Times*, the *New Yorker* considers these news quizzes as part of its humour section.

If puzzles and quizzes really do offer mental relief in addition to information, and if newspapers have been a major source of such puzzles, perhaps even the primary source, then a question rears its head: how many newspaper subscribers buy the paper just for the puzzles? The truth is startling: 54 per cent of 3,500 surveyed at About.com's puzzle section buy a newspaper 'all the time' just for the puzzles, finding their way to news, columns and features along the way (Fisher, 2009). *New York Times* crossword editor Will Shortz shares another hopeful statistic: 1 per cent of all people surveyed about 'their favourite thing to do' named crosswords as their top pick (Ryan, 2004). If these and other studies are to be believed, there's a very real possibility that the news industry has underestimated the importance of puzzles to the business.

Today, it's not just puzzles and crosswords that provide routine, mental exercise, a break from work or a distraction during a boring conference call. In fact, this is precisely what many online casual games offer. In the fifteen years of the commercial Internet, numerous sources for online games have arisen, from commercial powerhouses PopCap to independent portals like Newgrounds to new social network-oriented start-ups like Kongregate.

According to the International Game Developers Association, the market for casual games was worth US$2.25 billion in 2007, and growing at a rate of 20 per cent annually (IGDA Casual Games SIG, 2009, p. 9). Twenty-five per cent of Internet users play casual games, amounting to 200 million users. The addition of mobile game portals like the iPhone App Store demonstrates significant additional growth in this sector.

When seen in this light, the entire casual games industry could be understood as a threat, poised to do the same thing to the newspaper puzzle that eBay and Craigslist did to local advertising. Perhaps casual games like Tetris and Zuma are actually endemic, rather than tangential affairs for the news.

Literacy

Journalism comprises a set of values and skills that must be learned somehow – it is a literacy, or set of rules for reading, writing and critiquing a particular domain of knowledge (Gee, 2007, p. 17). The earliest steps in learning to do journalism traditionally take place in the classroom or on school newspapers, but certain qualities of videogames make them ideal supplementary media for a journalistic education.

One service that videogames can provide is that of media literacy, by explaining in part the role journalism provides to society. Mainstream games such as *Dead Rising* (Capcom, 2006) and *Beyond Good & Evil* (Ubisoft, 2003) illustrate the purpose of the profession by showing positive and negative examples of journalists in virtual worlds, often in a context where the freedom of the press has been suspended. *Beyond Good & Evil* presents the plight of an independent photojournalist living in a world where the news comes from two antagonistic and propagandising sources: an intergalactic military and its underground opposition. In-game news sources – non-player characters such as Three-Dog in *Fallout 3* (Bethesda Softworks, 2008), who reports on events taking place within the virtual world – tell us how the designers of these games view the profession. When they are played critically, players can come to understand or question how the game designers have modelled the work of journalists in their game.

Journalistic education games, by contrast, attempt to directly teach the practice of working journalists through reportage simulations. These games allow a 'psychosocial moratorium' (Gee, 2007, p. 59) or removal of real-life consequences that goes beyond even the relatively low-risk environment of school newspapers. The *Global Conflicts* series (Serious Games Interactive, 2007, 2008), designed to teach interviewing skills to middle and high schoolers, places players in low-trust environments where non-player characters have reasons to withhold vital information. These games track the emotional state of interview subjects, allowing players to coax information out of them by 'pushing their buttons' and sometimes learning when they've gone too far – at which point the interview ends and information is lost to them forever. *Global Conflict: Palestine* complicates this by forcing the player to choose whether to represent an Israeli or Palestinian news source, by which they can come to understand how ideological bias influences reportage and access to interviews. *Global Conflict: Latin America* climaxes in an interview with a corrupt political leader, and the player must build a case against him based on reports gleaned from earlier successful encounters with other non-player characters.

Both kinds of game advocate for the profession because players create 'projective identities' (Gee, 2007, p. 62) – a middle ground between who they are in real life and who they play in a virtual world – that help them to plan whether or not they might want to be a journalist in the future. A connected strength is that humans are proven to learn better within an embodied and situated context (Gee, 2007, p. 71). This is why school newspapers are so popular – the core ideas and skills of journalism cannot be adequately taught in a textbook. But games can also take their players to worlds and situations that a school newspaper could never provide.

Many of the people designing journalism literacy games are experienced reporters or educators. In fact, learning how to design games can help journalists to gain a new grasp of how to design the news. First, procedural literacy – the ability to understand and critique sets of rules – can help journalists to learn novel ways to engage with the complex networks of information and trust that they deal with on a daily basis while reporting. Game design can also inform understandings of key forms of transparency, a principal value of journalism. *Transparency of influence* means dealing with recognising one's ideological or economic bias, and in games this means making one's opinions of the system modelled apparent. *Transparency of construction* in journalism means dealing with being clear which information is available and what has been left out, and in game design this comes into play when one reveals which parts of the issue have been encoded and which have been left out. *Transparency of reference* means formally recognising the sources that one has drawn upon in research or through interviews; this is the most difficult form of transparency for game designers, because all information requires some form of modification in order to be encoded. In the end, game design can help to inform news design – traditionally the work of editors and layout artists – and perhaps help journalists to recognise new ways to interrogate and present information.

Community

In a blog report from May 2007, an unemployed woman named Rainey talks about the feasibility of reintroducing coal-fired locomotives for regional passenger and freight transport in the United States. Given the efficiencies of steam, she reasoned, and the local availability of both coal and steel in the USA, it might be possible to counteract the high price of diesel fuel, which, at $5 per gallon, still looked like a bargain compared to ordinary gasoline's price of nearly $7 per gallon.

The problem, it turned out, was not one of material but one of industrial feasibility. Steel mills long-closed would have to be reopened, as would erection shops on rail lines still servicing major destinations. Worse, qualified personnel to manufacture and service steam locomotives had nearly vanished. Even though some violence had already erupted around the country in response to the high cost of oil, truly widespread civil unrest would need to erupt before the governmental support required to revive the steam railroad might become a reality. In the meantime, the idea was a dead end.

Of course, gasoline never hit $7 per gallon in 2007, nor did any civil unrest erupt, nor did anyone consider reviving the steam rail as a salve to a logistics collapse that summer. But the blog just described was real, one of many incredibly detailed scenarios proposed over the thirty-two days of *World without Oil*, an alternative reality game run that summer by writer Ken Eklund and collaborators.

The game set up a hypothetical global oil shortage of the kind often described by 'peak oil' commentators. As with most alternative reality games, play took place not on a game board or a computer screen, but in the world, on streets and in gardens, and through a variety of online media channels like blogs and YouTube. Rainey was actually a fictional character, played by one of many real human 'puppetmasters' who pull the proverbial strings of the game, seeding scenarios and problems for its players to solve.

When we think of games, from table-top games like *Dungeons and Dragons* to board games like chess and *Risk* to videogames like *Super Mario Bros* and *The Sims*, we normally think of them as private affairs. We play games indoors, at tables or televisions or computers. Even if we play with others, it is only in small groups. And while recent innovations in massively multiplayer online games (MMOGs) can support many hundreds or thousands of simultaneous players at a time, those players are usually widely distributed geographically.

In the United States, industry consolidation, reductions in advertising revenue and massive competition online have de-emphasised the role of the local newspaper in creating a common perspective for communities, particularly in smaller cities and towns. Can games connect and motivate people to participate in and improve their local communities, especially at a time when local journalism is suffering so much? While still nascent, recent trends in games that blend fictional scenarios, Internet communication and player participation in the real world, on the street and in public might have the potential to do so. These games are often characterised by player discourse and collaboration features that also characterise successful journalism. In *World without Oil*, for example, players experiment with and discuss ways to reduce reliance on fossil fuels in a fictional peak oil-addled future. While their creators have called them 'alternate reality games' and 'big games', perhaps a better name for these games is simply 'community games', thanks to their potential to inspire players to better both themselves and their communities.

Platforms

A platform, at its most basic, is something that is built to make it easier to build other things (Monfort and Bogost, 2009, pp. 2–6). The newspaper itself is a platform that supports research, writing, printing, distribution and feedback from the public. The format of the evening news is a platform that describes how to order stories in a useful or compelling way, how to integrate advertising and how to consistently produce a televised show. As technology changes, new platforms change the very form of the news. We see news formatted for mobile devices and passed around as links on social media networks, and even on videogame consoles like the Nintendo Wii. Part of the development of newsgames involves envisioning new platforms for game-based journalism itself.

Fantasy football provides a good model for a platform's potential to engage an audience. In general, fantasy sports take data and turn them into points. Importantly, these data already exist in the world sport statistics ready to be manipulated and referenced. To play a fantasy sport, a player assembles a team of real-life athletes who, based on their performance during competition, earn the player points. Fantasy sport relies heavily on sport news, an infrastructure that already collects the massive amounts of data produced each week by sporting events themselves. Fantasy sports show how creating a news platform is just a matter of looking at what an organisation already possesses and applying some out-of-the-box thinking to see it in a new light.

The availability of simpler tools for software creation has made it easier to produce games. Aspiring designers need not create their own graphics or physics engines. Instead, they can build atop existing systems. Modding, for example, is the practice of taking a game and manipulating the assets (graphics, sound, characters and so on) and gameplay to create a new experience. *Escape from Woomera* was built using the popular *Half-Life* game engine, which freed the design team from the time-consuming process of writing complicated software so that they could instead focus on the mechanics, environment and models. However, these tools do have their downsides: a game designer's imagination is limited to what is permitted by the software.

Kuma Reality Games harnessed the potential of the platform for distribution of their episodic *Kuma\War* games. These short games based around recent military operations in the Middle East can be downloaded and played for free through a computer application that acts as a hub for finding new content, managing downloads and game installation. Kuma's games are built using Valve's Source engine (successor to the aforementioned *Half-Life* engine), which means they can share application, game and network resources. Using this platform has enabled them to quickly produce high-quality looking games so that they may respond to current events.

Ideas for new platforms (or how to employ existing platforms) range from the familiar to the bizarre, the serious to the silly. What if a news organisation released a documentary game 'yearbook' about the changes in a local community? What if Yoshi the dinosaur in *Super Mario Land* needed healthcare, and he had to buy insurance at the going rates? What if the dynamics of New York City racketeering laws could be operationalised in *Grand Theft Auto*? Whether good or bad on first blush, these ideas suggest how journalists need to think about what they do in new ways, not just translate old media for digital distribution.

Conclusion

All the categories discussed in this chapter rely on the traditional news media embracing new modes of production. Rather than just tacking on a 'games division', newsrooms must integrate games at a fundamental level if valuable contributions are to come. Most news organisations already have graphic artists who transform data visually, creating graphic assets, and ask readers to explore their infographics and visualisations. Current event games could be produced in tandem with or instead of text/radio/television stories, as editors and game designers collaborate to express ideas through game mechanics. The availability of 3D game engines allows events to be reconstructed spatially, situating documentary material in a realm of new potential. The print industry need only look inwards to its strong history of puzzles to recognise the potential of games in the news. Established journalistic conventions can be taught in games to both news producers and consumers. The communities of news viewers and readers exhibit untapped potential as tools for social good. These are just some possible ways the news media can use games to grow their editorial and publishing interests.

Nick Diakapolous, Sergio Goldenberg, Adam Rogers, Ray Vichot and Doug Wilson contributed to this article, as a part of their participation in the Georgia Tech Newsgames research group: http://jag.lcc.gatech.edu. Generous support for this research was provided by the John S. and James L. Knight Foundation.

REFERENCES

Arnot, Michelle (1981) *What's Gnu? A History of the Crossword Puzzle* (New York: Vintage Books).

Atomic Games (unreleased) *Six Days in Fallujah* (videogame).

Bethesda Game Studios (2008) *Fallout 3* (Bethesda Softworks LLC).

Bogost, Ian (2007) *Persuasive Games: The Expressive Power of Videogames* (Cambridge, MA: MIT Press).

Capcom (2006) *Dead Rising* (videogame) (Capcom Co. Ltd).

Chittum, Ryan (2009) 'Newspaper industry ad revenue at 1965 levels', *Columbia Journalism Review*, 19 August, http://www.cjr.org/the_audit/newspaper_industry_ad_revenue.php, accessed 8 October 2009.

C-Level (2003) *9/11 Survivor* (videogame), self-published.

Conde Nast Digital and Smallbore Webworks (2009) *Cutthroat Capitalism* (videogame), *Wired* Magazine, http://www.wired.com/special_multimedia/2009/cutthroatCapitalismTheGame, accessed 8 October 2009.

Eklund, Ken (2007) *World without Oil* (San Jose, CA: Writerguy), http://www.worldwithoutoil.org, accessed 8 October 2009.

Fisher, Dave (2009) 'Have you ever bought a newspaper just to do the crossword puzzle?', About.com, http://puzzles.about.com/od/crosswords/qt/PuzzlePollNews.htm, accessed 8 October 2009.

Frasca, Gonzolo (2003) *September 12th* (videogame), Newsgaming.com, accessed 8 October 2009.

Frasca, Gonzolo (2004) *Madrid* (videogame), Newsgaming.com, accessed 8 October 2009.

Frasca, Gonzalo (2006) 'This just in: playing the news', Vodafone receiver 17.

Game Show Network (2006) *So You Think You Can Drive, Mel?* (videogame), http://www.splashworks.com/pgame.php?id=5, accessed 8 October 2009.

Gee, James Paul (2007) *What Video Games Have to Teach Us about Learning and Literacy* (New York: Palgrave Macmillan).

Hall, Justin (2003) 'Newsgaming: September 12', *Game Girl Advance*, 23 September, http://www.gamegirladvance.com/archives/2003/09/29/newsgaming_september_12.html, accessed 8 October 2009.

Hatch, Joshua and Thomassie, Juan (2008) 'Delegate Tracker', *USA Today*, 11 February, http://www.usatoday.com/news/politics/election2008/delegate-tracker.htm, accessed 25 February 2009.

IGDA Casual Games SIG (2009) 'Casual games white paper', http://www.igda.org/casual/IGDA_Casual_Games_White_Paper_2008.pdf, accessed 8 October 2009.

Jackson, Tom and Tse, Archie (2008) 'Is it better to buy or rent?', *New York Times*, 2 June, http://www.nytimes.com/2007/04/10/business/2007_BUYRENT_GRAPHIC.html, accessed 8 March 2009.

Kuma Reality Games (2004) *Kuma\War* 'Mission 24 – John Kerry's Silver Star', 3 March.

La Molleindustria (2009) *Faith Fighter*. Self-published.

Monfort, Nick and Bogost, Ian (2009) *Racing the Beam: The Atari Video Computer System* (Cambridge, MA: MIT Press).

New York Times (1924) 'Topics of the times', *New York Times*, 17 November, 18.

Puzzlability (2003) *New York Times*, 5 July, http://www.nytimes.com/2003/07/05/opinion/05PUZZ.html, accessed 8 October 2009.

Rohrer, Jason (2008) *Gravitation* (videogame). Self-published.

Ryan, Laura T. (2004) 'He knows all the answers (2 words): Will Shortz', *Syracuse Post-Standard*, 5 December, http://www.primate.wisc.edu/people/hamel/heknows, accessed 20 August 2009.

selectparks (2003) *Escape from Woomera* (videogame). Self-published.

Serious Games Interactive (2007) *Global Conflicts: Palestine* (Copenhagen: Serious Games Interactive).

Serious Games Interactive (2008) *Global Conflicts: Latin America* (Copenhagen: Serious Games Interactive).

Sicart, Miguel (2008) 'Newsgames: theory and design', International Conference on Entertainment Computing, Pittsburgh PA.

Slansky, Paul (2008) 'Shouts & murmurs' (column), *The New Yorker*, http://www.newyorker.com/humor/2008/02/11/080211sh_shouts_slansky.

Tufte, Edward R. (1983) *The Visual Display of Quantitative Information* (Connecticut: Graphics Press).

Ubisoft Montpellier Studios (2003) *Beyond Good and Evil* (Ubisoft Entertainment SA).

'Who's Who and What's What?', *New York Times*, updated weekly, http://www.nytimes.com/learning/students/quiz.

Wittekind, Don and Horner, R. Scott (2000) '2000 butterfly ballot: see how the Palm Beach County ballot confused voters', SunSentinel.com, 10 November, http://www.sun-sentinel.com/broadband/theedge/sfl-edge-n-butterfly ballot,0,4467323.flash, accessed 15 July 2009.

CHAPTER 6

The intimate turn of mobile news

GERARD GOGGIN

In mid-June 2009, like many around the world, I avidly followed the popular uprising after the Iranian elections – what was called the Green Revolution. In doing so I was struck by the significance of mobile news in how this was reported, represented and shaped. Being someone still wedded to the habits of old media – tuning in to the seven o'clock nightly news, small children permitting – it seemed that much of the footage that was featured, capturing the latest events, was shot on mobile phone cameras, by individual protesters and witnesses, and also by journalists. To add to this, the role of mobile phones, and mobile and online media, featured prominently in other ways in how this news was created, listened to and watched, and circulated.

One well publicised example of this may be found in a terrible instance that occurred on 20 June 2009. A young Iranian woman, Neda Agha-Soltan, was taking part in a protest march on Karegar Avenue, in Tehran, with her father, when she was shot and fatally wounded by members of the Basiji militia. Her death was filmed on a mobile phone, by an anonymous bystander. Two videos of this were circulated on the Internet through YouTube and Facebook. Neda quickly become a symbol of the Iranian Green Revolution, through main media, such as the *New York News* (Kennedy, 2009), as well as Twitter (#Neda). The shocking videos of Neda dying as she lies on the roadside can still be viewed on a number of online sites at the time of writing ('Death of Neda', 2009).

This kind of use of mobile news became a particular theme of the Iranian uprising. In particular the mobile messaging system Twitter – operating across mobiles and the Internet – itself became a key actor in Iranian media and politics, just as earlier forms of media have been. The apogee of Twitter's starring role in the revolution was the plea by a young official at the US State

Department to delay a scheduled outage and maintenance to keep the system up and running (Landler and Stelter, 2009).

Timothy Garton Ash's column sums up the mood:

> Details of demonstration venues, tactics and slogans are passed round via Twitter, social networking sites like Facebook and text messages. Videos of demos and shootings are uploaded on to YouTube and other websites, whence they can be accessed from outside the country and broadcast back into it. Digital David fights theocratic Goliath . . . Probably the single most important thing the US state department has done for Iran recently was to contact Twitter over the weekend, to urge it to delay a planned upgrade that could have taken down service to Iranians for some crucial hours of people power–protest. Welcome to the new politics of the 21st century. (Ash, 2009)

Iran has been celebrated for its vibrant blogosphere, which has flourished precisely because of media restrictions (Khiabany and Sreberny, 2009) so it is no surprise that the authorities were ready and willing to counter the use of new technologies (Borger, 2009). The international backlash against Iran's interception and interdiction extended beyond the country's government to the leading mobile phone vendor Nokia too, which was squarely criticised by human rights activists and cultural jammers for its role in providing the top-down technology of surveillance as well as the grassroots handsets of hope.

While we are still to fully understand the significance of what occurred in Iran, and how new media and cultural practices actually did play a role in it, what is clear is that mobile news is a very important and potent facet of contemporary news and journalism, as it is, in particular situations, of the larger forces of culture and politics.

News conceived for and delivered on mobile phones has built on predecessor forms such as the pager. With the popularity of text messaging, new forms of news have developed, especially around customised modes of alerts and short new items. With the rise of the mobile Internet, mobiles offer a conjunct but distinct form of online news, using web and other convergent media applications. Then there is the arrival of mobile television, where news produced for television is transmitted, broadcast, abbreviated, customised or specifically conceived for mobile phones and new forms of mobile media (such as iPhones, smartphones, portable digital assistants and ultra-mobile personal computers).

With these new kinds of channels, genres and affordances for news construed for mobile technologies, and their patterns of consumption, come also new forms of production of news. There is the culturally significant role of the mobile in the gathering and construction of news. We find the incorporation of the mobile-wielding citizen-journalist into the practices of reporting. Then there are the ways that mobiles have been incorporated into the consumption of mainstream media.

Against this backdrop, this chapter considers the extent to which mobile news can be understood as an 'intimate turn' in online news. Here I am interested in seeing how the personal and portable technology of the mobile is bringing about a distinctive form of news that is playing a strategically important role in how contemporary media works.

To do this, I first shift the focus from the celebration of mobiles in protest, social change and citizen journalism, which the Iranian case highlights, and which is perhaps the reflex way in which mobile news is approached. Instead, I start with a brief look at how the mobile has been deployed by leading media organisations internationally, as part of their cross-platform strategy for distributing news. After this, I consider how mobiles are figuring in the reporting, news gathering and construction process, and how this co-creative process has been incorporated into the evolving genres and forms of online news, as well as the devising of new, independent news platforms and media. So I consider the rather more prosaic kinds of mobile news, as well as those celebrated for their spectacular, revolutionary potential. My argument is that this double constitution of mobile news rather complicates this new form.

Mobile news and its emerging patterns of consumption

Mobile news as a viable media form began with SMS alerts and news, though its potential had been discussed and prototypes developed before this (for instance, see Pavlik, 2001). With the rise of premium rate mobile services, as well as mobile data and content services in general, a wide range of mobile news services become available. Major newspaper companies especially took an interest in the possibilities of mobile news, as part of their overall online news strategies (see, for instance, the discussion of the *Irish Times* in Cawley, 2008). Many newspapers make it easy to receive alerts and news via SMS. Most major newspapers now offer news via mobiles, and there are significant initiatives under way with mobile news in a range of countries (notably South Korea, where mobile television has been most popular). To give a sense of what is occurring in the Anglophone world, I briefly discuss how mobiles figure in some English-language newspaper online sites.

In Australia, the leading broadsheet, the *Sydney Morning Herald*, promises:

'Breaking News in your Hand'
With the SMH on your mobile, breaking news now happens everywhere you go. SMH Mobile is designed to give you the information you need quickly and easily, be it; breaking news, national and world news, sport, entertainment, business, weather and more. (*Sydney Morning Herald*, 2009)

The *Guardian*, something of a pioneer in online news (see Ofcom, 2009, p. 291–4), offers access either via a mobile website or via SMS despatch of particular sections of news of interest. The *Guardian* mobile website (http://m.guardian.co.uk/, viewed 13 May 2009) is customised for mobile Internet access, a by now familiar look and feel for consumers of mobile news, with a minimum of images, and most navigation by textual hyperlinks. As the excerpt from the *Sydney Morning Herald* promotion suggests, it is now common to offer a 'full' web version of the newspaper, rather than simply the stripped-down mobile optimised version. The images from the *Guardian*'s publicity feature a Blackberry, a Nokia and an Apple iPhone, all with relatively generous screen-space to allow fuller display of the online news site. Mobile news is being positioned as part of a suite of cross-platform media options.

The motto of the *New York Times* echoes the common refrain in contemporary media of user-control of time and mode of consumption: 'Enjoy the high-quality journalism of The New York Times whenever and on whatever device you desire' (*New York Times*, 2009).

A new development in which mobiles are now playing a prominent role is digital editions. The advent of the iPhone in 2007 meant that there was now a popular mobile phone that did function quite well as an e-reader or e-book device. The *New York Time*'s 'All the news that's fit to print' becomes 'All the news that's fit to go' in their iPhone application – 'A new way to take your news with you.' Here the iPhone offers to extend the mobile news browsing and selection experience, making it more customisable and higher resolution – rather than ushering in a radically different experience:

Enjoy features such as:
Offline reading ...
Simple navigation – view pictures and articles quickly
Photo view – browse the news in pictures and link to the related articles
Customize your display by selecting your four favorite news categories. (*New York Times*, 2009)

One subscriber benefit offered by many newspapers – for instance, the *Financial Times*, as well as the *Guardian* and others – is the facsimile of the paper made available online, including a mobile version. The urge to 'See the paper exactly as it was printed' would appear to be a confected artefact of continuity in the midst of the new media ecology being created here (Boczkowski, 2005). The third version of the Amazon Kindle e-reader, announced in May 2009, featured a much wider screen, especially customised for newspaper reading (PDA, 2009). For his part, however, media proprietor Rupert Murdoch did not envisage such e-readers forming part of his plans to charge for *Times Online* and *Sun Online* content: 'I can assure you, we will not be sending our content rights to the fine people who created the Kindle . . . We will control the prices for our content, and we will control the relationship with our customers' (PDA, 2009). The interesting thing about this turn is how it illustrates the importance of mobile devices and networks for the development of online news and their business models. Not for the first time in the history of the Internet, Murdoch claimed that the 'current days of the internet will soon be over' (PDA, 2009). Thus far charging for online news content has not been generally successful. However, mobile devices may well be helpful for selling content. Mobiles offer new affordances, forms and content, but they especially provide systems for billing and licensing content.

So far I have focused on some of the ways in which well established newspapers are incorporating mobiles into their news offerings. Of course, third-generation mobiles are very much multimedia platforms, so they offer the potential for broadcast news to be extended, or conceived, for mobiles. Many media companies, broadcasters, mobile companies and handset vendors have made available television news programming for third-generation mobiles, although outside the case of South Korea, there is little reliable information on how widely these have been used – especially as mobile television is still in its infancy. In addition, new technologies, such as iPhones and smartphones, offer the potential for hybrid news services that cross previous computing and broadcasting divides. Take, for instance, the trajectory of the UK ITN television channel's digital division:

Back in 2003, ITN ON pioneered video news on mobile in Europe, launching with 3, and became the first UK company to create made-for-mobile news and weather channels. This year, it used its skilled developers to create an application that provides news to the ever-increasing iPhone audience. In the two weeks since its launch, the app had 65,000 downloads from the iTunes App Store, making it the number-one free news app globally. Who ever said the younger generation isn't interested in news? The key is making it available in a format that they want to use. (Smith, 2009, pp. 24–5)

This brings us to the general question about what information or research is available on the consumption of mobile news in its various forms. There is almost no dedicated research on this topic, but some general data is beginning to appear in national surveys. For instance, the Australian users surveyed in 2007 confirmed that the Internet is their most important source of information, and about six in ten users 'would visit an online news service if either a large international or large local story was breaking' (Ewing et al., 2008, p. vi). Pertinently, this survey also found that just over a quarter of respondents access news over a wireless or mobile device – though in the case of mobiles, this was less than one hour per week (Ewing et al., 2008, p. 10). A 2008 Australian mobiles industry survey found news, weather and sport to be the most heavily used information types (AIMIA, 2008). Otherwise, surveys in a number of countries indicate growing use of mobiles for Internet, the necessary condition for consuming news on mobiles (Ofcom, 2009; Pew, 2009).

Such national surveys establish the fact of growing use of mobiles for gaining information. However, specific research that better comes to grips with the forms of mobile news consumption is sorely needed. Nonetheless, it is clear that while in its infancy mobile news is also an important, if still minor, part of consumers' media habits and preferences – especially the customisation and personalisation of news (Deuze, 2007, p. 157). Further, as my earlier discussion indicates, mobile news is a firm and prominent part of the strategies of newspaper organisations, and other media organisations too – and there is a body of scientific and technical research and development focused on designing mobiles and handheld devices for mobile news.

Mobile news innovations and citizen journalism

While news is being redesigned for, and consumed on, mobile devices, much of this activity, as we have observed, is evolutionary in nature, and continuous with, or at least forms part of, the ecology being created by other forms of online news. However, there are some distinctive innovations emerging that see particular features of mobile cultures and networks being utilised to fashion new kinds of news. There are now a wide range of such forms of mobile news, mostly still in experimental or pilot form, but very interesting nonetheless. They are especially interesting because of their base in co-creation, spanning and combining consumption and production. They are also fascinating because many of the celebrated projects are located in the vast and fast growing mobile markets of developing countries.

With the rise and endurance of SMS across the world, this has become an important form of what Jonathan Donner (2009) has termed 'mobile media on low-cost handsets'. SMS has become central for a number of innovative news ventures, especially in the developing world. An oft-mentioned example is the Sri Lanka-based JasmineNews (JNW):

> JNW provides timely, well-sourced news headlines via text messages to reach you on your mobile phone wherever you may be. ... At all times, JNW aims to be a facilitator of sharing news, views and experiences by citizens, i.e. JNW aims to be driven by public news priorities and needs. Started by a group of journalists, JNW reports Sri Lankan news for Sri Lankans and those who want to be informed of happenings in the island.

Here those consuming JasmineNews are receiving alerts and messages via SMS, as well as being able to read and follow news on the JNW website. JasmineNews has a statement of ethics that stresses accuracy, clear sourcing and checking – but also balances traditional objectives of journalism, and maintaining the financial basis of the profession, with a broader conception of news. It includes the following:

4) Make news available to those who request it on a pay-what-you-can basis . . .
7) We believe news gathering is not independent of the people around whom news is centered and their needs come first.
8) Pay an adequate salary to journalists.
9) At all times, facilitate a sharing of information and experiences by subscribers and public alike. (JNW, 2009)

The JasmineNews case is rather reminiscent of the use of mobile telephony, SMS and mobile video for sending information and news from situations where media are suppressed. This role of mobiles has been highlighted in the well publicised cases of Burma – notably the brutally suppressed uprising of the Buddhist monks (Jimenez, 2007) – and Tibet (with the unrest in March 2008). These uses of mobiles for human rights and activism have attracted widespread interest, building as they do on existing developments in media and activism (for instance, Gregory, 2006) and also community development (Goggin and Clark, 2009). What is notable about JasmineNews is that it is an ongoing news venture, run by freelance journalists, independent from other news organisations. While the news items can be viewed on the JasmineNews website, to receive 'breaking news to your mobile phone' a user needs to subscribe via his or her mobile phone company, paying 30 Sri Lankan rupees per month.

Another oft-discussed venture is the *Voices of Africa* project, launched in May 2007, with the support of the Voices of Africa Media Foundation based in Haarlem, in the Netherlands. *Voices of Africa* involves the use of mobiles for newsgathering: it 'Equips African reporter trainees with mobile telephones, offers them a training programme and financial support so as to enable them to make video, photo and written reports about Africa and for online publication' (*Voices of Africa*, 2009). As well as offering concrete training and development opportunities for aspirant journalists, the project also hopes to make a contribution to media and democracy:

> it is now possible for Africans to send articles and images (still and moving) about events taking place in their countries without using a computer and without having traditional internet connection. Under those circumstances, the bigger the number of people expressing their opinions through that technology, the stronger becomes democracy, and the more valuable is the contribution to good governance efforts in Africa. (Nyirubugara, 2007)

In these two cases, and in many other innovations emerging through mobile news – consistent with online news generally – we can observe a broadening of what we understand by journalism.

Elsewhere mobiles have received most attention, and valorisation, for highly publicised moments, where cellular citizens are believed to be taking news creation into their own hands. For instance, mobile journalism has been celebrated as a species of 'citizen' journalism – as in the London bombings of 7 July 2005 (Allan, 2006; Gordon, 2007). Citizen journalism builds on various traditions of reforming, democratizing and opening up news and journalism, including the stalled movements of public and civic journalism (Rosen 1999; Allan & Thorsen 2009; Dahlgren 2009). In such conceptions, mobiles play an emblematic, if under-theorised, role, as in this representative claim:

> This is the idea that traditional journalism opens itself up to the public . . . it will also require a participatory revolution in the way we make the news. Blogging is the least of it. Much more important, for example, is the use of camera phones by citizens, capturing news as it happens and sending it to news organisations around the world. This produced the images of demonstrations by monks in Tibet or police beatings in Zimbabwe that would otherwise have been out of the range of the professional photographers' lens. That is media freedom. (Beckett, 2008)

Certainly the capacity of mobiles to capture news events and quickly make such images available has now become a common feature of television and online news. However, the implications of such developments, and the potency of citizen journalism, have been widely questioned. A 2008 Harvard Berkman Center for Internet and Society report contends that the significance of such a shift remains limited: 'it is very rare for reporting by amateur eyewitnesses to do more than supplement professional coverage of significant events' (Miel and Faris, 2008b, p. 17). In this view, existing models of news and journalism will endure, underpinned by refurbished publishers and news agencies: 'Participatory and online substitutes do not appear to be viable substitutes for this broad news gathering role, though able to supplement and expand this coverage' (Miel and Faris, 2008a, p. 10).

While this critique may be accurate as a general summation of mobiles in news to date, I think it overstates the case – and also underestimates the scope and depth of the shift under way. While mobiles have been associated with new forms of news and also expanded forms of journalism that put citizens in the frame alongside journalists, consolidating and extending such now common concepts has proved rather tricky. I have already introduced one case study, which seeks to put mobile technology into the service of training and providing opportunities for people wishing to enter, or be recognised, in the profession of journalism – namely the *African Voices* project. This project also shares objectivities of participatory, public and citizen journalism, to open up news production and distribution to a more diverse, grassroots range of actors. In order to approach this debate from a different angle, it is useful to consider a more limited but clearer idea of mobile journalism.

Mobile journalism

Mobile journalism is handy for this discussion, because it is a concept aimed directly at professional journalists, their identity, changing practices, conditions and processes of work. While still nascent, mobile journalism has become a particular set of practices in its own right under the name of 'mojo'. 'Mojo' is the use of mobile phones by journalists for reporting. Prominent blogs such as Norwegian journalist Frank Barth-Nilsen's *Mojo Evolution* (http://mojoevolution.com) and Australian journalist, educator and academic Stephen Quinn's *GlobalMojo* (http://globalmojo.org/) are popularising mobile journalism and making resources available. In short, mobile journalism amounts to an intervention in the profession of journalism.

There is an enthusiastic, technophilic discourse associated with this variety of mobile journalism. Exponents keenly report the latest uses of mobiles for journalism, and swap notes on mobile cameras and software. As well as the capabilities of video cameras, able to despatch images via the mobile phone network, what is essential to the early phase of 'mojo' activity is the existence of video sharing and broadcasting sites on the Internet. Sites such as Qik, Bambuser and Mogulus – to name the three best-known providers – allow live mobile streaming. That is, they enable someone with a camera phone to upload video directly for viewing on the Internet. Qik promises that it 'enables you to share your moments live with your friends, family and the world – right from your mobile phone!' (http://qik.com). The likes of Qik have also inserted themselves into the interstices of viral, social media, adding mobile video to Facebook in April 2009: 'Twitter is so ten minutes ago. Now there's Qik – an application that allows you to stream live video from your cell phone directly to the web or your Facebook account or to another phone' (Balkam, 2009). And, of course, the future is not just incrementally better, the revolution has arrived (again):

> The implications are mind boggling. Think political rallies, weather events, live births, slow deaths – all of these and more will be instantly available with a helpful Google map to show you exactly where the video is being streamed from, thanks to inbuilt GPS capabilities of most phones. We are heading for an unedited, unmediated, live view of everyone and everything, inside and out, whether we like it or not. (Balkam, 2009)

Like Qik, the Swedish start-up Bambuser is also trying to cover the mobile video bases from Windows mobiles to iPhone (http://bambuser.blogspot.com/).

As well as the social media mavens, the live mobile video companies are also providing a ready-made infrastructure for the 'mojos', who are able to broadcast their reportage to these emergent platforms as well as providing content for established media companies. Already there would appear to be certain assumptions about the future of news and journalism that colour 'mojo': first, that the future of news will lie in its claims to immediacy; second, that good reporting needs to be able to quickly find its place on online platforms.

> Thanks to networked technologies – and RSS in particular – there is no reason why newsgathering cannot also be news production, or news distribution. . . . You film some raw material on your mobile phone using Qik. It's published on Qik, with an update posted to Twitter too. The video feed is embedded on your blog or news site, and once again RSS distributes it anywhere you or someone else wants. (Online Journalism Blog, 2009)

As yet the mojos have not established anything to warrant parallels to be drawn with 'j-blogging', or blogging by journalists (Robinson, 2006). Like rhetorics of citizen journalism, it is difficult to see how widespread mobile journalism is, and what its significance will be. One place to observe this is in the sites of industrial transformation in the organisation of news and media industries.

Currently there is much attention being given to the use of information and communications technologies to re-engineer work practices in new gathering, redaction, production and distribution. Systematic approaches are being taken, for instance, in relation to the 'online newsroom'. This is also the case with mobile journalism, of which a leading example may be found in the initiatives of mobile phone manufacturer Nokia.

Nokia Research Labs has worked for some years on mobile journalism, as part of its comprehensive approach to exploring forms of everyday, personal mobile media:

> Have you ever found yourself experiencing something extraordinary without having any means to capture and share it? You become the eyewitness to dramatic events or you want to share a special moment with the people that matter to you.
>
> Now all you need to do is grab your Nokia device from your pocket. Mobile devices free us to capture stories where and as they happen. Your mobile enables you to be always connected, so you can capture and share the stories you see as they happen, where they happen. (Technowire, 2009)

Nokia's strategy here has been twofold. The first part is to recognise and key into the new developments in mobile and digital culture, such as citizen journalism. So Nokia researcher Timo Koskinen notes:

> The term 'citizen journalism' has been in use for several years, but technological innovations – particularly the introduction of mobile multimedia computers – have transformed the concept. 'Citizen journalism' is beginning to embrace a wide range of public engagement with the media, from groups of contributors organized around subject or geographic areas to the casual participation of observers who are lucky – or unlucky – enough to be at the scene of a newsworthy event. (Nokia, 2007)

At the same time Nokia has squarely targeted professional journalists. So with its October 2007 mobile journalism kit, developed with Reuters, professional users:

> made use of the mobile journalism application in their everyday work to edit, combine and file text, images, sound and live and recorded video streams,

producing and publishing multi-media stories of broadcast quality without needing to return to the studio or office. (Nokia, 2007)

What is interesting is how mobile journalism is being framed – especially in terms of what contribution it suggests this may make to practices of journalism and news-reporting. Reuters Media Chief Scientist Nic Fulton claims that:

> By running on handheld devices, rather than on bulkier laptop computers, the mobile journalism application enables us to create complete stories and file them for distribution, without leaving the scene. This saves us time and benefits our audience by ensuring that they receive high quality news that is absolutely up-to-date. (Nokia, 2007)

The Nokia–Reuters toolkit combined a number of things: the multimedia capabilities of smartphones; video streaming; text editing; a new user interface; and metadata that brings together all the device's information about context (including location, time and date) (Nokia, 2007). A less prominent but still vital feature was the inclusion of editorial capability, with a 'mobile editorial interface that links the toolkit developed by NRC [Nokia Research Centre] to the in-house editorial process, allowing stories to be published almost instantly from the field' (Nokia, 2007). While there was not a lot of critical examination of the Nokia–Reuters mobile journalism kit, at least one blogger did note with interest the attention being paid to the reconfiguration of the newsroom and its technologies in such developments: 'Stuff like this makes me think that investment in developing for equipment may be just as valuable as investing in the kit itself' (Dickinson, 2007).

Following on from its mobile journalism kit, Nokia turned its attention from retooling the handset to conceiving and building a network platform. In its beta version in June 2009, this platform was based on open content principles, and with it Nokia sought to create a mobile journalism assignment system that would be of use to news editors, professional journalists and the new mass of potential citizen journalists and interested mobile phone users.

Conclusion

In early 2010, the thing called mobile news is clearly a work in progress. As part of the mediascape of online news, its importance is already well demonstrated, and its potential is manifold. Yet it remains very much unformed, and relatively open to different trajectories that could see mobile news mean quite different things to diverse groups of interested consumers, producers and users.

From the perspective of established, mainstream media organisations and brands, cellular mobile devices are being steadily incorporated, as part of the intricate fashioning of news offerings and delivery – as the examples of well known newspapers and television broadcasters reveal. From the standpoint of new actors in news, whether small organisations, groups of interested journalists, citizens or communities, the affordances of mobile technologies and networks offer new possibilities for devising and circulating news – illustrated by quite a number of experiments, especially in Africa, Asia-Pacific and Latin America. Inflected by the professional, social and political investments of those engaged in the reform and envisioning of future notions, institutions, newsrooms and workplaces of journalism, mobile journalism is playing an emerging role – like blogging and video journalism before it – as an emblem, harbinger and practical solution to difficult tensions and rich possibilities.

Mobile news, then, is very much implicated in broader developments and debates attendant to online news and the mediascape that Graham Meikle characterises as 'News 2.0' (Meikle, 2009). Mobile news does entail changed practices of news consumption and production, and the redrawing of relationships and boundaries between various types of journalism – 'professional' and 'amateur', not to mention the co-minglings of public, civic, community and citizen journalisms. There is an intimacy in this personalisation of news (see Kate Crawford's chapter in this volume). Surprisingly, the intimate turn also offers new possibilities for how media, their audiences and publics are created and connected – in which large commercial media companies (television broadcasters; Internet and mobile phone companies) and small commercial interests (small software companies; mobile media start-ups; freelance journalists; bloggers) interact in dependent ways with public broadcasters, community media and organised and disorganised citizen media. Its futures, however, are also bound up in the fate of global mobile media, and how these develop, beyond the mobile phone – and what cultural centrality and social significance they garner. Thus small-screen, short-text, little video, mobile news is a ductible, inchoate, incomplete yet powerful form still in the mix.

My thanks to Caroline Hamilton for her research assistance in preparing this chapter.

REFERENCES

Allan, Stuart (2006) *Online News: Journalism and the Internet* (Maidenhead and New York: Open University Press).

Allan, Stuart and Thorsen, Einar (eds) (2009) *Citizen Journalism: Global Perspectives* (New York: Peter Lang).

Ash, Timothy Garton (2009) 'Twitter counts more than armouries in this new politics of people power', *Guardian*, 17 June, http://www.guardian.co.uk/commentisfree/2009/jun/17/iran-election-protests-twitter-students, accessed 15 May 2009.

Australian Communications and Media Authority (ACMA) (2009) *Digital Media Literacy in Australia: Key Indicators and Research Sources* (Sydney: ACMA), http://www.acma.gov.au/webwr/_assets/main/lib310665/dml_in_aust-data_available_and_key_sources.pdf, accessed 15 August 2009.

Australian Interactive Media Industry Association (AIMIA) (2008) *Australian Mobile Phone Lifestyle Index* (Sydney: AIMIA), http://www.aimia.com.au/enews/events/AMPLI%202008/AIMIA_ReportAugust2008_FULL_Final.pdf

Balkam, Stephen (2009) 'Qikker than Twitter', *Huffington Post*, 27 April, http://www.huffingtonpost.com/stephen-balkam/qikker-than-twitter_b_191262.html, accessed 18 May 2009.

Beckett, Charlie (2008) 'Networked journalism', *Guardian*, 3 May, http://www.guardian.co.uk/commentisfree/2008/may/03/networkedjournalism, accessed 13 May 2009.

Boczkowski, Pablo (2005) *Digitizing the News: Innovation in Online Newspapers* (Cambridge, MA: MIT Press).

Borger, Julian (2009) 'Iran election fallout: on the streets, in cyberspace, protest faces tough opponent,' *Guardian*, 17 June, http://www.guardian.co.uk/world/2009/jun/17/iran-election-results-protests

Cawley, Anthony (2008) 'News production in an Irish online newsroom: practice, process, and culture', in Chris Paterson and David Domingo (eds) *Making Online News: The Ethnography of New Media Production* (New York: Peter Lang), pp. 45–60.

Dahlgren, Peter (2009) *Media and Political Engagement: Citizens, Communication, and Democracy* (Cambridge and New York: Cambridge University Press).

'Death of Neda' (2009) *Wikipedia*, 13 August, http://en.wikipedia.org/w/index.php?title=Death_of_Neda_Agha-Soltan&oldid=307779138, accessed 15 August 2009.

Deuze, Mark (2007) *Media Work* (Cambridge: Polity Press).

Dickinson, Andy (2007) 'Reuters mobile journalism toolkit', 25 October, http://www.andydickinson.net/2007/10/25/reuters-mobile-journalism-toolkit/, accessed 13 May 2009.

Donner, Jonathan (2009) 'Mobile media on low-cost handsets: the resiliency of text messaging among small enterprises in India (and beyond)', in Gerard Goggin and Larissa Hjorth (eds) *Mobile Technologies: From Telecommunications to Media* (New York: Routledge), pp. 93–104.

Ewing, Scott, Thomas, Julian and Schiessl, Julianne (2008) *CCi Digital Futures Report: The Internet in Australia* (Melbourne: ARC Centre of Excellence for

Creative Industries and Innovation, Swinburne University of Technology), http://cci.edu.au/publications/digital-futures, accessed 20 April 2009.

Goggin, Gerard and Clark, Jacqueline (2009) 'Mobile phones and community development: a contact zone between media and citizenship', *Development in Practice*, 19: 4/5, 585–97.

Gordon, Janey (2007) 'The mobile phone and the public sphere: mobile phone usage in three critical situations', *Convergence*, 13: 3, 307–19.

Gregory, Sam (2006) 'Transnational storytelling: human rights, WITNESS, and video advocacy', *American Anthropologist*, 108: 1, 195–204.

Jimenez, David (2007) 'With mobiles and internet, protesters battle to keep eyes on Burma', *Guardian*, 29 September, http://www.guardian.co.uk/world/2007/sep/29/burma.topstories32, accessed 13 May 2009.

JNW (2009) 'About JNW', http://www.jasminenews.com/about-jnw, accessed 13 May 2009.

Kennedy, Helen (2009) 'Neda, young girl brutally killed in Iran, becoming symbol of rebellion', *New York Daily News*, 22 June, http://www.nydailynews.com/news/us_world/2009/06/21/2009-06-21_neda_young_girl_killed_in_iran.html

Khiabany, Gholam and Sreberny, Annabelle (2009) 'Internet in Iran: the battle over an emerging virtual public sphere', in Gerard Goggin and Mark McLelland (eds) *Internationalizing Internet Studies: Beyond Anglophone Paradigms* (New York and London: Routledge), pp. 196–213.

Landler, Mark and Stelter, Brian (2009) 'Washington taps into a potent new force in diplomacy', *New York Times*, 16 June, http://www.nytimes.com/2009/06/17/world/middleeast/17media.html?_r=2&scp=2&sq=Twitter&st=cse

Meikle, Graham (2009) *Interpreting News* (Basingstoke: Palgrave Macmillan).

Miel, Persephone and Faris, Robert (2008a) *A Typology for Media Organizations* (Boston: Berkman Center for Internet Society, Harvard University), http://cyber.law.harvard.edu/pubrelease/mediarepublic/downloads.html, accessed 15 May 2009.

Miel, Persephone and Faris, Robert (2008b) *News and Information as Digital Media Come of Age* (Boston, MA: Berkman Center for Internet Society, Harvard University), http://cyber.law.harvard.edu/sites/cyber.law.harvard.edu/files/Overview_MR.pdf, accessed 15 May 2009.

New York Times (2009) 'A new way to take your news with you on the iPhone and iPod Touch', http://www.nytimes.com/services/mobile/iphone.html, accessed 13 May 2009.

Nokia (2007) 'Nokia and Reuters team up to transform how journalists file stories in the field', 23 October, http://www.nokia.com/A4136001?newsid=1161557, accessed 13 May 2009.

Nyirubugara, Olivier (2007) 'About Voices of Africa', http://voicesofafrica.africanews.com/site/page/about_voices_of_africa, accessed 13 May 2009.

Ofcom (2009) *The Communications Market 2009* (London: Ofcom), http://www.ofcom.org.uk/research/cm/cmr09/, accessed 15 August 2009.

Online Journalism Blog (2009) 'Newsgathering-is-distribution ...', 9 February, http://onlinejournalismblog.com/2009/02/09/newsgathering-is-production-is-distribution-model-for-a-21st-century-newsroom-pt1-cont/, accessed 13 May 2009.

Pavlik, John (2001) *Journalism and New Media* (New York: Columbia University Press).

PDA: The Digital Content Blog (2009) 'Rupert Murdoch's plans for an ebook reader', *Guardian*, 7 May, http://www.guardian.co.uk/media/pda/2009/may/07/rupert-murdoch-news-corporation, accessed 13 May 2009.

Pew Internet and American Life (2009) *Wireless Internet Use* (Washington, DC: Pew), http://pewinternet.org/Reports/2009/12-Wireless-Internet-Use.aspx, accessed 15 August 2009.

Robinson, Susan (2006) 'The mission of the j-blog: recapturing journalistic authority online', *Journalism*, 7, 65–83.

Rosen, Jay (1999) *What Are Journalists For?* (New Haven, CT: Yale University Press).

Smith, Zoe (2009) 'Introducing multimedia to the newsroom', in Charles Miller (ed.) *The Future of Journalism* (London: BBC College of Journalism), pp. 18–24, http://www.bbc.co.uk/blogs/theeditors/future_of_journalism.pdf, accessed 15 August 2009.

Sydney Morning Herald, 'Fairfax Digital Mobile Services', http://mobile.fairfax.com.au/smh/, accessed 13 May 2009.

Technowire (2009) 'Share your Special Moments with Nokia', http://www.tecnowire.com/2009/06/share-your-special-moment-with-nokia.html

Voices of Africa (2009) 'Voices of Africa wins World Summit Award', 29 April, http://voicesofafrica.africanews.com/site/VoicesofAfrica_wins_World_Summit_Award/list_messages/24614, accessed 29 April 2009.

Zucker, Ethan (2008) *International News: Bringing about the Golden Age* (Boston: Berkman Center for Internet Society, Harvard University, http://cyber.law.harvard.edu/pubrelease/mediarepublic/downloads.html, accessed 15 May 2009.

CHAPTER 7

News to me: Twitter and the personal networking of news

KATE CRAWFORD

What does Twitter mean for news? Or, to put it another way, if we are to take Twitter seriously as a platform where news and information circulate, what role does it play in the wider news ecology? The company behind Twitter does not see itself as a news channel, but as something far more dispersed and organic. As revealed after a security breach in mid-2009, when over 300 sensitive documents were hacked and released to the public, Twitter Inc. is well aware of how its network is used to send updates, news and alerts. But the founders see a larger potential. 'Twitter is not an alert system', noted CEO Evan Williams in a strategic planning document. 'Maybe more of a nervous system', added Twitter's co-founder Biz Stone. Another note reads: 'if we had a billion users, that will be the pulse of the planet' (Schonfeld, 2009a).

This is a revealing insight into the ambitions of Twitter, which reached 44.5 million unique visitors to its site in June 2009 (Schonfeld, 2009b). There are millions more who access the service and post their own 140-character messages via desktop clients and mobile phones. It does not constitute a truly global 'pulse' yet, but neurological metaphors remain compelling, evoking McLuhan's claim that 'electric technologies' act as extensions of the human nervous system (1964, p. 3). Social media systems have many tendrils around the world, densely clustered in some regions, only delicately threaded through others, constantly receiving and transmitting thousands of electrical signals per second. Akin to a neuron, each user can receive and transmit information, and – when a network is functioning well – can be highly efficient at rapidly relaying information throughout the system.

The kinds of information shared through Twitter vary markedly. Some messages are personal and quotidian: about a meal, a train ride, a queue or a software problem. Others share links to news stories, sporting results, a trailer for a film or a report about a celebrity death. Media organisations themselves are also participating: sending breaking news updates, teasers for feature stories and commentary on the events of the day. The rate at which any signal is then relayed – or in Twitter parlance, retweeted – by other users depends on a range of factors, including what is seen as its interest or entertainment value, or the newsworthiness of the message (boyd, 2010).

As James Carey (1989, p. 15) describes, communication is commonly understood as a transmission of messages in space, but it can also be a ritual: a ceremonial process that draws people together through shared beliefs. Twitter is a network where rituals and transmissions are imbricated: communities of interest form clusters, and messages pass between them, with the occasional message being circulated to a much wider group. The death of Michael Jackson, for example, travelled rapidly throughout the network, becoming a top trending topic and at high volume: accounting for over 30 per cent of all messages, according to the tracking service Twist (Cashmore, 2009a). As the *New York Times* noted, for many people their first contact with the news of Jackson's death was on Twitter, before any coverage by newspapers, television or radio (Wortham, 2009).

But such large pulses through the entire system are rare. Many posts will never be relayed beyond their immediate network, and the majority of users on Twitter are not even regularly updating, preferring instead to listen in to the updates of others (Cheng et al., 2009). The experience of the social network is entirely determined by the selection of people that users elects to 'follow', or whose updates they will receive. Thus, what would be considered traditional news is often filtered through a nominated set of friends, associates and strangers: designed by each user to predetermine the kinds of updates they will receive. The almost infinitely customisable nature of Twitter means that communities will determine what is important to them and retweet topics of interest, in what Manuel Castells (2007, p. 248) has described as a 'mass self-communication'. The selection of people one follows on Twitter function collectively as a highly subjective filter that prioritises and re-orders the news agenda as it is understood by a newspaper or a TV network, influencing what is heard, and when.

At another level, the kinds of Twitter updates that are most often pilloried for being irrelevant to a wider audience (for example, when a person's cat dies) may constitute significant news to an inner circle of friends. The concept of what counts as news differs between individuals, and varies according to a multitude of factors, including geographical location, nationality, age, interests and profession. This, of course, is not a new phenomenon. The definition of what is news, as opposed to trivia, or rumour, or everyday chatter has always been hazy and mutable. As the journalist A. J. Leibling wrote in 1965, 'People everywhere confuse what they read in newspapers with news' (cited in Brighton and Foy, 2007, p. 2). Newspapers once held the dominant position of determining what, in the main, would be considered the news of the day. But within social media services, the ability to tailor exactly what is heard by selecting individuals and organisations results in individually specific experiences of a news landscape. This has implications for the creation, consumption and very definition of news as it is shared and recycled through Twitter.

This chapter considers the news practices that are emerging through Twitter, starting with a brief account of the various ways it is used to create, distribute and consume news. Are terms like 'citizen journalism' usefully applicable to Twitter practices to date? How do the immediacy and the subjectivity of networks like Twitter change the way news is understood? In particular, the critical reception of CNN's coverage of Iranian election protests in 2009 offers a case study of how Twitter users are able to access rapid and directly personal experiences of news, and how this changes expectations of media organisations and their capacity to listen. These events are examined as part of a broader question: does Twitter contribute to a reconsideration of news and its audiences, and how do emotions shape the social space of news?

When is Twitter journalism?

There are several archetypical moments of news breaking on Twitter. They are retold as dramatic narratives, and often become stories in their own right. 'There's a plane in the Hudson. I'm on the ferry going to pick up the people. Crazy.' Those fifty-seven characters, written by eyewitness Janis Krums, became the first news that US Airways Flight 1549 had ditched into the Hudson River. They were accompanied by an image of a floating plane, photographed from a ferry, with passengers clustered along the wings. As the news of the plane incident spread, Twitter itself became a news story, and Krums was held up briefly as a kind of 'citizen journalist' star (Mackey, 2009). Similarly, when bombs exploded in Jakarta in July 2009, the first reports came via Twitter (ABC News, 2009) and then continued as a major source of images and updates, as occurred during the Mumbai terror attacks and the bushfires across southern Australia in 2008. The social media site Mashable observed, 'it's remarkable to think that this form of instant news distribution, unheard of 3 years ago, is now commonplace' (Cashmore, 2009b).

Certainly, Twitter is becoming established as a short-form news platform. In terms of news distribution, a wide range of media outlets already have a presence, including the BBC, CNN, ABC, the *New York Times* and the *Wall Street Journal*. The major networks attract substantial audiences around the world, with CNN's breaking news service (twitter.com/cnnbrk) approaching three million followers. The most common style adapted by news agencies is to treat Twitter like another broadcast outlet: delivering dozens of updates per day, but not receiving updates from others in turn, or tracking how the news is received, or responding to any feedback. Despite CNN's large follower count, fewer than twenty people are followed in return.

This asymmetry is in itself interesting, as it reveals how closely the engagement with social media has been modelled on traditional broadcast models. In practice, CNN is merely using Twitter as another pipe to push down news feeds. As Mark Deuze has observed, the news industry has treated online spaces as just an advertisement for the offline product, while 'journalism still depends on its established mode of production, through which it largely (and unreflexively) reproduces the institutional contours of high ... modernity (Deuze, 2008, p. 856). The belief was maintained that the primary role of the online population was to behave just as people were expected to behave offline: as an audience (p. 856). Thus, while Twitter may be a new space, this does not mean that news companies have as yet developed particularly novel ways to engage with it.

Further, it remains unclear that terms such as 'citizen journalism' or 'participatory journalism' can map comfortably against the kinds of activities that occur on Twitter. Even in the case of Janis Krums, he had no intention to adopt the codes and processes that are associated with journalism: his message was not an attempt to tell an objective story, nor to conduct an investigation at arm's length by following leads or making enquiries (Herzog, 2009). The Twitter message Krums sent was immediate, subjective and emotional: he was on the ferry that would soon be collecting the stranded passengers. He was in the middle of a rescue mission and was sharing a dramatic experience with his set of followers. His message, however, was immediately retweeted and dispersed widely through the Twitter system. If a piece of information is widely circulated by a large international network, it may be considered to have reached the status of major news. But does that make the process that generated it 'journalism'?

In its most broad definition, the concept of participatory or citizen journalism is one where the role of reporting is taken on by those who are not professional journalists. Bowman and Willis define it as:

the act of a citizen, or group of citizens, playing an active role in the process of collecting, reporting, analysing and disseminating news and information. The intent of this participation is to provide independent, reliable, accurate, wide-ranging and relevant information that a democracy requires. (Bowman and Willis, 2003, p. 9)

For a non-journalist using Twitter, the intentions can be quite different. Addressing a few dozen, or even a few thousand, followers, a Twitter user may occasionally seek to share relevant information, but they may also wish to amuse, to vent, to capture a personal moment or to converse. The concepts of reliability, accuracy and providing objective commentary do not provide the common motivation for a Twitter message. The first tagline for the service was quite intimate – 'What are you doing now?' – suggesting that users contribute in an impressionistic, subjective style.

But in November 2009, more than three years after launching, Twitter's founders changed this introductory question to 'What's happening?' This was a clear and acknowledged shift towards a different mode. As Biz Stone explained, the service has 'long outgrown the concept of personal status updates', as people are also 'witnessing accidents, organizing events, sharing links, breaking news, reporting stuff their dad says, and so much more' (Stone, 2009). News, links and the witnessing of events are now characterised as a critical part of what people do on Twitter.

Certainly, Twitter is a platform that can lend itself to the speedy delivery of breaking news headlines, a capacity that is already being harnessed by services such as BNO News, the BBC, ABC and CNN. As the managing director of ABC, Mark Scott, has argued:

I think Twitter may emerge as the outstanding way of disseminating surprising breaking news. In my experience in newsrooms, the biggest stories always arrived in 140 characters or less: 'Princess of Wales dead', 'Plane hits World Trade Center'. (Scott, 2009)

But does the penning of a headline-like update, drawn from an eyewitness experience, constitute an act of journalism? Journalism has been defined as an occupational ideology, one that is defined and patrolled by those who self-identify as journalists (Deuze, 2005). This description would immediately delimit the description of non-journalist Twitter users as contributing to any conscious form of journalism – it may not be their intent or even desire. Janis Krums, for example, had been using Twitter for business reasons, to post links that related to his nutrition company. As he explained in an interview, 'the posts before and after the US Air photo were mainly random things that I think are interesting' (Herzog, 2009).

This raises the question of how a plane on the Hudson river is different: it was something interesting to Krums, and certainly something that became of interest to large numbers of other people. But his use of Twitter did not fundamentally change in that moment: he was sharing an experience, expressing a feeling about what he saw, not necessarily aspiring to be a journalist or to provide 'accurate, wide-ranging and relevant information'. Describing these moments as journalism is retrofitting an established mode of practice onto something that is materially different.

How are we to characterise these contributions, if not necessarily as journalism, citizen or otherwise? On networks such as Facebook and Twitter, millions of messages circulate every day, a series of tiny, experiential observations. Occasionally, one will be considered significant, and will rapidly move through the system, from one cluster of associates to the next. It moves from being personal news to something larger, in a shared recognition of interest and relevance. But while there are moments of eyewitness reporting occasionally shared en masse on Twitter, they can also fall outside the usual spectrum of citizen journalist activity or definitions of news. 'Journalism' may be an unnecessarily restrictive framework to apply to these experiential accounts, which often relate an affective, impressionistic moment of what was seen and felt, designed to be shared with a distributed social group. A more granular understanding is needed of the emergent habits and practices within social media spaces.

As Carey has noted, the concept of news is grounded in a historical period and represents the interests of a specific class:

> [News] is a form of culture invented by a particular class at a particular point of history – in this case by the middle class largely in the eighteenth century . . . [it] does not represent a universal taste or necessarily legitimate form of knowledge . . . but an invention in historical time, that like most other human inventions, will dissolve when the class that sponsors it and its possibility of having significance for us evaporates. (Carey, 1989, p. 17)

Twitter was produced by a class that differs from the middle class of the eighteenth century in key ways. It began as a network for information elites and early adopters, 'no collar' desk workers with an interest in scanning a wide range of sources and staying in touch with friends and family, regardless of the physical realities of long working hours. It has been adopted by a wider demographic, yet its emergence in the early twenty-first century needs to be understood in connection with particular labour practices and desires for information that also skew the way news is defined and received.

The case of CNNfail

It is important from the outset to understand emerging social media technologies in their historical context, as growing from and drawing upon the energies of major media companies as well as the tropes of broadcast media forms such as radio, TV and newspapers. If we are to return to the idea of Twitter as a nervous system, then traditional news companies act as a cortex, while the majority of users are dispersed like dendrites, connected to the cortex, reacting and responding to it and to each other, but also sending new signals of their own.

However, these signals are not necessarily received by media organisations. Many journalists and news agencies continue to see Twitter simply as a dissemination tool to deliver news to an audience. Certainly, by examining the updates of CNN, the BBC, ABC and the like, we can see that the major broadcast networks are being followed by millions, but few are following people back in return. This failure to be receptive to incoming signals, be it commentary or tips or criticism, has already generated public embarrassment for news networks.

A notable example occurred in June 2009, on the weekend of the Iranian election. After the announcement that Mahmoud Ahmadinejad had been returned to office, Tehran erupted into mass protests, with claims of fraud and voting irregularities. The election occurred on a Friday, and by Saturday there were images of street clashes and demonstrations appearing on the photo sharing site Flickr, as well as 140-character descriptions appearing on Twitter. These eyewitness account were circulated widely, to the point where Twitter users were receiving regular updates about the crackdown on protesters, while some mainstream news networks were only lightly covering the events (Morozov, 2009).

CNN, as a 24-hour cable news broadcaster, came under particular criticism for its slow response to the Iranian protests over the weekend. As described by the *New York Times*, the network seemed to have taken the weekend off, offering only occasional reports rather than the kind of rolling live coverage that made its name during the first Iraq war and the political crackdown in Tiananmen Square (Stelter, 2009). This laxity of coverage generated thousands of critical responses from Twitter users, who were receiving dramatic accounts online, but only sporadic coverage from CNN, MSNBC and Fox

News. The result was the emergence and widespread use of the tag *#CNNFail*, which then became a trending topic on Twitter. At points during the weekend, new criticisms were appearing on Twitter at least once per second (Stelter, 2009). Soon after, a website was created called CNNfail.com, with a live stream of all tweets relating to CNN's coverage. In the words of Andrew Sullivan, a blogger for *The Atlantic*, 'There's a reason the MSM [mainstream media] is in trouble' (Sullivan, 2009).

While CNN sought to defend its reporting, the damage had already been done to its reputation as the best source of around-the-clock news during a political crisis. A host of newspaper and television reports focused on Twitter taking its place as the service for immediate and diverse first-hand accounts (see Cohen, 2009; Morozov, 2009; Taylor, 2009). This perspective, however, overlooks the fact that Twitter and cable news channels are complementary forms, responding to each other as they cover different kinds of responses to an event, similar to the interaction between many blogs and the mainstream media. In the case of the Iranian election, one provided live television and web-based coverage within the genres of traditional news journalism, while the other offered instantaneous, emotional accounts of the lived experience of Iranians in the streets.

What was striking was how easily networks such as CNN could have avoided the situation. For example, by Sunday morning, Twitter users had already commenced tracking CNN's oversights in detail. One user, called Alierakieron, wrote: 'Tehran is burning, and CNN's headline is about a theme park.' Indeed, on that morning of the second day of protests, CNN's Twitter update read: 'Theme park chain Six-Flags files for bankruptcy.' Alierakieron responded with a comment directed straight to CNN: 'You're a disgrace to journalism.' However, as CNN does not follow her, or many of the millions of others who tune into CNN's Twitter channels, her comment received no response. Many thousands of similar comments were being written on the same day. Yet with no established process to 'listen in' to the feedback, CNN appeared slow and thoroughly disconnected from the news ecology on Twitter that it sought to influence as a news provider.

In all, it was a vivid study of the limitations of importing a broadcast news model from television and applying it to Twitter with little recognition of the importance of paying attention to the other users of the network. In the case of the Iranian protests of 2009, CNN would have been a stronger news network if it had tracked the comments and criticisms of the thousands of users who were interested in the developing events. As I have previously argued, the metaphor of listening is a particularly apposite one for the kinds of online activity that occur in social media spaces like Twitter (Crawford,

2009a). Had CNN been listening to the stream of small pulses of information, from Iranians, from news watchers in the West and from other news networks such as PBS (which had more detailed and sustained coverage), it could have deepened its coverage of the significant events in Tehran.

The capacity to listen in to hundreds, if not thousands, of people through their Twitter updates could be particularly powerful for news media companies. Of course, only a small percentage of updates may be directly useful to a story. But around certain issues and news events, updates can form very noticeable patterns, as with the Iranian protests. Yet there are few examples yet of media companies developing an ability to listen in order to strengthen their own news services. Some see Twitter as a kind of competitor to traditional news services (see Solis, 2009), without acknowledging its interdependence, or the way it enhances and expands the spread of traditional news services, while also contributing to the news ecology with millions of personal and subjective accounts. The case of CNNFail demonstrated the importance of listening as well as broadcasting.

Personal news network

The value of listening to Twitter users is still regularly disparaged, however. The service has been criticised as banal since its inception, without recognition that the 'conversations about nothing' are cementing forms of social connection and intimacy (Crawford, 2009b). Not only is phatic communication an important part of Twitter's utility, it also has ramifications for how we understand the concept of news.

In what became a much publicised study, US market research company Pear Analytics reported in 2009 that 40 per cent of the messages relayed on Twitter were 'pointless babble' (Kelly, 2009). Only 3.6 per cent were deemed to be news-related. There are considerable limitations to the study, which sampled 2,000 Twitter messages across a two-week period. But one of the most significant was definitional. News was defined as: 'Any sort of main stream [*sic*] news that you might find on your national news stations such as CNN, Fox, or others. This did not include tech news or social media news that you might find on TechCrunch or Mashable' (Kelly, 2009, p. 4). Babble constituted anything that 'did not appear to be useful to a large percentage of your visitors (more than 50%)' (Kelly, 2009). Ignoring technology and social media news immediately discounted an information genre that has been highly popular on Twitter ever since the service was widely adopted at the media and technology conference SXSW in 2007.

Pear Analytics received many queries about how its study had been conducted, including how pointless babble was detected: what could be important news to someone may be unrecognisable to another. The company responded on its blog: '[Babble] became very easy to spot in the public time-line – tweets like "I just saw a raccoon" or "I need to buy some shoes today" fall in this category.' But a Pear analyst later added that 'if you are a hunter or the owner of a shoe store, you would argue that those tweets are not irrelevant' (Kelly, 2009).

This study points to a wider misunderstanding of the concept of news as it is developing within social media spaces. The definition of news has been reduced to a narrow, corporate-centric information genre that is produced by major media groups. The observations of non-journalists are then consigned to babble, unless they capture a moment that is significant enough to be categorised as citizen journalism. This produces a seesawing of opinion about Twitter as news platform versus Twitter as mindless banality. As danah boyd wrote in a blog post:

> Far too many tech junkies and marketers are obsessed with Twitter becoming the next news outlet source. As a result, the press are doing what they did with blogging: hyping Twitter up as this amazing source of current events and dismissing it as pointless babble. (boyd 2009)

As I have argued, broadly defining much activity on Twitter as citizen journalism is problematic, as it over-emphasizes Twitter's role as a news source in opposition to the existing broadcast and online outlets, and fails to engage with the ways Twitter alters traditional understandings of news. Conversely, simply considering Twitter as little more than a noisy channel for meaningless streams of chatter downplays the significance of the emotional dimension of the technology. A more detailed engagement is needed with the emergent practices on Twitter to attend to the blurring between everyday personal updates and news, and to observe how they are different from pre-existing definitions of journalism. Of the many ways in which news functions differently within Twitter, three deserve mentioning here: reordering, flatness and shared feeling.

Reordering

Newspapers order stories in a hierarchical sequence that accords more weight to some – such as the lead story at the top of a broadsheet page. News broadcasts on radio and television similarly rank stories in a taxonomy that begins with what is deemed most important and runs on to the least, played in order through the course of the programme. But Twitter radically unsettles a pre-ordered experience of mainstream news. Users might read their friends commenting on what they think is the interesting news of the day, which could include links to stories, YouTube videos, blogs and photographs. If news organisations are followed on Twitter, they will offer updates in the order in which they are reported. The organising principle is temporal and linear, sent when it is received, not ranked in order of significance.

For example, BNO News (twitter.com/breakingnews) delivers news updates to its Twitter stream regularly throughout a day, but will signal a major news story with a prefatory 'urgent', or by capitalising the entire message. It does not have the ability to package together news, or reorder throughout the day – it aims to reach users as quickly as possible. When a news story is deemed to be of particular interest, it may be expanded upon with several messages. For example, after an earthquake off the coast of New Zealand, BNO first reported the earthquake, then forwarded an alert from the Pacific Tsunami Warning Centre, and followed with a warning to Australian residents on the coast of New South Wales. The threat dissipated a few hours later. But BNO was one of the earliest organisations to release the information about the quake and tsunami warning, which it proudly noted on its blog. 'This particular event, even though no destructive tsunami was generated and no one died from the earthquake, just shows the lack of coverage from the mainstream media at times' (BNO, 2009). Meanwhile, television news programmes reported the risk of tsunami later in the day, and were unable to update as regularly as Twitter news services.

Furthermore, many users will get their first access to a news story indirectly, when it is retweeted by someone they follow. The tsunami warning was immediately and widely retweeted, particularly by New Zealand and Australian users, radiating outwards from those who receive BNO updates to their followers, and beyond. This intense social reordering of news operates through communities of interest: groups with a particular focus (be it related to their profession, leisure activities, location or age) will prioritise the sharing and retweeting of news that will be of direct relevance to them and their followers (boyd 2010).

Flatness

The distinctly unhierarchical nature of Twitter generates other effects. Messages are not ranked in order of importance, and unless a software client such as Tweetdeck is used, there is little to prioritise or even distinguish one over another. This generates a kind of 'flatness', particularly in the web-based interface of Twitter. A message from a friend about lunch will arrive with the same format as an update about a bombing: neither will be highlighted or marked out as more important.

Further, if news headlines are particularly well suited to the 140-character limit, personal Twitter updates can easily assume the general form of news headlines. This is a kind of newsification of the everyday, where users are voluntarily contributing headline-style reports of their daily activities. This is to suggest not that there is no distinction between news headlines and personal updates from friends, but that the shared form of Twitter messages has the effect of blurring and flattening each: personalising the news and headlining the personal. Miller (2008, p. 388) has argued that social media tend to flatten communication 'towards the non-dialogic and non-informational', creating a phatic culture. But this is not a unidirectional tendency: affective and phatic exchanges can enhance and add dynamics to information streams.

For example, personal commentary can overlay and intensify mainstream news events, heightening the emotional experience. Writing about broadcasting live events on television, Dayan and Katz (1994, p. 97) draw together the relationship between rumour and flatness:

> Rumours reinject depth into a televised event, differentiating those who know from those who do not know yet. They suggest the existence of physical volume in the event: they counterbalance its pedagogic cool, its ironed out flatness.

If rumour can be understood as the general circulating wash of discussion and story telling, then the discussions on Twitter about a news event add to its depth in a similar way to watercooler discussions of television events. A story can be seen immediately having an impact on people, whether they are directly affected, or just sharing the news, or critically engaging with it.

Shared feeling

Twitter is well suited to augmenting live events, through 'live tweeting' and discussions occurring in real time during sporting events, elections or television shows. These exchanges can be full of suspense, joy, horror and disappointment. These everyday exchanges have their own complex emotional currents.

Expressions of shared feeling are particularly evident around celebrity death. In a study by the Web Ecology Project called 'Detecting sadness in 140 characters: sentiment analysis and mourning Michael Jackson on Twitter', it was found that record numbers of people went to Twitter to express their sorrow. In the space of the first hour, 270,000 tweets were about Jackson, at a rate of approximately seventy-eight per second (Kim et al., 2009). As a popular kind of digital mourning practice, the outpouring of emotion on Twitter also serves to deepen the experience of the death as event: its physical volume increases as it passes through a social space where grief is personalised and immediate, not televised or edited after the fact.

In her description of the ordinary, Kathleen Stewart (2007, pp. 2–3) writes:

> Ordinary affects are public feelings that begin and end in broad circulation, but they're also the stuff that seemingly intimate lives are made of. They give circuits and flows the forms of a life . . . they do not work through 'meanings' per se, but rather in the way that they pick up density and texture as they move through bodies, dreams, dramas, and social worldings of all kinds.

Stewart's nuanced and attentive account is about broader 'structures of feeling', drawing on Raymond Williams's concept, but her work also offers a way to consider the undertow of affect in spaces such as Twitter. At once public in reach and private in effect, Twitter moves between the space of the communal and the intimate. When a significant news event is shared, and moves quickly through the nervous system, it has no singular or containable meaning. It is rendered and re-rendered through thousands of discrete, subjective viewpoints. With great velocity and on a large scale, major news events are processed in public: the textures and inflections shift between individuals and communities.

Unlike traditional journalism, with its in-principle attachment to objectivity, networked media spaces are steeped in the subjective and the social. Mainstream news is filtered through the individual's own experience and associations. In Stewart's terms, this constitutes a kind of 'contact zone' where events, technologies, and emotions move and take place (Stewart, 2007, p. 4), and no neat divisions exist between news and the personal, meaningful accounts and 'babble'.

Conclusion: molecular news

In an interview with the *Columbia Journalism Review*, Clay Shirky observed that news is a very incoherent category, with considerable overlap into the terrain defined as 'gossip'. The dividing line between the two used to be defined in reference to news organisations. Now, he argues, it is suffering 'a kind of breakdown':

> [The model of] a group of accredited professionals deciding what becomes news and what doesn't become news has now been set aside in favor of a much more soft-focus, kind of permeable membrane-oriented way of handling or thinking about the news. (Juskalian, 2009)

In significant ways, the role of deciding what counts as news and what does not is diffusing, and moving into a more dispersed social ecosystem of news, gossip, personal headlines and shared feelings. In the gradual destabilisation of the functions of news organisations such as ranking stories, determining what is important and dividing the personal and the objective, Twitter is one space where we see the molecules passing through the membrane. Short news updates move through social filters, and personal messages can just as easily pass back through the membrane to become mainstream news. The now common use of Twitter updates in mainstream news stories as a kind of networked vox pop is the most obvious example of this counterflow, but the more interesting question may be how Twitter's communities of users are effecting a more gradual pressure that shapes how news organisations operate and determine their coverage.

One of the significant ways in which this may occur is the gradual alteration of the dominant model of news broadcasting to include a greater emphasis on listening. News stories will be circulated, but discussions they generate will also become part of the story itself, and go on to generate further stories. This increased emphasis on tuning in to the social circulation of news will also have ramifications for the work of journalists, in what I have called elsewhere the 'labour of listening' (Crawford, 2009a, p. 531). Further, it may raise new kinds of concerns and entrench inequities. Not the least of these is the question of who is being listened to: social networks are themselves skewed, with the majority of Twitter users currently under 35 years old, living in developed countries and well educated (Cheng et al., 2009).

McLuhan drew on biological analogies to depict what he saw as the 'disorganization of social networks' (Genosko, 2005, p. 86). But the metaphors of cellular osmosis and the functioning of nervous systems also evoke a kind of effortlessness within complexity. Certainly, there is an ease with which millions of people are already communicating over Twitter, sending messages and listening in to what they find of interest. Yet the wider cultural effects are complex, requiring us to stretch beyond established understandings of news, or gossip, or sharing, or community. Bonding rituals and information transmissions in such networks are not easily demarcated, but operate coextensively: as both information and emotion. Viewed in this light, Twitter underscores the ways in which news itself is a shifting and organic category, something that both forms and reflects communities, and moves within shared structures of feeling.

REFERENCES

ABC News (2009) 'Terror on Twitter: users break Jakarta story', *ABC Online News*, 17 July, http://www.abc.net.au/news/stories/2009/07/17/2628983.htm, accessed 17 July 2009.

BNO (2009) 'Powerful earthquake off southern New Zealand coast', 19 July, http://bnonews.tumblr.com/post/144685596/powerful-earthquake-off-southern-new-zealand-coast, accessed 22 July 2009.

Bowman, Shayne and Willis, Chris (2003) *WeMedia: How Audiences are Shaping the Future of News and Information* (The Media Centre, American Press Institute).

boyd, danah (2009) 'Twitter: "pointless babble" or peripheral awareness + social grooming?', Apophenia blog, 16 August, http://www.zephoria.org/thoughts/archives/2009/08/16/twitter_pointle.html, accessed 17 August 2009.

boyd, danah (2010) 'Tweet, tweet, retweet: conversational aspects of retweeting on twitter', in *Proceedings of Hawaii International Conference on System Sciences* 43 (HICSS).

Brighton, Paul and Foy, Dennis (2007) *News Values* (Los Angeles and London: Sage).

Carey, James (1989) *Communication as Culture: Essays on Media and Society* (Boston: Unwin Hyman).

Cashmore, Pete (2009a) 'Michael Jackson dies: Twitter tributes now 30% of tweets', *Mashable*, 25 June, http://mashable.com/2009/06/25/michael-jackson-twitter, accessed 26 June 2009.

Cashmore, Pete (2009b) 'Jakarta bombings: Twitter user first on the scene', *Mashable*, 16 July, http://mashable.com/2009/07/16/jakarta-bombings-twitter, accessed 17 July.

Castells, Manuel (2007) 'Communication, power and counter-power in the network society', *International Journal of Communication*, 1, 238–66.

Cheng, Alex, Evans, Mark and Singh, Harshdeep (2009) 'Inside Twitter: an in-depth look inside the Twitter world', Sysomos research report, June 2009, http://www.sysomos.com/insidetwitter, accessed 28 June.

Cohen, Noam (2009) 'Twitter on the barricades in Iran: six lessons learned', *New York Times*, 21 June, 4.

Crawford, Kate (2009a) 'Following you: disciplines of listening in social media', *Continuum*, 23: 4, 525–35.

Crawford, Kate (2009b) 'These foolish things: on intimacy and insignificance in mobile media', in G. Goggin and L. Hjorth (eds), *Mobile Technologies: From Telecommunications to Media* (New York, Routledge), pp. 252–65.

Dayan, Daniel and Katz, Elihu (1992) *Media Events: The Live Broadcasting of History* (Cambridge, MA: Harvard University Press).

Deuze, Mark (2005) 'What is journalism? Professional identity and ideology of journalists reconsidered', *Journalism*, 6: 4, 442–64.

Deuze, Mark (2008) 'The changing context of news work: liquid journalism and monitorial citizenship', *International Journal of Communications*, 2, 848–65.

Genosko, Gary (2005) *Marshall McLuhan: Theoretical Elaborations* (London and New York: Routledge).

Herzog, Ari (2009) 'Twitterville notebook: Janis Krums', *Global Neighbourhoods*, 13 March, http://redcouch.typepad.com/weblog/2009/03/twitterville-notebook-janis-krums.html, accessed May 23 2009.

Johnson, Bobbie (2009) 'Twitter news service taken over by MSNBC', *Guardian*, 1 December, http://www.guardian.co.uk/technology/2009/dec/01/twitter-bno-msn bc, accessed 2 December 2009.

Juskalian, Russ (2009) 'Interview with Clay Shirky, part II', *Columbia Journalism Review*, 22 December, http://www.cjr.org/overload/interview_with_clay_shirky_par_1.php, accessed 26 July 2009.

Kelly, Ryan (2009). 'Twitter study part 2 – continuing the conversation', Pear Analytics Blog, 24 August, http://www.pearanalytics.com/2009/twitter-study-continuing-the-conversation, accessed 25 August 2009.

Kim, Elsa, Gilbert, Sam, Edwards, Michael and Graeff, Erhardt (2009) 'Detecting sadness in 140 characters: sentiment analysis and mourning Michael Jackson on Twitter', *Web Ecology Project*, August, http://www.webecologyproject.org/2009/08/detecting-sadness-in-140-characters, accessed 5 September 2009.

Mackey, Robert (2009) 'Can a tweet be a scoop?', *New York Times Online*, 16 January, http://thelede.blogs.nytimes.com/2009/01/16/can-a-tweet-be-a-scoop, accessed 3 June 2009.

McLuhan, Marshall (1964) *Understanding Media* (New York: Mentor).

Miller, Vincent (2008) 'New media, networking and phatic culture', *Convergence*, 14: 4, 387–400.

Morozov, Evgeny (2009) 'Iran elections: a Twitter revolution?', *Washington Post Online*, 17 June, http://www.washingtonpost.com/wp-dyn/content/discussion/2009/06/17/DI2009061702232.html, accessed 2 August 2009.

Pear Analytics (2009) 'Twitter study – August 2009', Pear Analytics white paper, http://www.pearanalytics.com/2009/twitter-study-reveals-interesting-results-40-percent-pointless-babble, accessed 12 August 2009.

Schonfeld, Erik (2009) 'Twitter reaches 44.5 million people worldwide', *TechCrunch*, 3 August, http://www.techcrunch.com/2009/08/03/twitter-reaches-445-million-people-worldwide-in-june-comscore, accessed 4 August 2009.

Schonfeld, Erik (2009) 'Twitter's internal strategy laid bare: to be "the pulse of the planet"', *TechCrunch*, 16 July, http://www.techcrunch.com/2009/07/16/twitters-internal-strategy-laid-bare-to-be-the-pulse-of-the-planet, accessed 20 July 2009.

Scott, Mark (2009) 'Meet the CEO', speech given at the Australian School of Business, UNSW, 23 July.

Solis, Brian (2009) 'Is Twitter the CNN of the new media generation?', *TechCrunch*, 17 June, http://www.techcrunch.com/2009/06/17/is-twitter-the-cnn-of-the-new-media-generation, accessed 25 August 2009.

Stelter, Brian (2009) 'Real-time criticism of CNN's Iran coverage', *New York Times*, 14 June, B5.

Stewart, Kathleen (2007) *Ordinary Affects* (Durham, NC: Duke University Press).

Stone, Biz (2009) 'What's happening?', Twitter blog, 19 November, http://blog.twitter.com/2009/11/whats-happening.html, accessed 21 November 2009.

Sullivan Andrew (2009) 'The blogosphere's moment', *The Atlantic Online*, 13 June, http://andrewsullivan.theatlantic.com/the_daily_dish/2009/06/the-blogospheres-moment.html, accessed 25 June 2009.

Taylor, Marisa (2009) 'Twitterers protest CNN's coverage in Iran', *Wall Street Journal Online*, 15 June, http://blogs.wsj.com/digits/2009/06/15/twitterers-protest-cnnfail-on-iran-coverage, accessed 17 June 2009.

Wortham, Jenna (2009) 'Michael Jackson tops the charts on Twitter', *New York Times Online*, 12 August, http://bits.blogs.nytimes.com/2009/06/25/michael-jackson-tops-the-charts-on-twitter, accessed 13 August.

Chapter 8

News produsage in a pro-am mediasphere: why citizen journalism matters

Axel Bruns

The rise to prominence of citizen journalism is usually described as a paradigm shift in the relationship between news organisations and their audiences – 'citizen' or 'amateur' journalists are positioned as inherently different from, and possibly in competition with, 'professional' journalists. Some journalists in the industry have taken up this theme, and are at pains to distinguish their professional, supposedly objective and accountable practices from what they describe as the opinionated and partisan 'armchair journalism' of amateurs, while some citizen journalists, in turn, give as good at they get and describe the professionals as lackeys of their corporate masters who (willingly or unwittingly) fall prey to political and commercial spin. In fact, the very terminology we use to describe both sides creates the impression that professionals are not also citizens, and that citizen journalists are incapable of having professional skills and knowledges; in reality, of course, the lines between them are much less clear.

Stories of conflict between 'citizens' and 'professionals', though sometimes entertaining, generally tend to be unproductive; they obscure the fact that mutually beneficial cooperation between the two sides is possible, and beginning to take place, and keep us from exploring those opportunities. At a time when many mainstream news organisations are struggling to remain financially viable, and when various citizen journalism outlets are striving to develop long-term organisational structures of their own, it is important to examine the zones of overlap and contact between the two, and to highlight what is possible here. Neither professional nor citizen journalism is going to disappear any time soon (though the same cannot be said with confidence about any one specific publication in either camp), and it is likely that the best opportunities for sustainable journalistic models lie in an effort to combine the best of both worlds – in the development of hybrid, 'pro-am' journalism organizations, which may substantially transform journalistic practices while maintaining continuity with a long history of (professional *and* citizen) journalistic efforts. Some such models are now emerging, in fact.

Citizen journalism

In Jay Rosen's famous formulation, citizen journalism is fuelled by 'the people formerly known as the audience' (Rosen, 2006) who now actively engage in the journalistic process themselves. While media and cultural studies have long established that even in previous times, audiences were never merely passive and uncritical recipients of media messages, but already actively engaged *with* what they read, heard and saw, the main difference is that now they are able to engage *in* the process itself: that they have access to means of content creation and dissemination that no longer necessarily constitute a system secondary to the technologies available to mainstream media organisations.

At the same time, significant differences between citizen and industrial journalism remain, of course. By and large, individual participants in citizen journalism sites and projects commit only what JD Lasica (2003) has described as 'random acts of journalism': contributing news and commentary only occasionally and on selected topics rather than achieving a comprehensive coverage of the news; similarly, most citizen journalism websites focus only on specific news beats, or cover the news from particular ideological perspectives. Except perhaps for *OhmyNews* in the South Korean context, which itself is hardly representative for citizen journalism as such, there is no single citizen journalism site that manages to rival a major (or even minor) commercial or publicly funded mainstream news organisation in the breadth and depth of its coverage. However, the number of citizen journalism sites is vast, and though each covers only a particular slice of the news, in combination this flotilla of large and small sites and projects nonetheless manages to address virtually all the beats covered by mainstream news organisations. Its ability to do so is a result of citizen journalism's inherent openness to any participant able to make a meaningful contribution: as Clay Shirky (2008) has put it, 'here comes everybody'.

A further major point of difference between industrial and citizen journalism is their style of coverage: citizen journalism focuses mainly on providing opinion, commentary and evaluation of current events, rather than reporting these events first-hand (Bruns, 2006; Singer, 2006). This is a necessary result of the non-professional, random nature of citizen participation in journalistic practices, of course: by and large, citizen journalists have neither the accreditation or resources, nor necessarily the equipment and skills to gain access to and report from major or minor events as they happen – for the most part, they are unable to attend press conferences, travel to the scene, engage in lengthy investigations or secure high-profile interviewees. Well-publicised exceptions from that rule occur where people unexpectedly find themselves at the scene of major events (such as the 2004 Indian Ocean tsunami or the 2005 London bombings) or privy to as yet undisclosed information (such as Trent Lott's praise for Strom Thurmond's 1948 segregationist policies, or Barack Obama's lament that small-town Americans clung to god and guns in times of hardship), and commit a 'random act of (citizen) journalism' by reporting such events.

Other than in the case of such unforeseen scoops, however, citizen journalism relies mainly on a process of what can be described as gatewatching (Bruns, 2005). The role of industrial journalism especially in a pre-networked age has long been understood as one of gatekeeping or filtering: of all the news of the day, reported by in-house staff or arriving over the wire services, journalists and editors would select only the 'news that's fit to print' (as the *New York Times* slogan famously puts it), according to internal selection policies and their own idealised (and often somewhat condescending) image of what 'the man on the street' was interested in. Journalists, in other words, positioned themselves as keepers of the gates that controlled a steady flow of relevant news to their audiences, and prevented readers from being overwhelmed by a flood of reports from which it would have been difficult to pick those reports seen as most important.

But today's vastly greater direct access to a variety of news sources and reports now available to news audiences has made it necessary to acknowledge that any one news organisation's gatekeeping choices provide only one 'first draft of history', with many alternative versions also readily available; journalists must concede that the users of news are both very well able to make choices between them for themselves, and that a growing awareness of the many sources available to them has also increased their interest in doing so. We have entered a massively multichannel environment in which 'keeping the gates' to save users from the flood of information is no longer possible. To acknowledge this, journalists could link, for example, to reports by their competitors about the same event (as *BBC News Online* now occasionally does), and to the wire stories and press releases that provided source material for their reports; the popularity of the *Google News* service is a clear indicator of users' interest in such services.

Born into this multichannel environment, citizen journalism sites bypass the old gatekeeping logic altogether. Rather than ignoring the existence of alternative news sources and sticking to the claim that *their* collection of news is all their users need (as many mainstream news sites continue to do even now, by refusing to link to other sources), citizen journalism sites overtly acknowledge such sources and use them as input for their own coverage – though they may claim that their own *interpretation* of the news is the most correct and convincing. This is the essence of *gatewatching*, then (Bruns, 2005): participants in such sites observe on a continuous basis what information passes through the gates of other news organisations, they serve as watchdogs alerting their fellow participants to relevant items of information that may make useful contributions to the debate. They do so, for example, by posting articles that comment on stories in mainstream and niche online news publications, by analysing government and non-governmental organisations reports, by providing links to a range of documents relevant to current debates and by engaging in sometimes lengthy discussion threads that explore the implications of a news event from various perspectives.

While this difference in approaches is sometimes used to justify a classification of citizen journalism as secondary to and derivative of professional or 'real' journalism, this substitutes an idealised version of professional journalism for an accurate picture of day-to-day journalistic practice. Although it is true that there is a greater amount of first-hand research and reporting in professional journalism, it must also be acknowledged that in reality, the (technological, financial, staff) resources available for such reporting are strictly limited, and unevenly distributed both within and across news organisations (there exists what Shirky (1999) has described as a 'resource horizon', beyond which professional work is no longer feasible). Many major news organisations will have a number of dedicated correspondents in specific national and international locations, for example, but rely on wire services for other material; minor news services (including especially regional and local newspapers) employ an even smaller number of journalistic staff, or have even removed any boundaries between their news and advertising departments. Additionally, long-term investigative reporting has become a luxury that only a handful of internationally leading news organisations can still afford.

Any general claim that professional journalists report the news, and citizen journalists merely add commentary, is unsustainable, therefore. As John Quiggin notes for journalism in his field of economics, for example,

the distinction between news and analysis is largely meaningless. The information from which journalists and bloggers work consists mainly of official statistics and statements put out by governments, companies and organizations of various kinds. . . .

Bloggers typically go on from here by briefly stating, or linking the relevant facts and then providing some analysis. Added value, beyond the analysis itself, is likely to consist of more links to relevant information or to further commentary.

By contrast, the typical straight news story would consist mainly of (what are presented as) quotes from government ministers, and reactions from the opposition, business and so on. Even when simply restating the government's announcement, journalistic convention requires that it be presented in the form of a series of statements, presented as if taken down by reporters. Press releases are routinely written to facilitate this. (Quiggin 2009)

Indeed, the claim that professional journalism constitutes an inherently higher order of news and analysis than citizen journalism (still made by some journalists, and expressed at its most hyperbolic in the work of Andrew Keen (2007), for whom citizen journalism is part of an emerging and deleterious 'cult of the amateur') remains a key reason for the sometimes testy relationship between the two forms of journalism. Sustained (and sustainable) criticism by citizen journalists of the work of their counterparts in the industry has led a number of industry figures to lash out against their critics. In Australia, for example, such a reaction was visible against the backdrop of the 2007 federal election campaign, when the country's only national newspaper, *The Australian*, was embarrassed over its interpretation of opinion poll data by bloggers specialising in the science of psephology, the statistical analysis of elections; while *The Australian*'s journalists claimed that their election predictions were inherently better than those of the 'armchair journalists' because parent company News Ltd also owns Newspoll, in the end it was the psephologists who accurately predicted the election results (see, for example, Bruns, 2008b). Additionally, a number of citizen journalism sites and news blogs have been established specifically to highlight and correct perceived systematic biases in the mainstream news media – sometimes with very specific targets, as in the case of *Bildblog*, the citizen journalism site tracking misinformation in the popular German tabloid *Bild*. (Though not citizen journalism as such, US news parody TV programmes such as *The Daily Show* and *The Colbert Report* also deserve mention here – in their use of footage from mainstream television news to critique the performance of professional journalists, they can certainly be understood as engaging in citizen journalism-style gatewatching.)

In spite of the often antagonistic relationship with the mainstream news media that such examples highlight, however, citizen journalism ultimately also continues to depend on such news media content – at the very least as a basis for its critical function, but more broadly also for general background information, as impetus for its own work and (where views and debates in citizen journalism are in turn again picked up by the mainstream media) for the wider dissemination of its ideas. In particular, the problem remains that citizen journalism has only limited access to first-hand information (except for locally and hyperlocally sourced material, or in the specific areas of expertise of its individual contributors); while the gatewatching approach enables it to make useful contributions even in spite of such restrictions, citizen journalism's inability to engage in original reporting and especially in longer-term investigative journalism is a significant limitation. Beyond this input stage, it is possible to highlight other limitations for citizen journalism at the further stages of journalistic activity: at the process stage, the overall media agenda is still set by the mainstream media organisations, and at best corrected by citizen journalists drawing some degree of public attention to other issues and alternative views, while at the output stage, the work of citizen journalists has the greatest impact only when it manages to filter back into mainstream media coverage.

At the same time, such limitations should not be seen as fatally undermining the citizen journalism idea – it has become evident over the past decade that citizen journalism can make an effective, successful and important contribution to news coverage in a number of ways. The central point in this context is that (except perhaps in the dreams of some of its most ardent advocates) citizen journalism aims not to replace its industrial counterpart outright, but instead to challenge, complement and extend it wherever possible and necessary. It is able to do so in three key dimensions (see also Bruns, 2008c):

- It can extend the *breadth* of journalistic coverage by reporting (first-hand) from areas that mainstream journalism is now too underresourced and inflexible to cover. This includes analysis in specialist fields such as economics and psephology, as well as reporting about issues that have been ignored by the news media for various reasons, especially on the local and hyperlocal home front.
- It can improve the *depth* of journalistic coverage by offering a more detailed evaluation of current affairs, incorporating a greater variety of critical voices and thereby achieving a more multiperspectival coverage of the news (Gans, 2003).
- It can extend the ongoing journalistic coverage of issues over *time*, by being able to exist outside the 24-hour news cycle and utilising web technologies to compile growing dossiers of information about specific topics (e.g. in the form of expanding *Wikipedia* entries).

From citizen journalism produsage to pro-am news

In its potential ability to extend and add to the products of industrial journalism across these three dimensions, citizen journalism can be seen as part of a growing number of other user-led initiatives that similarly pick up their own content development processes where (for a variety of organisational reasons, mostly related to limited resources or diminishing returns from further investment) professionals leave off. Open source software development communities, for example, address a greater breadth of software uses by developing software for what the industry regards as niche applications (at one point including web servers and web browsers, in fact), and their non-commercial approach enables them to investigate in greater depth the best solutions for specific programming problems and to invest more time into finding and eradicating remaining bugs and errors. Similarly, *Wikipedia*'s open collaborative model has enabled it to beat its commercial contributors in both breadth and depth of coverage, and to both cover emerging topics more speedily and update existing entries more frequently. Each of these projects, and many more like them, manages to extend industrial models on the three dimensions of breadth, depth and time. In each of these cases, too – as in citizen journalism – users are no longer simply consumers of or audiences for content, but are able to become active producers too: they take on a hybrid role as *produser*.

In these collaborative projects that engage in such work, the creation of shared content takes place in a networked, participatory environment that breaks down the boundaries between producers and consumers and instead enables all participants to be users as well as producers of information and knowledge. These produsers engage not in a traditional form of content production, but instead in *produsage* (Bruns 2008a) – the collaborative and continuous building and extending of existing content in pursuit of further improvement, of further extending their work in all three dimensions. Participants in such activities are not producers in a conventional, industrial sense, as that term implies a distinction between producers and consumers that no longer exists; the artefacts of their work are not products existing as discrete, complete packages; and their activities are not a form of production because they proceed based on a set of preconditions and principles that are markedly at odds with the conventional industrial model.

Produsage projects – from citizen journalism through open source and *Wikipedia* to the many more emerging user-led content creation initiatives – build on a set of four universal principles:

1. Open participation, communal evaluation: produsage is based on the collaborative engagement of (ideally, large) communities of participants in a shared project.
2. Fluid heterarchy, ad hoc meritocracy: produsers in a community of produsage participate as is appropriate to their personal skills, interests and knowledges; such participation further changes as current points of focus for the produsage project change.
3. Unfinished artefacts, continuing process: content artefacts in produsage projects are continually under development, and therefore always unfinished; their development proceeds along evolutionary, iterative paths.
4. Common property, individual rewards: produsage adopts open source- or creative commons-based licence schemes that explicitly allow the unlimited use, development and further alteration of each user's individual contribution to the communal project.

However, participation in produsage is necessarily limited by individual users' 'interest horizons': in analogy to industrial production's 'resource horizon', produsage will take place only up to the point where 'a problem simply isn't interesting enough to attract a group of developers' (Shirky, 1999). Additionally, there are challenges to be overcome at each stage of the longer-term produsage process. To begin with, for many produsage projects it is difficult simply to begin from scratch, out of thin air: even a major success story like the operating system Linux began only with Linus Torvalds's donation of his early work to the wider development community, and even *Wikipedia* built in part on an early-1900s version of the *Encyclopædia Britannica*, which had become public domain after the expiration of its copyright term. Further, many projects rely on more or less elaborate support systems that require server resources and dedicated management staff – and few such projects are able to attract donations from 'angel investors' or the general public to the same extent that *Wikipedia* and a handful of other produsage leaders are able to do. Finally, while the informational content generated by produsage communities is usually readily available from their websites, in many cases there also remains a need for additional distribution mechanisms that are able to make this material available to larger audiences or through media channels other than the web.

The need for such support of produsage projects at input, process and output stages provides an important opportunity for the development of hybrid, pro-am models combining industrial production and communal produsage. Indeed, Leadbeater and Miller (2004) see the emergence of a new group of leading 'Pro-Am' users right at the interface between industry and community, between production and produsage; they are 'innovative, committed and networked amateurs working to professional standards. This emerging group ... could have a huge influence on the shape of society in the next two decades', they suggest (ibid., p. 9), and they fill a key role of being 'disruptive innovators': 'disruptive innovation changes the way an industry operates by creating new ways of doing business, often by making products and services much cheaper or by creating entirely new products' (ibid., p. 52). An industry aiming to engage in the exploration of pro-am models must particularly seek to involve these Pro-Ams themselves, as pathways to building relationships with the wider communities of produsage.

Given the challenging financial circumstances currently experienced by the journalism industry, such disruptive innovation at the pro/am interface – now visible in a few early projects – may be just what it needs. From these projects aiming to bridge the gap between citizen and industry journalism it is already becoming clear what professional journalists are able to bring to the table. Their contributions can, again, be distinguished across the three stages of publishing activity. At the input stage, dedicated journalistic and editorial staff are especially important during the early phases of pro-am journalism projects. Citizen journalists rarely arrive at such projects fully formed, and even in that rare case would have to adjust substantially to the intellectual, social and technological frameworks of the specific projects; professional staff are crucial both in attracting produser communities to such sites and in acting as role models for subsequent produser participation.

This was obvious for example in *Youdecide2007.org*, an independent project accompanying the 2007 Australian federal election that aimed to attract citizen contributors covering the local election contest across the 150 Australian federal electorates, and employed a small number of staff to encourage and facilitate citizen participation (the present author was a chief investigator of this Australian Research Council-funded project, which was run by Queensland University of Technology in collaboration with SBS, National Forum and Cisco Systems). *Youdecide*'s editor, Jason Wilson, has adopted Miller's (2007) term 'preditor' – that is, producer/editor – to describe his role in the site (see Wilson et al., 2008; Bruns and Wilson, 2009), and distinguishes four key areas of responsibility:

- *content work*, editing citizen content (for quality and legal issues) and producing professional 'seed' content to attract produsers;
- *networking*, involving both making and maintaining contacts in the mainstream and independent media, and procuring and republishing content across the networked news environment;

- *tech work*, both running the online services and using appropriate technologies to syndicate content, communicate with users and assess the performance of the service;
- most important of all, *community work*, gathering and serving an online newsmaking community (Bruns and Wilson, 2009).

What is immediately obvious from this description is that the professional staff member's contribution is designed to take on the tasks that citizen journalists cannot be relied upon to perform, both because of limits to their interest horizons and due to their limited integration into the wider mediasphere. So, for example, the tasks described as content work take place beyond the interest horizon of citizen contributors, while effective networking with the wider mediasphere – for example, to ensure that any scoops emerging through the site are taken up in the mainstream press – is possible for the most part only for legitimate site staff, not for 'average' citizens. Other tasks, especially community work, may be able to be transferred to the emerging community of contributors over time, as stronger community structures form and respected leaders emerge from within the community itself – but particularly in the early phases of a new project, professional staff are for the time being necessarily placed in a role of community leader themselves, and their performance in that role (that is, their ability to make the project appear welcoming and attractive) is a crucial factor in determining the success or failure of the project during that phase. For professional journalists, this poses an unaccustomed challenge – their work on the site must embody the spirit of citizen journalism (for example, a sense of openness and equipotentiality, an ease of participation and a communal approach to the project) even though their eventual role as professional staff on a pro-am undertaking places them somewhat at odds with these ideals.

This challenge continues beyond the formative phases of pro-am journalism projects – while with a project's growing maturity, its 'preditors' may be able to step back from generating seed content and managing the internal dynamics of the community, other aspects of their work (liaising with other media, managing the site technology) continue. In particular, pro-am sites that find themselves in direct competition with professional mainstream news organisations may now focus their energies on the process stage of journalistic work, deploying their professional staff to accompany the content creation processes of citizen contributors. South Korea's *OhmyNews* is perhaps the best-established example of pro-am collaboration in this context: here, all articles submitted by its tens of thousands of contributors are checked at least briefly for style and accuracy by a staff of some fifty editors. Instituting such professional oversight also constitutes a significant challenge for pro-am projects, however: especially for sites with substantial produser communities, handling the potentially substantial volume of incoming content without unacceptably slowing down the publishing process may be difficult.

A move towards pro-am models of this form may require a substantial investment in staffing, therefore – this is true both for news industry organizations (which may invite increased contributions of material by users, but often struggle to handle this material effectively) and for citizen journalism projects (which may be interested in pro-am opportunities in order to improve the quality of their content or the long-term sustainability of the project, but find themselves unable to afford to hire a sufficient number of professional staff). Much as in other industries where produsage provides an effective alternative to industrial production, and where pro-am production/produsage hybrids may be possible, the structural challenges in arriving at such hybrid approaches are non-trivial.

Other complementary approaches to professional support for citizen journalism processes are also possible – notably, for example, *OhmyNews* has recently opened a citizen journalism school aimed at improving the journalistic and content creation skills of its contributors. (*Youdecide*, too, provided some guides to basic journalistic practice, including advice on how to contact local authorities and how to conduct interviews with political candidates.) The relative scarcity of mature pro-am citizen journalism projects worldwide means that the full range of such approaches still remains to be explored – overall, any approach that provides professional assistance to citizen journalist practices will be relevant in this context.

Finally, however, for most citizen journalism and even pro-am journalism sites the problem of limited impact remains – *OhmyNews*, whose impact on Korean politics is by now well documented, remains an exception from the rule here. Pro-am journalism projects may make a welcome contribution to the journalistic coverage of the news, but it can be argued that this contribution remains of limited relevance unless such sites are able to gain an audience well beyond their own participants. This is a problem at the output stage of the journalistic process, which Wilson's 'networking' component of the preditorial tasks also touches upon – and here, too, the addition of professional support to citizen journalism processes can serve to provide a significant boost to the visibility and dissemination of their outcomes.

One important example for this model exists in the shape of the German citizen journalism site *myHeimat*. This project takes a hyperlocal approach that ultimately aims to attract participants from all over the country to cover events in their local area, and at present has managed to build strong produser communities especially around its initial base in the Munich–Augsburg region, and in the Hannover region in northern Germany. The project is strongest in local communities around major cities, where local attachment and history is important, and – by comparison with other citizen journalism projects – focuses remarkably little on covering political topics; its strengths lie in covering local cultural and community events instead. What is important for our present purposes is that in areas where it has achieved critical mass, *myHeimat* has begun to produce regular print magazines and newspaper inserts (either independently or in collaboration with local newspapers), which contain the best of the site's user-created content and are delivered free of charge to local households. Using this approach, *myHeimat* achieves vastly better penetration and brand recognition in the local news market than is possible for any other local or hyperlocal citizen journalism initiative; its print publications have also opened up a new market in hyperlocal advertising that remains inaccessible to larger local, regional or national magazines and newspapers (Huber, 2008). In this model, in other words, which in 2008 won a European Newspaper Award for its innovative pro-am approach, the professional harnessing and harvesting of citizen journalism content feeds back into the citizen journalism project by opening up new audiences and thereby improving its sustainability from both a financial and a community perspective.

Conclusion: next steps

In evaluating existing pro-am models and developing further approaches to combining professional and citizen journalism, the chief task is to understand clearly what contributions each side of the pro-am divide is best able to make. From the brief discussion of exemplary projects above, it becomes clear that professionals are often better placed to discharge the tedious tasks of journalistic work, such as reviewing the style and checking the facts of an article, and ensuring compliance of the site's content with applicable laws. Their contributions are also critical especially in the early stages of projects, where they are required to provide seed content and kickstart community processes; they may need to continue such work for some time in order to set the coverage agenda of a site, but must also be ready to step back and let the community take greater responsibility as it matures. Additionally, at least at present, the clout associated with journalists' professional status also continues to provide them with networking opportunities that remain inaccessible to citizen journalists – both the conduct of first-hand interviews with major public figures, and the maintenance of relationships with other newsmakers and news organisations (which is also important for ensuring the dissemination of scoops and other important stories through the wider mediasphere) therefore remain the domain of the professional for now. (It should also be noted, however, that some citizen journalists have now risen at least to Pro-Am status themselves, so that any inherent status advantages of professional journalists may be in decline – reporters from *Huffington Post* and other news blogs are now accredited members of the Washington press corps, for example.)

By contrast, this chapter has already outlined the key contributions that citizen journalists are able to make: their greater numbers, diverse views and lack of responsibility to commercial imperatives enable them to engage with the news in greater breadth and depth, and over a longer time, than is possible for the professionals. This can lead to a more detailed, more multiperspectival and longer-term tracking of issues than is possible in the mainstream news industry – it is possible to argue, for example, that mainstream coverage of long-term problems from the war in Iraq to the global financial crisis has been forced by the requirements of its 24-hour news cycle to focus largely on short-term events and report on process issues, while coverage by leading citizen journalism sites has returned more frequently and perceptively to exploring and critiquing the fundamental factors involved, while adding new information from the mainstream media to that bigger picture where useful.

Clearly, then, both sides of the journalistic divide have valuable contributions to make, and – in order for pro-am projects to be feasible – must come to respect one another more than is commonly the case. While citizen journalists already utilize the outputs of the news industry as a matter of course, and often highlight the work of professional journalists where it is of particularly high quality, the challenge here may be especially for journalistic staff in the industry, whose self-understanding must often still shift considerably to allow them to participate constructively in pro-am projects. Contrary to common industry practice in models where users may simply add comments or send in some other user-generated materials, in the pro-am models, as they have been discussed here, professional staff are no longer in a privileged position as moderators, but act simply as community guides supporting the pro-am journalistic process by addressing especially those tasks that would be difficult for the community to discharge on its own. In doing so, they must respect the necessary requirements for produsage processes (see Bruns 2008a) – they must allow community work to develop in sometimes unexpected directions, must allow users to rise to positions of leadership from within the community, must provide an environment where users may begin by making small contributions and graduate to more substantial forms of participation, and must respect user investment in and authorship over the content created in the process. Recent experience – from *OhmyNews* in Korea through *myHeimat* in Germany to *Youdecide* in Australia, and beyond this to a number of other projects – shows that on the basis of such mutual understanding, the creation of successful and sustainable pro-am models is possible.

In the context of current developments in the worldwide news industry, indeed, such a move towards pro-am models may be not only possible, but even necessary. Even before the global financial crisis showed any impact on the industry, existing business models were under pressure; newspapers around the world have begun to shed staff as advertising revenue in print publications declines, and the closure of long-running news magazines such as *The Bulletin* in Australia (Bruns et al., 2008) signals a growing unwillingness among proprietors to support especially the most expensive and risky forms of journalism, such as investigative reporting.

Such problems have emerged, however, in a context of continued and perhaps even increasingly strong citizen interest in the news – the emergence of citizen journalism itself, the success of news parodies such as *The Daily Show* and the ranking of *BBC News Online* and other leading news sites among the most accessed sites on the World Wide Web all point to this fact. The problem lies not in a decline in user interest, therefore, but in the content and business models favoured by the news industry; it may be attributed in part simply to the Internet generation's expectation that everyday information ought to be accessible free of charge, but partly also to the growing media sophistication of this 'Generation C' (*Trendwatching*, 2005) of content creators, who are no longer satisfied simply to access professionally produced news reports without also being able to engage with and publicly respond to them in meaningful ways. (A further factor in this development are the simultaneous improvements of the supporting media platforms and technologies that make such engagement ever more easily possible.)

Such developments are not at all unique to the news industry, of course – produsage approaches have emerged across a wide range of fields dealing with informational and even physical materials (Bruns, 2008a), and provide increasingly credible alternatives to industrial production. Much as in the news industry, the challenge in these industries is similarly to explore pro-am models for combining the best of industrial production and community produsage; today, however, due to the established histories of citizen journalism and open source software development the news industry – along with the software industry – is in a position to lead these disruptive but innovative developments towards the establishment of sustainable and successful pro-am frameworks that can also be adopted by other industry sectors.

REFERENCES

Anderson, Chris (2006) *The Long Tail: How Endless Choice Is Creating Unlimited Demand* (London: Random House Business Books).

Bauwens, Michel (2005) 'Peer to peer and human evolution', *Integral Visioning*, 15 June, http://integralvisioning.org/article.php?story=p2ptheory1, accessed 1 March 2007.

Benkler, Yochai (2006) *The Wealth of Networks: How Social Production Transforms Markets and Freedom* (New Haven, CT: Yale University Press).

Bruns, Axel (2005) *Gatewatching: Collaborative Online News Production* (New York: Peter Lang).

Bruns, Axel (2006) 'The practice of news blogging', in Axel Bruns and Joanne Jacobs (eds), *Uses of Blogs* (New York: Peter Lang).

Bruns, Axel (2008a) *Blogs, Wikipedia, Second Life, and Beyond: From Production to Produsage* (New York: Peter Lang).

Bruns, Axel (2008b) 'The active audience: transforming journalism from gatekeeping to gatewatching', in Chris Paterson and David Domingo (eds), *Making Online News: The Ethnography of New Media Production* (New York: Peter Lang), pp. 171–84.

Bruns, Axel (2008c) 'Beyond the pro/am schism: opportunities for collaboration between professional and citizen journalists under a produsage framework', paper presented at the CCi 2008 conference, Brisbane, 25–27 June.

Bruns, Axel (2009) 'Spore at 70', *Produsage.org*, 3 February, http://produsage.org/node/52, accessed 13 February 2009.

Bruns, Axel and Wilson, Jason (2009) 'Citizen journalism, social media and the 2007 Australian federal election', in Stuart Allan and Einar Thorsen (eds), *Citizen Journalism: Global Perspectives* (New York: Peter Lang).

Bruns, Axel, Wilson, Jason and Saunders, Barry (2008) 'Once were barons', *ABC Online*, 28 February, http://www.abc.net.au/news/stories/2008/02/28/2175431.htm, accessed 13 February 2009.

Flickr Blog (2008) 'Around the world and back again', 12 August, http://blog.flickr.net/en/2008/08/12/around-the-world-and-back-again/, accessed 13 February 2009.

Gans, Herbert J. (2003) *Democracy and the News* (New York: Oxford University Press).

Haklay, Mordechai (Muki) and Weber, Patrick (2008) 'OpenStreetMap: user-generated street maps', *IEEE Pervasive Computing*, 7: 4, 12–18.

Huber, Martin (2008) Interviewed by Axel Bruns, Munich, 28 October.

Keen, Andrew (2007) *The Cult of the Amateur: How Blogs, MySpace, YouTube, and the Rest of Today's User-Generated Media Are Destroying Our Economy, Our Culture, and Our Values* (New York: Doubleday).

Kovach, Bill, and Rosenstiel, Tom (2001) *The Elements of Journalism: What Newspeople Should Know and the Public Should Expect* (New York: Crown).

Lasica, JD (2003) 'Random acts of journalism: beyond "is it or isn't it journalism?" How blogs and journalism need each other', *JD's Blog: New Media Musings*, 12 March, http://www.jdlasica.com/blog/archives/2003_03_12.html, accessed 27 September 2004.

Leadbeater, Charles, and Miller, Paul (2004) 'The pro-am revolution: how enthusiasts are changing our economy and society', *Demos*, http://www.demos.co.uk/publications/proameconomy/, accessed 25 January 2007.

Miller, Toby (2007) 'Defining global media studies: content, control, and critique', roundtable discussion at the International Communication Association conference, San Francisco, 26 May.

Pink, Daniel H. (2005) 'The book stops here', *Wired*, 13: 3, March, http://www.wired.com/wired/archive/13.03/wiki.html, accessed 26 February 2007.

Quiggin, John (2009) 'Picking up the phone', *JohnQuiggin.com*, 8 February, http://johnquiggin.com/index.php/archives/2009/02/08/picking-up-the-phone/, accessed 13 February 2009.

Raymond, Eric S. (2000) 'The cathedral and the bazaar', http://www.catb.org/~esr/writings/cathedral-bazaar/cathedral-bazaar/index.html, accessed 16 March 2007.

Rosen, Jay (2006) 'The people formerly known as the audience', *PressThink: Ghost of Democracy in the Media Machine*, 27 June, http://journalism.nyu.edu/pubzone/weblogs/pressthink/2006/06/27/ppl_frmr.html, accessed 10 August 2007.

Rushkoff, Douglas (2003) 'Open source democracy: how online communication is changing offline politics', *Demos*, http://www.demos.co.uk/opensourcedemocracy_pdf_media_public.aspx, accessed 22 April 2004.

Shirky, Clay (1999) 'The interest horizons and the limits of software love', *Clay Shirky's Writings about the Internet: Economics & Culture, Media & Community, Open Source*, February 1999, http://www.shirky.com/writings/interest.html, accessed 24 February 2007.

Shirky, Clay (2008) *Here Comes Everybody: The Power of Organizing without Organizations* (New York: Penguin).

Singer, Jane B. (2006) 'Journalists and news bloggers: complements, contradictions, and challenges', in Axel Bruns and Joanne Jacobs (eds), *Uses of Blogs* (New York: Peter Lang).

Trendwatching (2005) 'Generation C', http://www.trendwatching.com/trends/GENERATION_C.htm, accessed 18 February 2007.

Trendwatching (2007) 'Top 5 consumer trends for 2007', http://www.trendwatching.com/trends/2007top5.htm, accessed 17 February 2007.

Von Hippel, Eric (2005) *Democratizing Innovation* (Cambridge, MA: MIT Press).

Wilson, Jason, Saunders, Barry and Bruns, Axel (2008) '"Preditors": making citizen journalism work', paper presented at the AMIC 2008 conference: 'Convergence, Citizen Journalism, and Social Change', Brisbane, 26–28 March, http://www.uq.edu.au/sjc/docs/AMIC/Jason_Wilson_Barry_Saunders_Axel_Bruns.pdf, accessed 13 February 2009.

CHAPTER 9

'Comment is free, facts are sacred': journalistic ethics in a changing mediascape

NATALIE FENTON AND TAMARA WITSCHGE

Introduction

Digital media present several challenges to the role of the journalist in society. The functions of inquiry, observation, research, editing and writing have had to adapt to the vast array of information available online, digital video footage, wire photos, amateur pictures taken with camera-enabled cell phones or digital cameras and the blogosphere, as well as the speed of 24/7 cable news. Since the mid-1990s a number of studies have explored the implications of the Internet for journalistic practice (for example, Reddick and King, 1997; Miller, 1998; Singer, 1998; Deuze, 1999; Garrison, 2000, 2001, 2003; Rivas-Rodriguez, 2003; Gillmor, 2004). They have looked at the nature of news content, the way journalists do their jobs, the structure of the newsroom and the shifting relationships between journalists, news organisations and their publics (Pavlik, 2001). In their quest to make sense of the impact of new media on the news they have considered the interactive nature of the Internet, the complexity of its content in volume and variety, its accessibility and its convergence across previously distinct media. The majority of these studies report that the Internet brings new ways of collecting and reporting information into newsrooms. This new journalism is open to novices, lacks established forms of editorial control, can stem from anywhere (not just the newsroom), involves new writing techniques, functions in a network with fragmented audiences, is iterative and delivered at great speed.

One challenge that is felt particularly keenly by professional journalists is the role of so-called citizen journalists and other writers online that offer their thoughts, witness statements and accounts of events freely and often for free, usually from non-institutionalised settings and without the pressures of news-room deadlines. These voices inhabit a vastly expanded world of news and current affairs online, often questioning the legitimacy of the privileged posi-tion of the professional journalist as chief interpreter and presenter of facts. The space available online for news and current affairs reportage and commentary, the speed at which news can be reported and immediately commented on, the accessibility of 'journalism' for anyone with a computer and the right software, and the interactive qualities of the Internet all pose a challenge to professional journalism that is felt throughout the news industry.

But a focus on the technology alone presents only one small part of the whole news picture. The technology may have created the means by which multiple stories can be told simultaneously, but it exists within a complex political economic context of deregulation, marketisation and globalisation – taken together, these factors have exerted multiple pressures on professional journalists and the mainstream news industry that are manifest in profit loss (Cohen, 2002; Singer, 2003; Scott, 2005; Freedman, 2009), redundancies, restructuring and closures (National Union of Journalists, 2007; Project for Excellence in Journalism, 2008; Nichols and McChesney, 2009). Journalists find themselves battling for credibility and the news industry fighting for economic survival.

In this chapter we examine how, in this changing mediascape, newsmakers view and evaluate online challenges to their professional authority. Through interviews and ethnographies in regional and national journalism in the UK – print, broadcast and online – we interrogate the response of journalists to the new online news providers. How do professional journalists perceive those that have been termed citizen journalists? What do they believe sets them apart from the often unpaid, untrained news reporter online? The research findings suggest that for journalists the main difference lies in perceptions of professional ethics and values. Whereas citizen journalists are perceived by the majority of journalists interviewed to be 'only' providing comment and opinion, trained and experienced journalists are felt to provide something more valuable: accurate and factual information that is legally sound and serves the public interest. Or as the title to this chapter states, 'comments are free, facts are sacred' (Scott, 1921). It is this contribution of the normative values of traditional journalism, the reassertion of objectivity and impartiality, that makes journalists convinced of the future of journalism: in their view the public will continue to need (perhaps now more than ever) the anchor that traditional news journalism provides in dealing with the abundance of infor-mation called news. The irony is that the circumstances that allow them to practise the journalism they believe sets them apart from the rest are precisely those that are being eroded by the contemporary structures and commercial constraints of news production (Phillips et al., 2009).

There is also another possible interpretation of journalism in the digital age that the journalists we interviewed were less willing to accept – as more people have access to more stories that claim partiality and subjectivity as their modus operandi and even as the route to 'truthfulness' so too might a different kind of journalism emerge that may better reflect the complexities and nuances of an increasingly diverse and pluralistic society. Through a consideration of the complex conditions of contemporary journalism we discuss the ways in which journalistic ethics are being reimagined in the digital age. First, we trace the arguments relating to the Internet and the new news environment it has created, and the subsequent desire by professional journalists to restate their value and reclaim their territory by recourse to the skills and ethos of their profession. Then we argue that the opportunity to practise the skills and enact the ethics that are claimed to distinguish journalists from non-professional generators of news content is being threatened by largely commercial factors that have construed new technology and squeezed professional journalism in particular ways. Finally, we consider whether professional journalism matters in an age when anyone can lay claim to being a journalist.

The new news environment: speed and space

Objectivity and its close relative impartiality have become the holy grail of professional journalism (Sanders, 2003). Their pursuit came out of the institutionalization of news (Friend and Singer, 2007; Allan, 2009) and they now constitute part of what has been referred to as 'a powerful occupational mythology' (Aldridge and Evetts, 2003, p. 547) that characterises much of the profession. The normalisation of these terms emerges from the Enlightenment and distinguishes journalism from other writing as rational and truth seeking. But in an online environment these normative anchors appear to become dislodged or at least threatened as the abundance of voices, all offering potentially conflicting interpretations of news, favours the acknowledgement of the impossibility of objectivity and an increased awareness of subjectivity. Both academics and practitioners claim that the Internet provides a space where interested readers can check the validity of one news report against another and even access and verify information from the news sources referred to (see, for example, Gillmor, 2004; Beckett, 2008). Furthermore, the ability of audiences to go online and check reports and substantiate mainstream news perspectives for themselves is argued to lead to increased media literacy and critical capacity. The possibility of audience interrogation of the validity and viability of news reporting is argued to expose the nature of news gathering like never before (in particular where journalists get their information from and whom they choose to talk to), undercutting the conventional notions of journalistic objectivity and impartiality (Hargreaves, 2003; Ofcom, 2007b).

The interactive and participative characteristics of the web mean that potentially anyone with the right tools can claim to be a journalist through the sharing of news and information. This impact comes in three main forms. First, civic journalism is increasing; second, citizen access to public information and government services is expanding; and, third, citizens are more and more able to get direct contact with news sources themselves (Pavlik, 2001). As a result, citizen journalism bleeds into mainstream journalism and vice versa. Boczkowski (2004) argues that because of the interactive and participatory characteristics of the web the content and form of news (in his case, news that originates from American mainstream newspapers) is becoming more audience-centred, which in turn changes the nature of journalism. In this vein, Andrejevic (2008, p. 612) notes how the successful blogger Andrew Sullivan has portrayed the power of the digital media in revolutionary terms, arguing that the Internet allows citizens to 'seize the means of production', wresting power from institutionalised journalism.

In this context, the distinguishing qualities of professional journalism become increasingly blurred amidst a morass of information. Journalists are keen to preserve that which sets them apart but are unsure whether this is possible:

> anybody can publish, but I don't know. I suppose the sort of ethics of journalism they do still exist. They exist here. They exist at the BBC. They exist wherever, but I am not sure the public understand that any more.
>
> Interviewer: So what is the ethics of journalism?
>
> The sort of judgement and balance I suppose, balance is a particular thing, and that lack of opinion. (Web editor, regional newspaper)

Journalism has, of course, always had formal and informal manifestations. The more formal are exemplified by mainstream, traditional news outlets that conform to established professional ethics and guidelines. The more informal have often been described as alternative news and journalism, such as radical community newspapers or pirate radio stations that may eschew normative notions of news in favour of more subjective, political styles of reporting (Atton and Hamilton, 2008). But the sheer multiplicity of online news sites, including many that provide critical commentary on mainstream news coverage (for example, www.mediachannel.org; www.fair.org), as well as those sites that seek to provide alternative news to the mainstream or at least alternative perspectives on mainstream news (for example, www.indymedia.org; www.alternet.org), are felt by professional journalists to place their work under constant review and open it up to perpetual potential challenge. It is worth noting, however, that many sites of citizen journalism actually seek to replicate formal qualities of journalism in order to gain journalistic credibility (Reich, 2008; Thorsen, 2008) and will frequently link back to mainstream news platforms (Messner and Watson Distaso, 2008). As a result, many of these interventions can lead to the duplication of the journalistic norms they often claim to be subverting. But this is not how these non-professional journalistic interventions are experienced by our interviewees. These professional journalists may accept that the Internet as an open platform for the practice and critique of journalism is not necessarily negative – public accountability of journalism is in itself to be welcomed – but untrained, non-professional journalists function to undermine the professional ethics of the trade. Objectivity and impartiality are felt to be displaced by perspective and point of view in striving to understand or make sense of what is fed to us as 'the news'.

It is these very forms of non-institutionalised journalism that are held in poor regard by professional journalists. Unbound by rules and ethics, they are felt to equate to 'bad journalism', where opinion masquerades as facts:

> It's not news; it's opinions. The most important thing in journalism is to make a totally innocent – and this is not an original thought whatsoever – to make a totally clear distinction between fact and opinion. . . . Well, what are these blogs? They are opinion masquerading as fact, very dangerous. I mean very dangerous. . . . They [blogs] are by definition self serving and biased, they can be nothing else. . . . So what are the features of proper journalism? Distinguish between fact and opinion, number one. Number two, distinguish between fact and opinion, and double, triple, quadruple, check the facts. If you've got something wrong factually, apologise immediately, don't try and argue about fact, you can argue about opinions, don't argue about facts. (Specialist correspondent, regional newspaper)

> I just think this idea that blogs are going to save the world seems to me to be . . . even worse than saying the Internet's going to save the world because at least there's some kind of checks and balances with what we do. What does a blogger have? He just writes what he sees and what he believes in. Believe me, a lot of our bloggers talk out their asses. (Reporter, national newspaper)

The Office of Communications (Ofcom, 2007a), the independent regulator and competition authority for the UK communications industries, which also undertakes informative research, states that there was a one hundred fold increase in weblogs from 2004 to 2007. This has been claimed as a positive enhancement of democracy – allowing citizens to break through the mainstream media's stranglehold on what is and what should be news (Beckett, 2008). The multiplicity of voices online is believed to exert pressure on journalists to keep abreast of new developments and websites and respond to readers' criticisms and counter-claims. News providers are argued to become 'in effect a network of a variety of news sources, rather than the undisputed bearer of "the news" or "the truth"' (Hargreaves, 2003, p. 53), thereby introducing a more relativistic view of what constitutes the 'facts'. The notions of objectivity and impartiality are clearly rattled in this environment and professional journalists are at pains to signal this as problematic:

> Blogs are an agenda, they're one person's point of view, and as I say you'll get a balance [in newspapers]. You'll also get inaccuracies filtered out. Blogs have inaccuracies in them. Journalism, of course there are always mistakes made but I don't think half the members of the public realise how we kill ourselves to make sure the story's balanced. We would always ask for an opposing view. (News editor, regional newspaper)

But retaining an emphasis on the traditional concerns of objectivity and impartiality is coming increasingly under challenge, even from official sources. In a recent report Ofcom (2007b, p. 2) notes that 'rules on impartiality serve to stifle the expression of views that are not part of the established mainstream' and links the issue of impartiality to the broader question of disengagement from mainstream news. It states that 'Impartiality, if applied across the board, may come to be seen as a possible hindrance to a truly diverse news supply and will, in any case, be increasingly difficult to enforce' (ibid.). This is not a view shared by the majority of the professional journalists we interviewed, who seek to retain and reassert their value through an emphasis on the acquired skills of their trade.

The production of news: interactivity and participation

In 1973 Sigal wrote 'News is consensible: newspaper audiences, by their responses to news, actively shape its content. Yet the average reader has little impact on the consensual process' (Sigal, 1973, p. 40). As noted above, in the online environment it is argued that readers can have a much greater impact on the news through an increase in the intensity of their exchanges with journalists or the presentation of their own views in online papers (for example, Gillmor, 2004; Beckett, 2008). News online is thus open to a higher degree of contestation than is typical of traditional news media. Were this true, then it would indeed be good reason for claiming radical positive benefits to deliberative democracy in an online world. However, our research suggests that this is a far from accurate depiction of news production in the digital age. On the contrary, journalists find it too time-consuming to sift through the abundance of e-mails each day, most of which they do not trust or respect as authoritative voices. As a result they rarely respond to readers' comments and only very occasionally find stories from the blogosphere (Phillips, 2009).

Similarly, Örnebring (2008, p. 783) finds that even when audience content is used as a means of generating stories, it is usually in a very restricted range of areas: 'the overall impression is that users are mostly empowered to create popular culture-oriented content and personal/everyday life-oriented content rather than news/informational content'. Traditional news organisations, he concludes, are not willing to hand control over news and informational content to the users.

Other experiments, such as at the *Daily Telegraph*, a broadsheet newspaper in the UK, that allow a greater role for the public, where articles are published by journalists online and the public are encouraged to take on the role of sub-editors (Ponsford, 2004), are driven by commercial motives rather than user empowerment or news benefit. Furthermore, even though journalists may view the Internet as holding the potential for the disruption of journalism as a static unchangeable entity, where articles can be amended and complemented by readers after publication, editors still apply the same normative rules and values to online news as they do to the paper edition (see, for example, Butterworth, 2008).

It would seem that the interactivity and participation characteristic of a web 2.0 environment have impacted upon the news process but our research suggests that professional journalists do not generally experience this as a positive development. Other changes to the professional practice of journalism and the production and consumption of news in the digital age also contributed to the sense of professional insecurity felt by our interviewees. The sheer space available for news and journalism has expanded exponentially (Fenton, 2009a; Witschge and Nygren, 2009). Mainstream news connects to a network of further online sources of information via hyperlinks supplying users with the potential to move directly between different news platforms and news types (although the extent of these hyperlinks is debatable: see Redden and Witschge, 2009). And at the same time, the modes of journalism are also expanding. Professional journalism now works via e-mail, text-messaging, multimedia story telling, blogging etc. Our research suggests that all these factors together destabilise the authority of the traditional news provider. So, rather than the expansion of space facilitating an increase in the range of news and diversity of perspectives on the same news stories, pressures of time and space result in news that is largely homogeneous across all mainstream platforms (Redden and Witschge, 2009). And although the blogosphere has been credited with taking on the major news corporations through instant feedback that is often lively, openly subjective and highly critical, in reality, these cases are few and far between.

As well as contributing to homogeneity of news content, a culture of pervasive journalism is also argued to have resulted in journalists being less trusted than they used to be and to have produced more cynicism towards the media (Mindich, 2005). This is not, however, simply related to technological advances. Instead, it follows closely on the heels of a history of the marketisation of news that has contributed to the culture of spin, as well as the close relationship of mainstream news to public relations machinery and the power of commercial pressures to guide news content (Overholser and Hall Jamieson, 2005; Love, 2007). As a result, according to Mindich (2005), news audiences have become more cynical about news, more questioning of claims to objectivity and more inclined towards entertainment. The annual *Public Affairs Monitor Omnibus Survey* by market research firm Ipsos Mori (2008) puts journalists at the bottom of a table of sixteen occupations (including doctors, teachers, scientists, business executives, civil servants, politicians and government ministers) measured in terms of (low) public esteem and trust.

Ofcom (2007b) reports that both the young and ethnic minority audiences in particular perceive bias and exaggeration in what the mainstream news tells them. There is a paradox at the heart of this debate: news users may not trust news professionals' claims of objectivity and impartiality but they also want more of it – they have less faith in the credibility of news generally and are less convinced of its actual objectivity and impartiality, but still want news to strive for it. This paradox allows journalists to retain faith in the future of their trade without fully confronting the systemic problems at the heart of the industry:

> If you've got an education policy, you're not going to trust Mrs Mop down the road to talk to you about education policy. Someone from the council is not likely to speak to anybody other than a journalist because they don't know what they're going to make of that information. (Web editor, regional newspaper)

Ultimately, the perception of the journalists is that readers, viewers and listeners will return to the professional trademarks of known outlets even though their confidence in journalism has been shaken:

> There are loads and loads of blogs out there, and these blogs will increase, but I still feel that people will go back to trusted brands for news and for reliability. . . . I think as long as things are clearly demarcated people are clever enough to know the difference between journalism and citizen journalism and blogging. (Specialist reporter, regional newspaper)

Professional journalism, therefore, is able to hold its ground and rebut criticism on the basis of the belief that it has a specific role in news production that cannot easily be taken over by others. Professional journalists consider their output to be more valuable than that of non-professional news producers because – in contrast to others – they provide 'reliable' and 'factual' information: 'If you want to get an authoritative, well researched, well written, unbiased report on the news, then that's something that we [traditional media] give you in the way that a blogger or citizen journalist can't' (Web editor, regional newspaper). On the contrary, the limitless opportunities online for anyone to have their say on anything are decreed by our interviewees to result in opinion and vitriol replacing the hard won gains of investigative journalism. One-off fragmentary commentaries are claimed to be the norm, rather than sustained analysis. 'Old news' values, they argue, are replaced by populist ranting or by those more interested in self-publicity than the ethics of public value. Spaces for online discussion blur into the wider provision of news. The lack of accountability and anonymity of those responding online is also felt to introduce concerns of verification, accountability and accuracy:

> Well I'm a journalist and I'm used to quantifying things, qualifying things before I put them on to paper, backing up what I say, with a bit of fact. Even if I write something about my views I'll always seek to back it up. I'll always seek to not have too much of an agenda and seek to be as objective and professional as possible. I'm also wary about law and libel and slander and defamation, and I think that's the difference. (Specialist reporter, regional newspaper)

News for the public, or news by the public?

The journalists in our study believed that professional journalism provides a valuable and unique public service: journalists do not merely give information that the public may find interesting, they also provide information that is important for public deliberation. In other words, they educate people by providing information that they should know, rather than simply want to know, thereby providing a critical public service of importance to democracy.

On the other hand, according to many of the journalists interviewed, online anything goes and bloggers can (and will) publish anything that pleases them. Bloggers, we are told, do not consider the consequences of their writings. This is not critical or reflexive subjectivity – most of what they publish, the journalists maintain, is slander and gossip devoid of the safety-checks of professional journalism:

> We wouldn't want to do what they [bloggers] do. . . . They're not journalism. When I say journalism I'm talking about something where standards apply, basically. That to me is the hallmark of professional journalism. Professional doesn't just mean that you're paid. It's something [to do] with standards. You have to make an effort to be fair and rigorous about what's happened. . . . I think it's also important to any sort of democracy that you have rigorous and professional journalism. (Reporter, regional newspaper)

Journalists embrace a public responsibility that they argue is absent among bloggers and citizen journalists. And they maintain that even though some bloggers may be very good, journalists still provide a more valuable contribution to society:

> There are people out there who are very good at blogging . . . [but] that doesn't necessarily mean you should respect them or trust them as much as you would a qualified journalist. I believe in my profession and I respect my profession. (Specialist reporter, regional newspaper)

In this way, journalists foresee a viable role for themselves in the future: producing impartial, objective and thereby credible news that serves the public interest. This is their manifesto for the future of professional journalism in the digital age. The blogger, the citizen-journalist, the writer-gatherer (Couldry, 2009) have become the virtual manifestation of their fears. What these anxieties disguise is a far deeper malaise related to the commercial imperatives of an industry in turmoil. Many of the journalists interviewed did not feel they had the time or resources to conduct the ideal of journalism embodied in the repeated ethical framework of objectivity, impartiality and public interest. They believed they were not given enough time to investigate stories properly and felt increasingly desk-bound – caught in the practice of regurgitating stories produced by the wires, and reproducing other existing material to fill the space in the time required. It is this, we argue in the section that follows, that presents the real threat to professional journalism.

News production in the digital age

The characteristics that were frequently identified by the professional journalists interviewed as the distinguishing markers of their trade – objectivity and impartiality and concern for the public interest – are precisely the aspects of journalism as practice that our research project found constricted by contemporary structures of news production. Phillips (2009) details how some journalists, subject to the need to fill more space and to work at greater speed while also having improved access to stories and sources online, are thrust into news production more akin to creative cannibalisation than the craft of independent journalism. Information available to all online is repurposed with minimal verification, particularly if it comes from another mainstream news site. Journalists find themselves in the business of slightly reorganising copy rather than generating original material, while assuming that other journalists have made the necessary checks before them. As a result, newsgathering remains anchored to traditional news values and established hierarchies.

The need to work at great speed in a vastly extended news environment also makes it more difficult for ordinary citizens to engage in direct contact with professional journalists in national news organisations, thereby reducing interactivity with the audience. Fenton (2009a, b) notes how, paradoxically, new media have reduced the interaction between journalists and other non-elite news sources such as non-govermental organisations. Whereas the instinct of a journalist trained prior to the Internet is to talk to someone, the instinct of the new breed of Internet-bound journalists is to send an e-mail. The increase in journalists' workloads and the increasing pressures on them all render a much thinner level of interactivity between journalist and source. So, as news production becomes more expansive, engagement with the public and news sources diminishes, becomes more symbolic and increasingly 'virtualised' (Davis, 2009), as this Labour Member of Parliament notes when talking about the Lobby in the House of Commons:

> They [journalists] don't even try to talk to you, they just watch breaking news upstairs. I pass them every day when I come in, I pass one of the rooms and I see them watching telly and they're banging away on the typewriters, all of them. . . .

When I first came here . . . it would be rare for that Lobby not to include some journalists, and sometimes it could be as many as ten or a dozen or twenty. Now, the only people you see in the Lobby are the fellas in the fancy breeches looking after the place . . . I think it's the advent of 24 hours news. (Labour MP, quoted in Davis, 2009)

If it were not for the hype of the ubiquity and connectedness that frequently accompanies debates on new media, this would come as no great surprise. News media are (mostly) businesses and the news is a product. As mainstream news providers plough more resources into online operations that are generally loss makers, further commercial pressures increase the temptation to rely on cheaper forms of newsgathering to the detriment of original in-depth journalism (Freedman, 2009). Cheaper forms include not only cut and paste journalism from other established news sites or from PR-generated material but also (largely free) material from citizen news producers. This material, however, is largely confined to the entertainment and personal sphere and rarely impinges on the public and informational sphere (Örnebring, 2008). In this vein Andrejevic (2008, p. 612) argues that 'the trumpeting of the subversive power of interactivity contributes to the deployment of what might be described as "the mass society repressive hypothesis" which pays lip service to revolution even as it stimulates the productivity of consumer labor.'

New technologies of production operate within the systemic (most often commercial) constraints of media institutions. They do not liberate these constraints but are seen more as a technical fix to the increasing problems of cutting costs and increasing efficiency (Lee-Wright, 2009). The utopian visions of a brave new world with everyone connected to everyone else, a non-hierarchical network of voices with equal, open and global access, is a far stretch from reality. The latest 'new' world of 'new' media has not transformed news values and traditional news formats; neither has it connected a legion of bloggers to a mass audience (Fenton, 2009a). But as the economic model for traditional news production stumbles and falls in the digital age, the response by news organisations has been to make professional journalism the first casualty.

For newspapers in particular, a decline in advertising revenues and reader figures since the 1970s has forced them to increase output while cutting back on staff and diminishing conditions of employment (Davis, 2009; Freedman, 2009). The material conditions of contemporary journalism do not offer optimum space and resources to practise independent journalism in the public interest. On the contrary, job insecurity and commercial priorities place increasing limitations on journalists' ability to function according to their stated professional ethical framework and fulfil the purposes they claim characterise their professional desire and identity. It is these structural constraints that provide the main challenge to journalists, rather than other non-professional journalistic voices online.

Conclusion

The codes and conventions of professional journalism are being challenged as they are being restated. Professional journalists are keen to guard the borders of their profession, and demarcate where journalism ends and something else begins. The main distinction between professional journalism and other spaces of news as perceived by the journalists lies in the differentiation between facts and opinion. Journalism generates facts, substantiated and verified; the other spaces provide opinions. Journalists reassert core journalistic values because of a range of external pressures. These may be felt as pressures that have transpired through new technology and non-professional journalistic voices online, but this is only one part of a complex picture.

The increasing presence of non-professional or citizen journalists is suggestive of a different type of journalism that may be able to disrupt and change institutionalised journalism in particular ways in certain circumstances. However, the balance of evidence to date suggests that these instances are rare and where they are more common they are confined to the entertainment and personal spheres and seldom have democratic intent. At the same time, the space and time to practise news journalism that seeks to support the public interest is being constantly diminished.

Commercial pressures of news production in the digital age prevent journalists practising much of what they value in their profession. And as the glut of information, opinion and commentary online expands daily, so too do the difficulties of establishing authenticity, source verification and accuracy. Objectivity and impartiality become the pseudo-science of the twenty-first century at a time where many question, but all still seek, the truth.

So, do we need professional journalists when news is everywhere? Yes we do. In a harsh commercial environment, news and current affairs journalism that purports to be for the public good and in the public interest, needs to be preserved and protected (Schulhofer-Wohl and Garrido, 2009); although this may mean that professional journalists have to acknowledge more readily a critical objectivity and reflexive impartiality that recognises the limitations of the institutional enactments of these terms. This is not the same as preserving and protecting news organisations or even the news as we know it. In a world of communicative abundance there remains, more than ever, a sense that there are many things that news journalism *ought* to be doing: to monitor, to hold to account and to facilitate and maintain deliberation; we neglect this at our peril. To ignore it is to accept that the market can be relied upon to deliver the conditions for deliberative democracy to flourish. Markets do not have democratic intent at their core. When markets fail or come under threat, ethical practice is swept aside in pursuit of financial stability. Professional journalism at its best defends the public's right to know – the structures that enable this ethical practice need to be reimagined and restated.

This research was funded by the Leverhulme Trust and forms one of the first thorough empirical investigations of journalistic practices in different news contexts in the UK. In addition to the authors of this chapter, the research team included James Curran, Nick Couldry, Aeron Davis, Des Freedman, Peter Lee-Wright, Angela Phillips and Joanna Redden. This project is part of a large programme of work at Goldsmiths Leverhulme Media Research Centre: Spaces, Connections, Control (http://www.goldsmiths.ac.uk/media-research-centre/index.php).

REFERENCES

Aldridge, M. and Evetts, J. (2003) 'Rethinking the concept of professionalism: the case of journalism', *British Journal of Sociology*, 54: 4, 547–64.

Allan, Stuart (2009) *News Culture*, 3rd edn (Maidenhead: Open University Press).

Andrejevic, M. (2008) 'Power, knowledge and governance: Foucault's relevance to journalism studies', *Journalism Studies*, 9: 4, 605–14.

Atton, C. and Hamilton, J. (2008) *Alternative Journalism* (London: Sage).

Beckett, C. (2008) *SuperMedia: Saving Journalism so It Can Save the World* (Oxford: Wiley-Blackwell).

Boczkowski, Pablo (2004) *Digitizing the News* (New Baskerville, MA: MIT Press).

Butterworth, S. (2008) 'The readers' editor asks: "Whose content is it anyway?"', *Guardian*, 19 May, http://www.guardian.co.uk/commentisfree/2008/may/19/1, accessed March 2009.

Cohen, E. (2002) 'Online journalism as market-driven journalism', *Journal of Broadcasting and Electronic Media*, 46: 4, 532–48.

Couldry, N. (2009) 'New online news sources and writer-gatherers', in N. Fenton (ed.), *New Media, Old News: Journalism and Democracy in the Digital Age* (London: Sage).

Davis, A. (2009) 'Politics, journalism and new media: Virtual iron cages in the new culture of capitalism', in N. Fenton (ed.), *New Media, Old News: Journalism and Democracy in the Digital Age* (London: Sage).

Deuze, M. (1999) 'Journalism and the web: an analysis of skills and standards in an online environment', *Gazette*, 61: 5, 373–90.

Fenton, N. (ed.) (2009a) *New Media, Old News: Journalism and Democracy in the Digital Age* (London: Sage).

Fenton, N. (2009b) 'NGOs, new media and the mainstream news: news from every-where' in N. Fenton (ed.), *New Media, Old News: Journalism and Democracy in the Digital Age* (London: Sage).

Freedman, D. (2009) 'The political economy of the "new" news environment', in N. Fenton (ed.), *New Media, Old News: Journalism and Democracy in the Digital Age* (London: Sage).

Friend, C. and Singer, J. B. (2007) *Online Journalism Ethics: Traditions and Transitions* (London: M.E. Sharpe).

Garrison, B. (2000) 'Diffusion of a new technology: online research in newspaper newsrooms', *Convergence: The Journal of Research into New Media Technologies*, 6: 1, 84–105.

Garrison, B. (2001) 'Diffusion of online information technologies in newspaper newsrooms', *Journalism*, 2: 2, 221–39.

Garrison, B. (2003) 'How newspaper reporters use the web to gather news', *Newspaper Research Journal*, 24: 3, 62–75.

Gillmor, D. (2004) *We the Media: Grassroots Journalism by the People, for the People* (Sebastopol, CA: O'Reilly Media).

Hachten, W. A. (2005) *The Troubles of Journalism: A Critical Look at What's Right and Wrong with the Press*, 3rd edn (London: Lawrence Erlbaum).

Hargreaves, I. (2003) *Journalism: Truth or Dare* (Oxford: Oxford University Press).

Lee-Wright, P. (2009) 'Culture shock: new media and organizational change in the BBC', in N. Fenton (ed.), *New Media, Old News: Journalism and Democracy in the Digital Age* (London: Sage).

Love, Robert (2007) 'Before Jon Stewart: the truth about fake news. Believe it', *Columbia Journalism Review*, 45: 6, 33–7.

Messner, M. and Watson Distaso, M. (2008) 'The source cycle: how traditional media and weblogs use each other as sources', *Journalism Studies*, 9: 3, 447–63.

Miller, L. C. (1998) *Power Journalism: Computer Assisted Reporting* (Fort Worth, TX: Harcourt Brace).

Mindich, D. T. Z. (2005) *Tuned Out: Why Americans under 40 Don't Follow the News* (New York: Oxford University Press).

National Union of Journalists (2007) *Sharing the Future: Commission on Multi-Media Working* (London: NUJ).

Nichols, J. and McChesney, R. W. (2009) 'The death and life of great American newspapers', *The Nation*, 6 April, 4, http://www.thenation.com/doc/20090406/ nichols_mcchesney/4, accessed March 2009.

Ofcom (2007a) *The Communications Market 2007* (London: Ofcom), http://www.ofcom.org.uk/research/cm/cmr07/tv/tv.pdf, accessed March 2009.

Ofcom (2007b) *New News, Future News: The Challenges for Television News after Digital Switch-over* (London: Ofcom), http://www.ofcom.org.uk/research/tv/reports/ newnews/newnews.pdf, accessed March 2009.

Örnebring, H. (2008) 'The consumer as producer of what? User-generated tabloid content in the Sun (UK) and Aftonbladet (Sweden)', *Journalism Studies*, 9: 5, 771–85.

Overholser, G. and Hall Jamieson, K. (eds) (2005) *The Press* (New York: Oxford University Press).

Pavlik, J. V. (2001) *Journalism and New Media* (New York: Columbia University Press).

Phillips, A. (2009) 'Old sources: new bottles', in N. Fenton (ed.), *New Media, Old News: Journalism and Democracy in the Digital Age* (London: Sage).

Phillips, A., Couldry, N. and Freedman, D. (2009) 'An ethical deficit? Accountability, norms, and the material conditions of contemporary journalism', in N. Fenton (ed.), *New Media, Old News: Journalism and Democracy in the Digital Age* (London: Sage).

Ponsford, D. (2004) 'Express staff call in PCC over anti-gypsy articles', *Press Gazette*, 30 January, http://www.pressgazette.co.uk/story.asp?sectioncode=1&storycode=24921, accessed March 2009.

Project for Excellence in Journalism (2008) *The State of the News Media 2008*, executive summary, http://www.stateofthenewsmedia.org/2008/chapter%20pdfs/PEJ2008-Overview.pdf?cat=9&media=1, accessed March 2009.

Redden, J. and Witschge, T. (2009) 'A new news order? Online news content examined', in N. Fenton (ed.), *New Media, Old News: Journalism and Democracy in the Digital Age* (London: Sage).

Reddick, R. and King, E. (1997) *The Online Journalist: Using the Internet and other Electronic Resources* (Fort Worth, TX: Harcourt Brace).

Reich, Z. (2008) 'How citizens create news stories: the "news access" problem reversed', *Journalism Studies*, 9: 5, 739–58.

Rivas-Rodriguez, M. (2003) *Brown Eyes of the Web: Unique Perspectives of an Alternative US Latino Online Newspaper* (London: Routledge).

Sanders, K. (2003) *Ethics and Journalism* (London: Sage).

Schulhofer-Wohl, S. and Garrido, M. (2009) 'Do newspapers matter? Evidence from the closure of the Cincinnati Post', Princeton University, discussion paper 236, http://free.convio.net/site/R?i=1HvQjKFBfa7h3rtbEDuiGA, accessed March 2009.

Scott, B. (2005) 'A contemporary history of digital journalism', *Television and New Media*, 6: 1, 84–126.

Scott, C. P. (1921) 'A hundred years', http://www.guardian.co.uk/commentisfree/2002/nov/29/1, accessed April 2009.

Sigal, L. V. (1973) *Reporters and Officials. The Organization and Politics of Newsmaking* (Lexington, MA: D. C. Heath & Co).

Silvia, T. (ed.) (2001) *Global News: Perspectives on the Information Age* (Des Moines: Iowa State University Press).

Singer, J. (1998) 'Online journalists: foundation for research into their changing roles', *Journal of Computer Mediated Communication*, 4: 1, http://www.asusc.org/jcmc/vol4/issue1/singer.html

Singer, J. (2003) 'Who are these guys? The online challenge to the notion of journalistic professionalism', *Journalism: Theory, Practice and Criticism*, 4: 2, 139–68.

Thorsen E. (2008) 'Journalistic objectivity redefined? Wikinews and the neutral point of view', *New Media and Society*, 10, 935–54.

Witschge, T. and Nygren, G. (2009) 'Journalism: a profession under pressure?', *Journal of Media Business Studies*, 6: 1, 37–59.

CHAPTER 10

Journalism without journalists: on the power shift from journalists to employers and audiences

MARK DEUZE AND LEOPOLDINA FORTUNATI

The key to understanding journalism's move online in search of a new business model is, according to industry observers such as Jay Rosen (2006), the fact that its audience is not really an 'audience' any more. Rosen's much-quoted 2006 analysis, titled 'The people formerly known as the audience' (TPFKATA), points towards a shift in access to reporting tools (news gathering, editing and publishing) for what used to be imagined by news workers as the audience. Beyond the tools of reporting now available to TPFKATA (such as blogging, podcasting, vodcasting and other forms of social or 'We' media; see Gillmor, 2004), emerging forms of legal protection (Creative Commons licensing; Lessig, 2004), and increased publication of user-generated content by professional media organisations, give the former audience a semi-official status as competitor-colleagues. TPFKATA have become special competitors, in the sense that their role is not to do a better and cheaper journalism but to do something different and for free. In other words, they contribute to the design of another system that, as Shirky (2008) argues, renders the traditional system of information, as it was in the pre-Internet epoch, obsolete. TPFKATA, in our opinion, become competitors despite not necessarily being willing to do so, since they do not seem to have any interest in destroying traditional news organisations or their websites. It is the publishers that have made them competitor-colleagues, by constructing them as playing this role, while at the same time aggressively 'depopulating' the field of journalism (as evidenced in recent years by accelerated mass layoffs, unpaid furloughs, forced early retirements, overreliance on agency feeds and freelance contri-butions, outsourcing and offshoring practices; see Deuze, 2007).

The examples and arguments put forward by Rosen, Shirky and others are not stand-alone or otherwise marginalised cases. Apparently in most, if not all, newsrooms today, a certain awareness of the productive behaviour of TPFKATA seems to be cultivated as an editorial and managerial strategy. However, studies carried out in Europe on online newspapers and on the influence of the Internet on journalism (Fortunati et al., 2005, 2009; Fortunati and Sarrica, 2006) show how far away the publishers (and the editors) often are in understanding how to manage the relationship with the audience on economic and organisational levels. A survey of journalists showed that the majority of the press has been characterised by the lack of a true interaction between newsrooms and the audience and a situation of 'dissociated' interactivity (that is, interactivity mainly between audience members, rather than between journalists and audience members). While journalists showed more sensitivity to this issue and became available to do a lot of additional and volunteer work in order to respond to audiences, editors were rather deaf to the necessity of reorganising newsrooms based on this new role played by TPFKATA. As a consequence, departments or sections of the news organisation charged with organising (and filtering) the contributions of consumer-citizens tend to be underfunded and understaffed (Deuze et al., 2007).

It must be clear, then, that we see a situation evolving in the field of jour-nalism where power is increasingly flowing in two directions: that of the owners, shareholders, business partners, editors and publishers of news organisations, and that of TPFKATA. In both instances, the power – to tell stories, to earn a living, to enjoy professional freedom and protections – is being sapped away from the people democratic societies used to rely on for their news and information: journalists. Hence our title's prediction of a jour-nalism without journalists emerging in the current context of news moving online. Our argument is structured in three parts. First, we explore the hopeful rhetoric around power redistribution in professional journalism by looking at the potential of flattening hierarchies (particularly in the relation-ships between editors, journalists and audiences). Considering the shift towards 'atypical' newswork (that is, contingent, precarious, subcontracted labour), we then move on to analyse the tactics and strategies of TPFKATE, that is 'the people formerly known as the employers' (Deuze, 2009). Third, we discuss the power shift from journalists to media organisations and audiences. These reconfigured power relationships in the field of journalism are then set against the prevailing economic models of the new media age in order to

assess potential business pitfalls and opportunities. Finally, we briefly analyse
the grand adventure of news in the online social network world.

Flat hierarchies

It is possible to understand properly the current attempt on the part of
publishers to reinvent a journalism without journalists only if we consider and
analyse the world of the press as governed by a network of power relationships: namely that between publishers and journalists, that between journalists and audiences and that between publishers and audiences. The power
relationships between journalists, employers and audiences have been transformed in the course of time by a series of concauses, such as the adoption of
the Internet, the more powerful status of audiences, the loss of prestige and
power by journalists, the concentration of media organisations and so on
(Deuze, 2007, pp. 141ff). The shift of power from journalists towards publishers might be characterised by two stages: the first has seen journalism's
domestication by publishers (and editors) who have subjected journalists to
the macrophysics of power and made them become their 'legitimators' and
'guardians' (as exemplified by journalism's overreliance on the ruling elite and
its spokespeople for setting the agenda and serving as sources for news). The
second stage has seen the publishers destructuring journalism by using the
Internet and deploying the utopian concept of the networked organisation –
redesigning the profession as simple, immaterial labour, as we will see later on.

This shift has been made possible by the particular features of the profession of journalism, which might be described as a profession characterised by
a double bind (Bateson et al., 1956; Bateson, 1972), and which is emblematic
of Foucault's (1973, 1977) analysis of power. Generally, double bind theory
explains a dilemma in the communication process in which an individual (or
a group of individuals) receives two or more conflicting messages. Journalists
represent a case of double bind since they receive two conflicting messages:
on the one hand, their self-policed professional ethics and occupational ideology require that they exercise a right/duty of writing news and facts, about
events, as watchdogs of democracy (Deuze, 2005); on the other, the enterprise of the outlet for which they work may conflict with the interest to
publish specific news or facts, because news organisations may prefer keeping
business and governments happy over creating controversy. In a nutshell,
journalists are required to survey and denounce the power that gives them the
money to live. While the first message is explicit (coming from schools of
journalism and its much-celebrated history of professionalisation), the second

is implicit. Thus, the essence of this double bind is two conflicting demands, each on a different logical level (the former on the level of freedom of information and the other on the level of obedience and loyalty to the employer), neither of which can be ignored or escaped. Journalists do not know how to respond to the conflict between journalistic ideology, rhetoric and ethics and the contrasting requests coming from their employers. If journalists succeed in responding to one message, this means failing with the other and vice versa. They can neither discuss publicly the conflict, nor resolve it, nor opt out of the situation. In this sense, journalists are no different from any other worker in the creative industries, perpetually caught between the competing claims of the market (and, in tandem, management) and the demands of artistic freedom (or professional autonomy).

This conflicting situation begs different solutions, located outside the newsroom: going out of the system and becoming freelance, opening a blog (or other social media publishing platform), becoming an entrepreneur. If a journalist wants to continue to work in a typical newsroom, the reporter may resolve this discomfort by modifying or renouncing his or her personal identity and integrity, applying self-censorship and pleasing the employer. This self-censure is realised to prevent censure by the editor and to apply in advance the editorial strategy of the outlet. Self-censorship in the journalists' world is a typical mechanism of the adaptation to the microphysics of power (Grabe and Bucy, 2009). Journalism can be seen as the locus where self-discipline, as it has been described by Foucault, has been applied with particular vehemence given that journalists work for the entrepreneur who controls them.

The decline of journalists' power *vis-à-vis* the industry can be retraced in the worsening of their working conditions (for a review see Deuze and Marjoribanks, 2009), which should push them to build a new relationship and alliance with audiences. At the heart of the argument for a co-creative relationship between professional journalists and TPFKATA lies the recognition of a new or modified power relationship between news users and producers, as well as between amateurs and professional journalists. It can be heralded as a democratisation of media access, as an opening up of the conversation society has with itself, as a way to get more voices heard in an otherwise rather hierarchical and exclusive public sphere. In this scenario, some of the traditional and generally uncontested social power of journalists now flows towards publics, and potentially makes for a flatter hierarchy in the gathering, editing, publication and dissemination of news and information of public interest. In fact, the power of journalists has traditionally been based on the complex labour they do, which required a high degree of specialisation. The decline of communication costs provoked by the use of the Internet by a mass of well educated users has undermined this exclusive status for the profession. The profession of journalists with its specialised knowledge and skills has become but one system of news and information gathering, editing and publishing among many. Forums, blogs and social networks (such as Twitter) are not only other means of online news dissemination, they also represent an alternative to the traditional publication of news (Bruns, 2005).

By all means, this is an important intervention on the audience side. But what Rosen and others tend to neglect or underestimate is another equally if not more powerful redistribution of power taking place in the contemporary media ecosystem: a sapping of economic and cultural power away from professional journalists to what can be called 'the people formerly known as the employers'.

The people formerly known as the employers

Employers in the news industry traditionally offered most of their workers permanent contracts, including healthcare and other benefits (near the end of the twentieth century sometimes including maternity leave), pension plans and in most cases even provisions sponsoring reporters to retrain themselves, participate in workshops and serve on boards that gave them a formal voice in future planning and strategies of the firm (Bierhoff et al., 2000). Today, most if not all of that has disappeared – especially when we consider the youngest journalists at work.

Today, the international news industry is contractually governed by what the International Federation of Journalists (IFJ) in 2006 euphemistically described as 'atypical work', which means all kinds of freelance, casualised, informal and otherwise contingent labour arrangements that effectively individualise each and every worker's rights or claims regarding any of the services offered by employers in the traditional sense as mentioned. This, in effect, has workers competing for (projectised, one-off, per-story) jobs rather than employers competing for (the best, brightest, most talented) employees.

Furthermore, news work, particularly in English, Italian, Spanish and German-speaking countries, is increasingly outsourced to subcontracted temporary workers or even offshored to other countries. Journalists today have to fight with their employers to keep the little protection they still have, and do so in a cultural context of declining trust and credibility in the eyes of audiences (the few 'audiences' that still exist given the Rosen formula), a battle for hearts and minds that they have to wage without support from those who they traditionally relied on: their employers. What is particularly salient here (given the IFJ report and studies among newsworkers in various countries) is the fact that most unions and trade associations do not include, or offer little representation for, the youngest professionals – those most likely to work in atypical labour contexts. Indeed, labour laws generally are much better at protecting those already 'in' (that is, enjoying the benefits of full-time or part-time contracted labour) than supporting those who, by necessity or choice, practise their craft outside of the walls of media organisations and newsrooms. Without all these people journalists (and their representing agencies) do not have sufficient critical mass to win the battle against the publishers.

Power shift

The radical changes that are occurring in the news world are, according to Agostini (2004), the result of a power shift among social actors who in the past had different levels of power and who, at this stage, see the quantity and quality of this power radically changing. Behind the restructuring of power relationships between publishers, journalists and audiences there is a series of trials of strength on a variety of issues. Central to these issues are the uses of (new) technologies, labour laws and even the definitions of what 'news' is in the service of power redistribution. Employers can take advantage of IT technology in the newsroom in order to reduce journalists' power and social prestige. First, computer systems allow control over the entire production process, use of machines included; second, much of the journalistic work gets relatively simplified and 'deskilled' (Bromley, 1997), so what was once the specialised competence required by this profession becomes superfluous; third, the simplification of many stages of the work necessary to produce a newspaper or broadcast allows the radical reduction of the number of professionals involved. It is in this context that the current shift to 'one man bands' in TV news and ongoing downsizing in print newsrooms should be seen. The power and social prestige of journalists is additionally reduced by an accelerated pace of outsourcing, and the managerial embrace of other forms of precarious, 'atypical' labour. Such workforce measures are further enhanced by the tendency for employers to diminish and discourage unionisation among journalists (McKercher, 2002), as unions contribute to shaping a class of journalists not sufficiently obedient towards editorial policies established by directors and management. At the same time, journalism unions struggle to reinvent themselves, caught between a rapidly growing number of (younger) contingently employed reporters and a generally much more senior, established and full-time employed editorial workforce.

In these trials of strength between media groups, journalists and audiences, the weakest actors are the journalists. Media groups have the capital and own the means of production, so they have command over the news organisational process. Audiences are fragmented and dispersed, so they do not have the power to demand a commodity tailored as they need or like, but they have purchasing power (which they are strongly exercising), so they have the power to not buy a commodity if they do not like it or have other alternatives. In the end, journalists have only their labour to sell, and they are forced to sell it at an increasingly lower price.

However, in this picture where at the end the last word is up to audiences (as it always is in market situations), we must state that an anomaly has developed. Audiences do not just exercise their purchasing power to prefer the generally 'free' news online (over paid newspaper subscriptions or watching TV news), but are also summoning the right to directly create 'their' own news. Becoming owners of the production means in the IT socio-technical system, they use these tools in order to access online news for free first, and then move on to make news about, and for, themselves. In other words, audiences take the opportunity to change their status in the 'market place of ideas' and have become also producers, instead of only consumers. The anomaly, articulated by Terranova (2000) and Manovich (2001), is that audiences, by producing news for free, supply unwaged labour. None of this is essentially new: audiences working for free throughout the news system start by simply performing their role as audiences to be sold to advertisers, but in a more creative role they (chronologically) write letters to the editor and participate in talk radio shows and TV opinion polls; this ranges from forms of public or civic journalism in the 1980s to today's so-called 'citizen' news. This unwaged labour is beneficial (because free) to media organisations, but at the same time it gradually changes the inner logic of news and of journalists' jobs, taking from media groups' hands the exclusive right to produce news and the prerogative to dictate the rules of the game.

This unwaged labour is apparently also beneficial to journalists, who may find on the web a precious source of information, stories and expertise – a potential exemplified by a communally edited information platform such as Wikipedia. This emerges in much research, such as that carried out in Europe (Fortunati et al., 2009; Hermans et al., 2009), in which journalists declare that the Internet is beneficial to them as it suits their professional skills, practices and purposes. They are convinced that this tool speeds up and facilitates their work, improves its impact on audiences, increases the diffusion of news and enables them to offer additional information and to organise a more visible, interactive and effective relationship with audiences. However,

European journalists fear the unreliability of online information and are aware of the greater difficulty of distinguishing credible content. In reality, journalists today enter into competition with the unwaged labour of TPFKATA for a chance to tell stories (and earn a living). Content created by citizen journalists is cheap, adds volume to news sites (and keeps them constantly updated) and offers materials (including photographs and videos) at a fraction of the cost of professionally produced content. The socio-technical system of news in fact takes advantage of this competition, with the consequence that the unwaged labour serves to devalorise the waged labour of news. As employers, if you can have news for free on the part of audiences, you try to pay increasingly less for journalists' news (including the work of photographers, sound engineers and other production-related labour in the journalism industry). It is a competition that makes journalists and audiences worse off instead of empowering them. This situation sees journalists losing a lot of power and prestige and audiences winning very few assets in terms of money, training or protection (for example, copyright), and only a few media groups benefiting economically from declining labour costs and increased market efficiencies. At the same time, today many media organisations are not better off in comparison to journalists and audiences, as a clear vision and development of business models based on these reconfigurations of power is yet to emerge across the media industries (Jenkins, 2006; Deuze, 2007). They are going through a financial and organisational crisis (van der Wurff and Lauf, 2005).

Immaterial labour workers

If we call publishers TPFKATE, and citizens TPFKATA, what can we call journalists? Just employees? We prefer not to use this term since it is an old Fordist category that refers to a world that hardly exists in the precarious context of labour today. But they are also not exclusively journalists any more, as today more and more news companies call their audiences journalists as well – for example, by starting dedicated divisions or segments for user-generated content and citizen journalism contributions (some telling examples are Yo Periodista at Spanish newspaper *El Pais*, iReport at CNN and STOMP, '*Straits Times* Online Mobile Print', in Singapore). Those journalists who choose to do their work professionally – to make a living, to work within the system of media industries – can perhaps best be labelled as immaterial labour workers (Fortunati, 2005, 2006, 2007). This category might have the merit of situating journalists inside the large stratum of workers engaged in abstract labour (Lazzarato, 1997; Hardt and Negri, 2000). The computerisation of journalistic work and especially the adoption of the Internet have developed its mechanisation and simplification and made journalists simple workers. This notion of immaterial labour workers also has the merit of including in the same category regular journalists and amateurs: both of them in fact share more or less the same situation of labour suppliers – the former inside a subordinated work relationship, the latter inside a scheme of voluntary work. The production of news is situated inside the variegated production of immaterial commodities, such as information, communication, education, entertainment, learning and so on. All these workers are subjected to a very strong policy of legal compression of their normative profile, economic impoverishment and loss of social status (Hesmondhalgh, 2007).

Considering journalists as immaterial labour workers puts what is happening in newsrooms in perspective. Journalists belong to those professionals, like academics, researchers, other media professionals and artists, whose professional profiles, labour content and skills are reshaped by new media, digital culture and ICTs. While an increasing part of the working population is joining these professionals in doing immaterial labour (public servants, service workers and so on), it becomes a priority for postmodern economic systems to break their power and reorganise all the sectors on a transnational scale (as that is the scale on which the industry operates in terms of financing and ownership) as a huge, horizontal working-class sector submitted to what Sennett (2006) has called the culture of the 'new' capitalism. In this restructuring of labour relations, workers are expected to continuously adapt, 'self-program', to flexible production processes and new technological demands – all without the support and investment of their employers, of course.

Beyond the cult of amateurs

We do not share the approach advanced by Andrew Keen (2008), who criticises audiences who produce news for being amateurish. We see his argument primarily serving as a self-defence elaborated by one of the professionals who are already on the way of decline. Keen's analysis, however, contains several pertinent points. As it takes place outside of a salaried and otherwise professionally sanctioned context, news production by bloggers, independent news website owners and so on is activity supplied during spare time, after the work day and on the basis of voluntary engagement. This type of activity can be configured as an affective activity – done when one can and wants, for the period one decides, in the way one decides. Of course, not being regulated by a waged work relationship that establishes duties and rights, this activity has boundaries, meanings and purposes that may not be standard. News provided in this framework might reach a very high quality, might be a bulwark of the truth and so on, but it might be, for example, not sufficiently verified. This unwaged newswork is a journalism that might work well locally, but, generally not being based on a financial investment, does not guarantee the structural production of news from abroad or from far away (while we recognise the successes of individual entrepreneurs and travelling reporters served by donations). Amateurs and professional journalists represent polarities of power, of (at times) different interests, yet in the current media ecosystem they are obliged to negotiate a new type of relationship between them, in which the power is less asymmetrically divided or aligned. At the heart of these opposite poles lies the issue of responsibility – as in the professionals' acceptance of responsibility for the editorial choices made (and the codified legal/ethical instruments available to enforce and enable such responsibility), and TPFKATA's lack thereof.

The widespread provision of unpaid labour exists across many other industrial sectors – particularly across the creative industries – including social services and scientific research, and also including the domestic sphere, where reproductive labour (making children, reconstructing the energy of labour forces, cleaning the house, cooking, taking care of family members and so on) has traditionally been supplied by unpaid subjects (mainly women). Voluntary participation is a kind of production without any formal safeguards or power over rewards for labourers (while it might seem progressive or rebellious).

From this point of view, unwaged work escapes from the formal and informal rules imposed at the socio-economic level, but in a way in which it pays all the prices of rebellion. In its final outcome – unpaid news labour – it summons the freedom to frame the news in an autonomous way but comes at the cost of indirectly cooperating with media organisations in their quest to cut the cost (and power) of labour.

News and social networks

As journalism moves online, its workers not only have to engage with the challenges of the new medium while at the same time negotiating by all means rather frail power relationships with employers and audiences – they also have to find answers to the age-old question of what news is. Nietzsche's (1987) reflections on the need to be untimely, to not be subjected to the tyranny of currents affairs (and so news), are like ghosts in the statute of the information world, which is based on news. News until the past two decades has been the result of a highly routinised, isomorphic and inter-institutionally coherent system that unilaterally decided what could become news – most memorably reflected in the *New York Times* tagline 'All the News that's Fit to Print', implying that the journalists of the newspaper can and should be the sole arbiters of what indeed is fitting (see Schudson, 2003). Given that media have always been part of the power system, in the tradition of news there has always been a concern about legitimating power (and being part of the powerful), to use a Weberian expression, and a certain level of smugness towards it. This, for example, is reflected in the way the informal hierarchy of the profession is organised around its most celebrated practitioners: those closest to (political) power, such as White House correspondents in the USA and parliamentary specialist reporters elsewhere.

On the part of the journalists, this system operated arguably with the best of intentions: to provide a voice for the voiceless, to inform the people in a way that would enable them to self-govern. However, such nobility equally constructs people outside of the profession of journalism as competent only to the extent of not having a voice, only the eyes and ears needed to consume the information provided to them. The relevant point was that people could not understand current affairs but instead should have a certain version and interpretation of what happened, which essentially served to occult reality. News thus acted to construct a specific kind of reality – but never a reality subject to consensus, as Luhmann (1996) would argue.

The only thing to which people could aspire to was to buy news without being able to intervene in any other way than as consumers. The big power consisted in the fact that the mass was huge enough to make media a lot of money, but fragmented enough to be unable to build power as consumers, because of being separated inside it, one from the other. The big novelty of the past two decades has been not only user-generated content, the coming to light of 'prosumers', but also the advent of networked audiences, audiences that are not necessarily separated any more, but can be (and often are) connected. The advent of networked publics represents an important development in the framework of media systems, since these are publics that can overcome fragmentation and isolation inside it, possibly interconnecting in a variety of ways. This element increases the power of audiences because it increases their ability to speak with each other – to 'bridge' and 'bond' as Pippa Norris (2002) distills from the character of online communities. Social networks can be the ideal tool to develop an informed, 'informational' (using Schudson's phrase), as well as informing audience, and to develop a bottom-up public opinion formation process. Of course these are processes that are in their infancy.

Conclusion

Hierarchies, both within the profession of journalism and between journalism and its audiences, are flattening. Employers in the news industry turn their organisations into 'shell' or 'zombie' institutions: a dying culture of paid producers. The work that journalists do in comparison to previous journalistic practice has become less specialised and rare, instead moving almost completely to the realm of affective and immaterial labour. This process must be seen in conjunction with the 'free labour' of news and information-producing 'networked publics', contributing to a power shift away from journalists towards employers and specific audiences: audiences disappointed with the news selected for them, frustrated with a news system that only speaks to them, or rich, educated and skilled enough to be able to produce their own news. Our discussion of journalism online therefore contains a cautionary tale of a journalism without journalists. Amplified by trends online, a journalism without journalists is, in a traditional sense, a source of concern indeed. However, when seen through the critical lens of journalism's cosy relationship with society's elite institutions (including itself) and the potential of re-engagement with a self-organising and self-producing citizenry, perhaps a journalism without journalists is exactly what we need. If so, we would need to study and support journalists in working for themselves and their communities, rather than for organisations. We would need labour laws, union structures and support organisations that primarily serve those wishing to work on the outside (of the corporate waged labour system), rather than those already in. We would need new theories of power in journalism that start from the premise and position of individual journalists, rather than from the system and culture of established news organisations. Unless these and other, more managerial and economic (such as the formulation of non-profit business models), demands are met, a journalism without journalists must be an inevitable critical sidebar to any consideration of journalism's potential and future online.

REFERENCES

Agostini, Angelo (2004) *Giornalismi. Media e giornalisti in Italia* [*Journalisms. Media and Journalists in Italy*] (Bologna: Il Mulino).

Bateson, Gregory (1972) *Steps to an Ecology of Mind: Collected Essays in Anthropology, Psychiatry, Evolution, and Epistemology* (Chicago: University of Chicago Press).

Bateson, Gregory, Jackson, Donald D., Haley, Jay and Weakland, John (1956) 'Toward a theory of schizophrenia', *Behavioral Science*, 1, 251–264

Bierhoff, Jan, de Vreese, Claes and Deuze, Mark (2000) 'Media innovation, professional debate and media training: a European analysis', http://www.ejc.nl/pdf/pub/mi.pdf.

Bromley, Michael (1997) 'The end of journalism? Changes in workplace practices in the press and broadcasting in the 1990s', in Michael Bromley and Tom O'Malley (eds), *A Journalism Reader* (London: Routledge), 330–50.

Bruns, Axel (2005) *Gatewatching* (New York: Peter Lang).

Deuze, Mark (2005) 'What is journalism? Professional identity and ideology of journalists reconsidered', *Journalism Theory Practice and Criticism*, 6: 4, 443–65.

Deuze, Mark (2007) *Media Work* (Cambridge: Polity Press).

Deuze, Mark (2009) 'The people formerly known as the employers', *Journalism Theory Practice and Criticism*, 10: 3, 315–18.

Deuze, Mark, Bruns, Axel and Neuberger, Christoph (2007) 'Preparing for an age of participatory news', *Journalism Practice*, 1: 4, 322–8.

Deuze, Mark and Marjoribanks, Tim (eds) (2009) 'Newswork', special issue of *Journalism Theory Practice and Criticism*, 10: 5.

Fortunati, Leopoldina (2005) 'Forme di interattività. Un'indagine sui quotidiani on line in Italia', *Problemi dell'Informazione*, 30: 1, 89–113.

Fortunati, Leopoldina (2006) *First Monday*, special issue 7, September, http://firstmonday.org/issues/special11_9/fortunati/index.html.

Fortunati, Leopoldina (2007) 'Ephemera. Theory and politics in organization', http://www.ephemeraweb.org/journal/7-1/7-1fortunati.pdf.

Fortunati, Leopoldina, Raycheva, Lilia, Harro-Loit, Halliki and O'Sullivan, John (2005) 'Online news interactivity in four European countries: a pre-political dimension. Comparing practices in Bulgaria, Estonia, Ireland and Italy', in Pere Masip and Josep Rom (eds), *Digital Utopia in the Media: From Discourses to Facts. A Balance*, volume 1 (Barcelona: Blanquerna Tecnologia I Serveis), pp. 417–30.

Fortunati, Leopoldina and Sarrica, Mauro (2006) 'Internet in redazione. Un'indagine in Italia', *Problemi dell'informazione*, 4, 510–40.

Fortunati, Leopoldina, Sarrica, Mauro, O'Sullivan, John, Balcytiene, Aukse, Harro-Loit, Halliki, Macgregor, Phil, Roussou, Nayia, Salaverría, Ramón and de Luca, Federico (2009) 'The influence of the Internet on European journalism', *Journal of Computer-Mediated Communication*, 14: 4, 928–63.

Foucault, Michel (1973) *The Order of Things: An Archaeology of the Human Sciences* (New York: Vintage Books).

Foucault, Michel (1977) *Microphysique du pouvoir* (Ithaca, NY: Cornell University Press).

Gillmor, Dan (2004) *We the Media*, http://www.authorama.com/book/we-the-media.html

Grabe, Maria Elizabeth and Bucy, Erik Page (2009) *Image Bite Politics: News and the Visual Framing of Elections* (Oxford: Oxford University Press).

Hardt, Michael and Negri, Antonio (2000) *Empire* (Cambridge, MA: Harvard University Press).

Hermans, Liesbeth, Vergeer, Maurice and Pleijter, Alexander (2009) 'Internet adoption in the newsroom: journalists' use of the Internet explained by attitudes and perceived functions', *Communications*, 34: 1, 55–71.

Hesmondhalgh, David (2007) *The Cultural Industries*, 2nd edn (London: Sage).

International Federation of Journalists (2006) 'The changing nature of work: a global survey and case study of atypical work in the media industry', http://www.ifj.org

Jenkins, Henry (2006) *Convergence Culture: Where Old and New Media Collide* (New York: New York University Press).

Keen, Andrew (2008) *The Cult of the Amateur* (London: Nicholas Breadley Publishing).

Lazzarato, Maurizio (1997) *Lavoro immateriale* [*Immaterial Labour*] (Verona: Ombre corte).

Lessig, Lawrence (2004) *Free Culture*, http://free-culture.cc

Luhmann, Niklas (1996) *The Reality of the Mass Media* (Cambridge: Polity Press, 2000 edn).

McKercher, Catherine (2002) *Newsworkers Unite: Labor, Convergence and North American Newspapers* (Lanham, MD: Rowman & Littlefield).

Manovich, Lev (2001) *The Language of New Media* (Cambridge, MA: MIT).

Nietzsche, Friedrich Wilhelm (1987) *Untimely Meditations* (Cambridge: Cambridge University Press).

Norris, Pippa (2002) 'The bridging and bonding role of online communities', *Harvard International Journal of Press/Politics*, 7: 3, 3–13.

Rosen, Jay (2006) 'The people formerly known as the audience', *PressThink: Ghost of Democracy*, 27 June, http://journalism.nyu.edu/pubzone/weblogs/pressthink/2006/06/27/ppl_frmr.html, accessed 6 August 2009.

Schudson, Michael (2003) *The Sociology of News* (New York: W.W. Norton & Co.).

Sennett, Richard (2006) *The Culture of the New Capitalism* (New Haven, CT: Yale University Press).

Shirky, Clay (2008) *Here Comes Everybody. The Power of Organizing without Organizations* (New York: Penguin).

Terranova, Tiziana (2000) 'Free labor: producing culture for the digital economy', *Social Text*, 18: 2, 33–57, http://www.uoc.edu/in3/hermeneia/sala_de_lectura/t_terranova_free_labor.htm

van der Wurff, Richard and Lauf, Edmund (eds) (2005) *Print and Online Newspapers in Europe: A Comparative Analysis in 16 Countries* (Amsterdam: Het Spinhuis).

CHAPTER 11

Web 2.0, citizen journalism and social justice in China

XIN XIN

Introduction

This chapter discusses the political and social implications of the rise of 'citizen journalism' (CJ) in China, a country where arguably social injustice is rising as quickly as the gap between rich and poor. China has been growing quickly in the past thirty years and economic growth has been accompanied by processes of urbanisation, industrialisation, marketisation and a gradual opening to the outside world. China's 'economic miracle', however, has been achieved mostly at the cost of social justice. Over 60 per cent of Chinese residents surveyed in 2007 were concerned about inequality and injustice in the distribution of income, welfare and job opportunities among different social groups and between urban and rural areas of China (Blue Book of China's Society, 2007). The rural population in inland China remains the most disadvantaged group in an increasingly stratified society and is vulnerable to violations of individual freedoms and civil rights (Li, 2008).

Most cases of social injustice in China are related, directly or indirectly, to corruption, governmental misadministration, merchant misbehaviour, property and labor rights violations and environmental problems (Blue Book of China's Society, 2005). According to China's official statistics, the number of massive protests increased sixfold in ten years, growing from 10,000 cases in 1993 to 60,000 cases in 2003 (ibid.). The population who took part in the protests jumped from 730,000 to three million in ten years (ibid.). Although official figures have not been updated since 2003, there is strong evidence that social conflict is intensifying (Zhu, 2009). Social injustice goes in parallel with uneven economic development. These problems are compounded by the lack of a rule of law and information transparency, and the inability of the media to act as a 'watchdog' checking on corruption and wrongdoing (ibid.).

As part of the country's modernisation package the Internet is developing quickly. China has the largest online population in the world: the total number of Internet users reached almost 180 million by the end of 2008 (Economist.com, 2009). Statistics provided by the China Internet Network Information Centre (CINIC, 2008) revealed an even higher figure – over 250 million Internet users in China by the end of June 2008. The vast majority of Chinese Internet users are based in urban areas. Only slightly over one in one hundred rural residents had access to the Internet in 2005 (Zhao et al., 2006).

With the rise of Web 2.0, media scholars have become concerned with the impact of CJ on mainstream journalism (MJ) and public participation in Western democracies. A central aspect of this academic debate concerns the extent to which MJ has adapted to CJ in order to enhance public participation. Most discussions associated with this debate are framed within a long-standing theoretical controversy over the relationship between journalism and democracy.

Here 'Web 2.0' is seen as a new range of Internet-based services, such as YouTube, Facebook, Flickr and MySpace, for social networking and sharing user-generated content (UGC) (O'Reilly, 2005). New technological means in the Web 2.0 environment have enabled grassroots-citizens to do the job that used to be done only by professional journalists (Gillmor, 2004). With the emergence of mainstream journalism weblogs, the divide between blogger-amateurs and journalist-professionals in the Web 2.0 environment is blurring (Robinson, 2009).

According to Gillmor (2004), CJ has an advantage over MJ in that it greatly enhances public participation. Stuart Allan's (2007) study of the eyewitness reporting of the London bombings in July 2005 by ordinary citizens shows that CJ has gained high public recognition in Western democracies. Some scholars suggest that CJ is posing challenges to and opportunities for MJ (Allan, 2007). In democratic societies the weblog community is growing and now attracts a sizeable audience, exerting political influence by reporting disasters and controversies (Chang, 2005; Nguyen, 2006; Allan, 2007). The Asian tsunami, the London bombings, Hurricane Katrina and presidential elections in the USA, Australia and South Korea are good examples of CJ's activism and of its media impact. Some scholars have also suggested that CJ has taught MJ how to communicate with the public, in and outside the newsroom (Chang, 2005; Nguyen, 2006). With self-generated content and self-managed distribution and reception, Web 2.0 applications in general and CJ in particular are transforming the traditional mode of communication (one to one and top-down) into 'mass self-communication' (many to many and bottom-up) (Castells, 2007, p. 248).

However, it is doubtful that such self-communication is really a mass phenomenon, as research on the 'digital divide' reminds us. Pippa Norris defines the 'digital divide' as a 'multidimensional phenomenon' consisting of three key aspects: 'global divide', 'social divide' and 'democratic divide'. In terms of Internet access, 'global divide' and 'social divide' apply to the gap between developed and developing countries and that between different social groups (differentiated by income, education etc.) in each country respectively. Within the online community, the 'democratic divide', as Norris suggests, 'signifies the difference between those who do, and do not, use the panoply of digital resources to engage, mobilize, and participate in public life' (Norris, 2001, p. 4). Even in affluent and technologically advanced democracies like Britain, in 2008 only 13 per cent of the population used the Internet for 'citizen participation', doing such things as 'giving views, getting in touch with elected representatives, joining organizations and taking part in surveys and consultations' (Ofcom, 2009). Moreover, some studies have shown that the adoption of UGC by the newsrooms of mainstream media is likely to be hindered by a combination of professional, organisational, socio-cultural and economic factors (Paulussen et al. 2007; Paulussen and Ugille, 2008).

Empirical research on the impact of CJ on MJ has been undertaken so far mainly in the context of Western democratic societies. We know very little about CJ and its impact on MJ in non-democratic societies like China, the country upon which this chapter focuses. What impact does CJ have on traditional media and on the level of public participation in debates on social injustice in China? What roles does CJ play in a society where the Internet, media and public participation remain subject to tight ideological control? What are the likely consequences of the fact that China is embracing Web 2.0 technology and digitalisation on the one hand, while being reluctant to relinquish its control over content distributed by traditional media and the Internet on the other? To explore these questions, this chapter provides four case studies of CJ practice in China in order to analyse the multifaceted relationship between CJ and MJ in China.

As a key component of the Chinese media and ideological system, content distributed over the Internet is still under tight control. A 'great firewall' is used to filter out all sorts of sensitive information that might challenge the rule of the Communist Party or address the issue of national unity and social stability (Zhang, 2006). During the 2008 Beijing Olympics this control over the Internet was loosened to a certain degree. The Chinese service of the BBC and other foreign news websites were unblocked and made available within mainland China. This was one of the outcomes of the continuing efforts of the International Olympic Committee and international communities, pressing the Chinese government to keep its promises as a host country. However, these websites were blocked again after the Olympics. The major social networking services, such as YouTube, Facebook, Twitter and Flickr, are also blocked in mainland China. The blockade of Twitter and Flickr began in the lead-up to the twentieth anniversary of the so-called 'Tiananmen event', which took place on 4 June 1989. Moreover, under a massive campaign to clear 'vulgar and harmful content' from the Internet, nearly 3,000 websites were forced to cease their service by 24 February 2009 (People.com, 2009). A bundle of popular blogs at bulloggers.com were forced to cease their activity in mainland China (Tan, 2009).

Against this background, I argue that the progressive role of Web 2.0 technologies, in empowering grassroots journalists to fight against the current political, economic and ideological establishment in an authoritarian society like China, should not be overstated. Instead, we need to realistically assess the role of CJ in relation to MJ bearing in mind China's complex socio-political context. China's economic prosperity, its technological advances and its increasing integration into the global capitalist economic system, I argue, do not necessarily lead to the development of a Western model of democratic society characterised by justice, press freedom, openness and tolerance. However, China's special socio-political context does not mean that the impact of the weblog phenomenon on the country's political and media system is less dramatic than in Western democracies. The impact of CJ in China is multifaceted and serves as a useful example of the complexity of the relationship between Web 2.0 technology, CJ and democracy/social justice.

This chapter explores this relationship from three main perspectives. It begins with an examination of the ways in which CJ influences the journalistic practices adopted by Chinese mainstream media. It then uses two case studies to show that CJ serves as a complementary news source for mainstream media as well as an alternative channel for releasing 'politically sensitive' news. The third case discusses how in some circumstances both CJ and MJ might fail to break through China's Internet and media censorship. Finally, this chapter discusses how CJ and the online community nurture Chinese neo-nationalism and tend to be more cynical towards foreign critics than towards domestic social problems. Drawing on a contextual analysis of these four case studies, I suggest that the weblog phenomenon and CJ in China are still far from becoming an engine of social change. CJ, just like MJ, is facing challenges posed by a combination of forces, including tightened ideological control, severe market competition and the rise of Chinese nationalism. In order to understand the complex reality of CJ in China, this chapter aims to go beyond those polarised accounts about the rise of CJ and the decline of MJ. Instead, it shows how complex the relationship between CJ and MJ is in a transitional society like China.

CJ is more than a source of information: the case of the 'nail house'

It is nowadays quite common for Chinese mainstream journalists, particularly investigative journalists, to use CJ or weblogs as a source of news and information (Zheng and Hao, 2008). In the case of the 'nail house' in Chongqing, CJ not only served as a source of information for MJ, but also involved the sort of field reporting traditionally associated with MJ. As I recount, the interaction between CJ and MJ was the key factor in explaining the effectiveness of the investigation into the 'nail house'.

'Nail house' is a term that was used to describe a household that disobeyed the official command to move out from a state-owned property. Here it refers to a modest two-storey brick building, which stood in the centre of a 10-metre deep pit as the only house left in a construction site in Chongqing, south-west China (Xinhua News Agency, 2007). The origin of the Chongqing nail house can be traced back to as early as 2004, before the existence of China's first property law, which came into effect three years later. It was associated with one of the disputes that are likely to occur in today's China between ordinary citizens and real estate developers – symbols of capitalism. The story of the Chongqing house began with its owners' refusal of the offer of compensation from a local real estate developer, who planned to demolish their home for business purposes. The house's owners were then sued by the real estate company. In a decision made on 19 March 2007, the local court ruled that the house owners must move out of their own house within three days.

The first image of the nail house appeared online in February 2007. The photo was taken by a local resident and was then posted on an online forum under the title 'The coolest nail house in history'. This photo spread among online forum participants and bloggers. The comments were supportive of those who spread the photo. Just twenty or thirty years ago, when nail houses were still owned by the government, such comments were inconceivable, as they were widely seen as being against the collective interest. The issue did not attract attention from the Chinese mainstream media until 8 March 2007, when the *Southern Metropolitan Daily* for the first time published the photo, attached to a small story about online discussions of house disputes. More coverage appeared after 19 March. On 2 April the house owners ultimately reached agreement with the real estate company through the mediation of the local government. On the same day, the building was demolished.

Zola Zhou, a young Chinese blogger, made a self-financed visit to Chongqing and reported the dispute over the nail house on site (Zhou, 2007). Zhou interviewed the house owners and he chatted with other house owners, who were likewise threatened with losing their own homes because of the urban development plans of Shanghai, Guangzhou and other cites. Zhou won the trust of interviewees and Internet users because of his independent stance and the role as a grassroots-blogger. Hundreds of readers and Internet users left favourable comments on Zhou's blog and other websites carrying his reports about the nail house (ibid.). Zhou's blog became an open platform for Internet users to comment on both sides of the house dispute, as well as to make a spontaneous response to any comment posted. This was something that the mainstream media failed to provide during the period of the house dispute.

Still, it is too early to conclude that bloggers, like Zhou, are able to replace professional journalists and undertake an entire investigation and fully inform the public. Having no journalistic training, Zhou did not know how to handle the field investigation and asked professional journalists and supporters for advice, as he admitted in his blog diary (Zhou, 2007; Zheng and Hao, 2008). Moreover, as an individual blogger, Zhou was in bad need of support from the mainstream media and relied heavily on the latter's coverage of his own story to justify the reliability of his reporting. Zhou posted a blog entry to the article published by the *Southern Metropolitan Daily* about him. In order to draw weblog hits, Zhou added an entry to the investigative report done by the *Southern Metropolitan Daily* about the 'nail house'. As an individual blogger, Zhou suffered from financial constraints. Zhou's trip to Chongqing was sponsored by a small family fund and some support from Internet users. Without adequate financial support, it is difficult for independent bloggers, like Zhou, to carry out field reporting. Although mainstream media may face the same problem, CJ practitioners are likely to suffer much more. Last but not least, Zhou seemed to lose interest in the nail house event immediately after the two sides of the conflict had reached an agreement, while professional journalists continued to report. Clearly, CJ is unable to function alone. In the case of the nail house, CJ with support from MJ carried out the investigation and made the public aware of the dispute.

To sum up, the case suggests that CJ is an important news source for MJ and that the slow response of Chinese mainstream media to social conflicts enhances CJ's investigative role. CJ played a watchdog role in unveiling violations of property rights (Zheng and Hao, 2008). Even though CJ had a positive impact on the exposure of social injustice and the presentation of grassroots opinion over the house dispute, it is still far from able to challenge, let alone change, the status quo in China. The main reason behind the mainstream media's silence before 19 March was that the 2007 annual conference of the National People's Congress (NPC) took place in March in Beijing. All mainstream media were focusing (very probably were forced to do so) on the conference, during which the property law was passed; it subsequently went into force on 1 October in the same year. Therefore, the sudden increased attention from the mainstream media after 19 March cannot be fully explained by CJ's influence. This means that the significance of CJ highlighted in the case of the nail house does not necessarily apply to other cases.

CJ as an alternative news distribution channel for journalist-bloggers: the case of the Loufan landslide

The case of the Loufan landslide indicates how a mainstream journalist-blogger used his weblog to expose the cover-up of an accident in north-west China. Work-related accidents due to poor safety measures are another important aspect of social injustice in today's China. The landslide took place at a local iron mine in Loufan county in the suburbs of the Shanxi provincial capital Taiyuan on 1 August 2008. Initially, the local authorities attempted to cover up the causes of the disaster by blaming the 'bad weather', and deliberately concealed the real number of casualties.

Sun Chunlong, a reporter for the *Oriental Outlook* news journal (a commercial affiliation of Xinhua News Agency), was not convinced by the information about the accident provided by Loufan local authorities (Sun, 2008). After Sun traced the record of the discussions in the 'Loufan online forum', run by the popular Chinese search engine Baidu, and consulted his local friends about the accident, he decided to undertake further investigation. The outcome of Sun's filed research is the co-authored article 'Loufan: the delayed truth', published in the *Oriental Outlook* in late August. The article explains the real cause of the disaster and reveals the real number of casualties. However, the article did not have as huge an impact as Sun expected, having failed to draw attention from high-level officials in charge of safety in the workplace. Then, Sun decided to write an open letter to a Chinese officer, who had just taken up the post of handling workplace-related safety issues. Sun posted his letter to his personal weblog on 14 September 2008. The letter quickly travelled among bloggers and online forums' participants. However, Sun's blog letter was soon blocked by some Chinese Internet portals, including Sina.com and 163.com.

To Sun's surprise, his blog, though it had been blocked, drew attention from Premier Wen Jiabao and State Councillor Ma Kai, who issued an order on 17 September demanding that Shangxi local authorities verify the number of casualties and reinvestigate the cause of the disaster. Three weeks later, the State Council announced the results of the investigation into the Loufan case on the website of the State Administration of Work Safety (2008). The investigation concluded that the disaster was a major liability accident, for which the managers of the iron mine and related local officers should take full responsibility.

The major implications of this case for CJ and MJ in China are at least threefold. First, the case of Loufan suggests that the boundaries between MJ and CJ are blurring. Sun Chunlong, a professional journalist, used both mainstream media (the news magazine) and citizen journalism channels (his individual blog) to present the outcomes of his investigations. The fact that the news journal in which Sun's investigative report was first published failed to draw public attention, while Sun's blog succeeded in this, suggests the increasing attention to CJ paid by Chinese decision-makers.

Second, the case shows that regardless of whether or not CJ gets involved, the approach to dealing with social injustice in today's China has not fundamentally changed. It is true that the appeal Sun made in his letter to the Chinese safety officer to reveal the covered truth is a demonstration of his efforts to play a watchdog role. And it is also true that Sun and his colleagues' efforts were partly aimed at informing the public about the Loufan accident and increasing public awareness about a social problem. However, Sun's main purpose was not to expose failures of the system but to draw the attention of the Chinese central government to ensure that the 'bad guys' would be punished. Blaming the 'bad guys' at lower levels of public administration with the support of the 'good guys' at higher levels is a strategy that has been widely used by mainstream journalists as a pragmatic approach to handling social injustice at local levels. This is because Sun and other journalists are not in a position to criticise the system in those circumstances where there are conflicting interests between the central government, local authorities and grassroots. Instead of using the rule of law, both Chinese journalists and the victims of accidents still prefer to turn to officials at higher administrative levels for a solution. From this perspective, CJ and MJ share the same approach to handling social injustice in China. Apart from the fact that Sun used a weblog to report the accident to top officials, there is not very much difference from the past in the way in which social injustice is currently handled. While CJ and Web 2.0 allow Chinese bloggers to have better access to their target audience, the way in which social injustice is handled has therefore not fundamentally changed.

Finally, in comparison with an amateur-blogger like Zhou, Sun was equipped with better journalistic training and was backed by a mainstream media outlet and his colleagues. However, this does not mean that Sun won the trust of grassroots-interviewees any more easily. In fact, as Sun claimed, at the beginning many victims of the Loufan landslide did not trust him (Xinhuanet.com, 2008). Surely, though, as a journalist-blogger, he used mainstream media resources and his individual blog to good advantage.

CJ and MJ's failure to empower grassroots-citizens to fight for social justice: the case of the 'milk scandal'

This scandal concerned Sanlu, the market leader (with nearly 20 per cent market share), and another twenty-one dairy brands, which were found to contain melamine, an industrial chemical used to produce coatings and plastics (Wang et al., 2009). Melamine was added by some suppliers to make the infant milk appear to be higher in protein than it actually was. These twenty-two companies were considered in good standing and were exempt from inspections by the General Administration of Quality Supervision, Inspection and Quarantine, the food safety watchdog in China (ibid.). The melamine-contaminated infant milk resulted in at least six deaths and sickened nearly 300,000 infants by the end of November 2008 according to statistics released by Chinese authorities (ibid.). More than 50,000 infants were hospitalised. Many of them had kidney stones or calculi after consuming melamine-tainted milk (WHO, 2008).

According to Hans Troedsson, WHO's China representative, the disastrous impact of the melamine-contaminated milk on affected children was 'aggravated by delays in reporting at a number of sources'. These delays were seen as 'a combination of ignorance and deliberate failure to report' (Spears and Lawrence, 2008). The melamine contamination had been detected in Sanlu's diary products as early as December 2007. The company received complaints about its infant formula in March 2008, when kidney stones were found in ten babies in a hospital in Nanjing, capital of Jiangsu province. All affected infants consumed Sanlu's milk. In July, more cases were diagnosed in Gansu province. Melamine was confirmed in Sanlu tests on 1 August 2008. The company reported the results only to the local authority of Shijiazhuang, capital city of Hebei province, where Sanlu was based. The decision made by the local authority and Sanlu in early August was to withhold the information about the contamination until the end of the Beijing Olympics. In order to cover up the scandal, Sanlu tried to buy off media, parents and even a popular

Internet search engine (Wang et al., 2009). The company did not order a full recall of its tainted milk until mid-September, when the full scandal was exposed by media and the State Council began its investigation into the scandal.

Both CJ and MJ failed to inform the public promptly about the food safety crisis in China. The first media coverage of the milk scandal, which pointed directly to Sanlu, appeared in the *Oriental Morning Post*, a Shanghai-based local newspaper, on 11 September 2008. It was written by Jian Guangzhou, a reporter for the newspaper. Before Jian's story about Sanlu's wrongdoing, A Gansu-based local newspaper, *Lanzhou Morning Post*, published an article about fourteen babies in Gansu who were found to be ill after consuming the same brand of tainted milk. However, the author did not identify the brand name of the milk. This story was available online. Newspaper readers and Internet users, including worried and angry parents, started demanding that the brand name of the tainted milk should be disclosed. In response to the 'overwhelming' reaction from the general public, Jian decided to reveal the name of Sanlu, as he recounts (Jian, 2008), believing that any journalist in his position would do the same thing in that circumstance. As early as late August, a media outlet based in Hubei province released a story about three babies suffering from kidney stones after consuming the tainted milk (ibid.). However, this report failed to alarm Chinese audiences (ibid.). Despite the fact that Sanlu and local authorities were trying to cover up the milk scandal, information delays were also due to the banning order from the Party's Propaganda Department, which considered the food safety issue as a sensitive topic during the Beijing Olympics (Fu, 2008). As Fu Jianfeng (or He Feng), a reporter for the newsweekly *Southern Weekend*, pointed out in an editorial note, he spotted the contaminated milk in late July. However, because of the banning order, Fu's investigative report was not allowed to appear on the website of *Southern Weekend* and *Southern Metropolitan Daily* until mid-September 2008 (ibid.). CJ and Internet users started reporting and discussing the milk crisis after the mainstream media's coverage appeared on 9 September (Lianhe Zaobao, 2008).

This case shows that both CJ and MJ failed to inform the public adequately about the tainted milk both before and during the Olympics. This also means that both failed to empower grassroots-citizens to fight for social justice. The banning order from the Propaganda Department, the lack of information transparency at the local level, Sanlu's attempts to cover up the scandal, the food safety watchdog's exemption and the local protection granted to a popular home diary brand – all these factors point to major flaws in China's communication and administration system. However, neither CJ nor MJ managed or dared to pinpoint the essence of the problem when the milk crisis broke out at the moment of national celebration of economic achievements and openness before and during the Beijing Olympics. In this respect, it is too optimistic to talk about the revolutionary role of CJ in the Internet age. It is true that in theory the Web 2.0 environment provides journalists and bloggers with a technologically advanced channel to inform the public. However, this channel can still be blocked by political and economic forces in a society where the rule of law and a mechanism for guaranteeing media and information transparency remain absent, as in China. This is particularly the case when political and economic interests combine together under the banner of national interest and pride.

CJ as a vessel for Chinese nationalism: the case of the new generation of 'angry youth' (*fengqing*)

With weblogs broadening the social geography of today's journalism activities, it is essential not to ignore their impact on national identity, particularly on the way in which 'we' and 'others' (those from outside the nation) are divided. The following case illustrates how young people use CJ to identify themselves and judge those 'others' in China. An 'online nationalism' with patriotic sentiments coexists with 'critical online realism' – a critical view of the country's social reality shared among the Chinese online community (Youth Journalist, 2004). The weblog phenomenon serves as a vessel for both.

According to Min Dahong, a Chinese communication scholar, 'critical online realism' and 'online nationalism' are adopted by the Chinese online community to handle domestic and foreign affairs respectively. Min sees moderate expressions of nationalistic sentiment and behaviour in a positive light. However, Chinese nationalism seems threatening to others, while the Internet is transformed into a vessel for nurturing a new generation of 'angry youth' (*fengqing*) (Osnos, 2008). According to Li Datong, an outspoken journalist, there is a difference between the new generation of 'angry youth' and the rebellious generation demonstrating in 1989. The latter demonstrated against corruption and social injustice, while the current young generation tends to adopt an opportunistic approach, blaming the West while turning a blind eye to the Chinese reality (ibid.). As the Chinese official statistics suggest, two in three Chinese Internet users are young people aged thirty and under (CINIC, 2008). There is a sizeable pool of potential *fengqing* growing up online. The following three episodes outline what we mean by 'angry youth' and how nationalistic sentiments are expressed by them via CJ and the Internet.

Episode I

Imperialism will never abandon its intention to destroy us.

Obviously, there is a scheme behind the scenes to encircle China. A new Cold War!

We [Chinese] will stand up and hold together always as one family in harmony!

These quotes come from a short video entitled '2008 China Stand Up!' (quoted by Osnos, 2008). The video was made by Tang Jie, a young Chinese graduate based in Shanghai. This video clip appeared on Sina.com, a popular Chinese portal, on 15 April 2008. According to *The New Yorker*, it 'captured the mood of nationalism that surged through China after the Tibetan uprising, in March, sparked foreign criticism of China's hosting of the 2008 Summer Olympics' (ibid.). The video was then posted on YouTube, which by then had been blocked in mainland China. It drew more than a million hits in the first ten days and very favourable comments (ibid.).

Episode II

Grace Wang, a Chinese student at Duke University, tried to take an approach different from Chinese patriots by mediating between pro-Tibet and pro-China protesters on campus in April 2008. Her photo and a video clip with her speech in front of two groups of people were posted on Chinese websites, labelled 'traitor' and 'the most ugly student' (Chen, 2008). People ferreted out her parents' address, workplaces and IDs, and then publicised them on the Internet. Wang's parents were called 'traitors' too (ibid.). After their home was vandalised, Wang's parents went into hiding (Osnos, 2008). However, as a journalist-blogger noted, a few Chinese Internet users paid attention to what she actually said in her speech made available online (Chen, 2008).

Episode III

Jin Jing, a disabled torchbearer, was praised at home for her courage and heroic behaviour in fending off pro-Tibet protesters, who were trying to extinguish the Olympic torch during the relay in Paris in April 2008 (Times Online, 2008). Later, after Jin had expressed her disagreement with the action of boycotting Carrefour, a French supermarket chain, in China, she began to be called 'traitor' on the Internet (Zhang and Chen, 2008).

These three episodes are representative of the 'online nationalism' phenomenon, which is arguably as widespread as is CJ's critical attitude to social injustice in today's China, if not more. The group of active citizen-bloggers is likely to be provoked by nationalistic sentiments and turn against not only Westerners who are critical of Chinese reality, but also people belonging to the same race as them but labelled 'traitors'. Under the name of national interest or patriotism, CJ is in danger of becoming a space not for rational public discussion, but for verbal insults and xenophobia. The slight difference between the first episode and the other two lies in the discourse to which they are accordingly connected. The first episode mainly reflects the old 'Cold War' discourse, which divides the West and the East by ideology. The latter two mostly address the discourse of national identity – anxiety about the crisis in national identity in the process of globalisation. Both discourses seem relevant to the rise of CJ in relation to social justice in the Web 2.0 environment. And few studies draw attention to them. However, the three episodes vividly demonstrate the complex nature of CJ in China. They also suggest that active online participation by a youth-dominated community in China does not necessarily lead to rational activism for a global civil society or social justice at home. Instead, it results in the rise of Chinese nationalism in a virtual world. CJ's impact is much more complex than simplified accounts of CJ-as-good and MJ-as-bad suggest, and it certainly deserves further research.

Concluding remarks

This chapter has examined the political and social context within which CJ is currently practised and tried to make sense of its complex relationship with MJ. In China, the Internet and Web 2.0 are growing quickly. In parallel, however, social injustice is still as widespread as ever, and traditional media as well as content distributed over the Internet continue to be tightly controlled and censored. At the same time, Chinese nationalistic sentiments are accumulating online, exerting an influence on offline activism. There are therefore competing factors: technological advances versus information censorship; journalism and blogging for social justice versus online activism for Chinese nationalism; political control versus economic interests. These factors are shaping the emergence of CJ and the role it plays in promoting or hindering social change in China. These factors sometimes neutralise each other, sometimes reinforce each other. Understanding the interactions between them is the key and most challenging task for researchers.

The four case studies presented in this chapter shed some light on the social and political implications of CJ for the debate about the relationship between journalism and democracy. The analysis demonstrates the complexity of CJ practice in China. It illustrates how in certain circumstances CJ is used by MJ as a news source as well as an alternative channel for distributing information. From this perspective, CJ appears to be performing a valuable function in aiding MJ to perform the sort of Fourth Estate role that liberal theories expect from the media. At the same time, however, CJ is establishing itself as a vehicle for the expression of nationalistic sentiments or hate speech. Moreover, CJ remains subject to the Party's control, similarly to MJ, and therefore might fail to provide the public with information they need (this was apparent in the case of the 'milk scandal'). In short, political, economic, social, journalistic and moral forces constrain the technological potential of the Web 2.0 environment. Therefore, CJ alone is unlikely to be a driving force in promoting social change in China, though it might work together with MJ to make it more diffi-cult for the Party to control online information flows within the country. In the long term, if CJ, MJ and other social forces continue to denounce social injus-tice, it is possible that a more democratic, but not necessarily a less national-istic, country will emerge. Undoubtedly, the relationship between democracy and nationalism, which lies outside the scope of this study, is a key but under-researched area, deserving serious investigation in future.

REFERENCES

Allan, Stuart (2007) 'Citizen journalism and the rise of "mass self-communication": reporting the London bombings', *Global Media Journal* (Australian edn), 1: 1, 1–20.

Blue Book of China's Society (2005) *Analysis and Forecast of China's Social Development in 2005* (Beijing: Social Science Academic Press).

Blue Book of China's Society (2007) *Analysis and Forecast of China's Social Development in 2007* (Beijing: Social Science Academic Press).

Castells, Manuel (2007) 'Communication, power and counter-power in the network society', *International Journal of Communication*, 1: 1, 238–66.

Chang, Woo-Young (2005) 'Online civic participation, and political empowerment: online media and public opinion formation in Korea', *Media, Culture and Society*, 27: 6, 925–35.

Chen, Yaowen (2008) Chen Yaowen's Weblog, 22 April, http://chenyaowen.blshe. com/post/943/191280, accessed 1 April 2009.

China Internet Network Information Center (CINIC) (2008) *Statistical Survey Report on the Internet Development in China*, abridged edn (Beijing: CINIC), http://www.cnnic.net.cn/uploadfiles/pdf/2008/8/15/145744.pdf, accessed 10 January 2009.

Economist.com (2009) 'Internet users: China is number one. More than a billion people are using the Internet', *Economist.com*, 26 January, http://www.economist.com/daily/chartgallery/displayStory.cfm?story_id=13007996, accessed 27 January 2009.

Fu, Jianfeng (2008) 'An editorial note about the investigation into the Sanlu poisoning milk', *Minzhuzhongguo.org*, 22 September, http://www.minzhuzhongguo.org/Article/wl/sj/200809/20080922120933.shtml, accessed 11 April 2009.

Gillmor, Dan (2004) *We the Media: Grassroots Journalism by the People* (Sebastopol, CA: O'Reilly).

Jian, Guangzhou (2008) 'The story behind the report about 14 Gansu babies caught kidney diseases because of consuming Sanlu milk', *blog. hsw.cn*, 14 September, http://blog.hsw.cn/139297/viewspace-345305.html, accessed 5 January 2009.

Li, Qiang (2008) *Ten Lectures on Social Stratification* (Beijing: Social Science Academic Press).

Lianhe Zaobao (2008) 'A national shock caused by babies with kidney stones', *Zaobao.com*, 12 September, http://www.zaobao.com/special/china/milk/pages/milk080912e.shtml, accessed 10 April 2009.

Nguyen, An (2006) 'Journalism in the wake of participatory publishing', *Australian Journalism Review*, 28: 1, 143–55.

Norris, Pippa (2001) *Digital Divide: Civic Engagement, Information Poverty, and the Internet Worldwide* (Cambridge: Cambridge University Press).

Ofcom (Office of Communication) (2009) Citizens' digital participation, a research reported released on 20 March 2009, http://www.ofcom.org.uk/advice/media_literacy/medlitpub/medlitpubrss/cdp/main.pdf, accessed 1 July 2009.

O'Reilly, Tim (2005) 'What is Web 2.0: design patterns and business models for the next generation of software', http://www.oreillynet.com/pub/a/oreilly/tim/news/2005/09/30/what-is-web-20.html, accessed 1 April 2009.

Osnos, Evan (2008) 'Angry youth: the new generation's neocon nationalists', *The New Yorker*, 28 July, http://www.newyorker.com/reporting/2008/07/28/080728fa_fact_osnos, accessed 1 August 2008.

Paulussen, Steve et al. (2007) 'Doing it together: citizen participation in the professional news making process', *Observatorio (OBS*) Journal*, 1: 3, 131–54.

Paulussen, Steve and Ugille, Pieter (2008) 'User generated content in the newsroom: professional and organizational constraints on participatory journalism', *Westminster Papers in Communication and Culture*, 5: 2, 24–41, http://www.wmin.ac.uk/mad/pdf/WPCC-Vol5-No2-Paulussen_Ugille.pdf, accessed 1 April 2009.

People.com (2009) '2962 Websites have been shut down since the campaign for clearing "vulgar content" over the Internet', *People.com*, 24 February, http://media.people.com.cn/GB/8862353.html, accessed 1 March 2009.

Robinson, Susan (2009) 'The mission of the J-blog: recapturing journalistic authority online', *Journalism*, 7: 1, 65–83.

State Administration of Work Safety (2008) 'The State Council began to investigate the landslide accident in Lofan on 1 August', *Chinasafety.gov.cn*, 6 October, http://www.chinasafety.gov.cn/gongzuodongtai/2008-10/06/content_288791.htm, accessed 11 October 2008.

Spears, Lee and Lawrence, Dune (2008) 'China delays in milk scandal "Deliberate", WHO says (update 1)', *Bloomberg.com*, 26 September, http://www.bloomberg. com/apps/news?pid=washingtonstory&sid=aNGZNTdtW5a8, accessed 1 March 2009.

Sun, Chunlong (2008) 'A letter to a Chinese safety officer', http://blog.ifeng.com/article/1727838.html, accessed 1 April 2009.

Tan, Renwei (2009) 'The popular weblog service, Bulllog.cn, got shut down', *Nanfang Metropolitan Daily*, 12 January, p. A24, http://www.nanfangdaily.com.cn/ epaper/nfds/content/20090112/ArticelA24003FM.htm, accessed 13 January 2009.

Times Online (2008) 'Sarkozy apologises to disabled torchbearer Jin Jing over torch melee', *Times Online*, 21 April, http://www.timesonline.co.uk/tol/news/world/asia/ article3788922.ece, accessed 25 March 2009.

Twigg, K. (2009) 'Twitterers defy China's firewall', *BBC News Online*, http://news. bbc.co.uk/1/hi/world/asia-pacific/8091411.stm, accessed 10 July 2009.

Wang, Heyan, Zhu, Tao and Ye, Doudou (2009) 'The "poisoning milk" trial opens in China', *Caijing Online*, 5, http://magazine.caijing.com.cn/2009-01-02/ 110057114.html, accessed 6 January 2009.

World Health Organization (WHO) (2008) *Expert Meeting to Review Toxicological Aspects of Melamine and Cyanuric Acid*, *WHO.int*, 8 December, http://www.who. int/foodsafety/fs_management/Exec_Summary_melamine.pdf, accessed 2 April 2009.

Xinhua News Agency (2007) '"Nail house" in Chongqing demolished', *Chinadaily.com.cn*, 3 April, http://www.chinadaily.com.cn/china/2007-04/03/ content_842221.htm, accessed 5 January 2008.

Xinhuanet.com (2008) 'The journalist-blogger exposed the covered truth in Lofan landslide', *Xinhuanet.com*, 18 October, http://news.xinhuanet.com/video/2008-10/ 18/content_10213544.htm, accessed 1 April 2009.

Youth Journalist (2004) 'Dialogues with Prof Ming Dahong: online opinion and public expression', *Xinhuanet.com*, 22 October, http://news.xinhuanet.com/ newmedia/2004-10/22/content_2115745.htm, accessed 26 March 2009.

Zhang, Lena (2006) 'Behind the "great firewall": decoding China's Internet media policies from the inside', *Convergence: The International Journal of Research into New Media Technologies*, 12: 3, 271–91.

Zhang, Xiong and Chen, Xuan (2008) 'Chinese anger: inconceivable boycotts', *New Century Weekly*, 28 April, http://news.sina.com.cn/c/2008-04-28/140615443763. shtml, accessed 29 April 2009.

Zhao, Jinqiu, Hao, Xiaoming and Indrajit, Banerjee (2006) 'The diffusion of the Internet and rural development', *Convergence: The International Journal of Research into New Media Technologies*, 12: 3, 293–305.

Zheng, Jiawen and Hao, Xiaoming (2008) 'The Internet and citizen journalism in China: a case study of Zola Zhou's blog', in Michael Bromley (ed.), *AMIC Conference Proceedings. Convergence, Citizen Journalism and Social Change: Building*

Capacity (Brisbane: University of Queensland), http://www.uq.edu.au/sjc/docs/AMIC/Zheng_Jiawen_and_Hao_Xiaoming.pdf, accessed 10 April 2008.

Zhou, Zuola Shuguang (2007) *Zou Shuguang's weblog*, March–April, http://www.zuola.com/weblog, accessed 10 November 2007.

Zhu, Li (2009) 'An analysis of Chinese social risks: the nature of the mass incidents in China', *Xuehai*, 1, http://www.minzhuzhongguo.org/Article/wl/sx/200904/20090409125730.shtml, accessed 10 April 2009.

CHAPTER 12

Marrying the professional to the amateur: strategies and implications of the OhmyNews model

AN NGUYEN

In the summer of 1950, during the early days of the Korean War, American soldiers machine-gunned hundreds of helpless South Korean refugees, including children, women and old people, under a railway bridge near Nogeun-ni. Forty-nine years later, the hidden massacre was uncovered in an Associated Press (AP) story and was quickly spread on the front pages of newspapers in Korea and around the world, forcing the US military to conduct a full investigation into the incident. The AP won a Pulitzer Prize for the investigation. But the honour should have gone to a then little-known Korean journalist named Oh Yeon-Ho (French, 2003). Five years before the AP, Oh had investigated the nightmare and reported it in a relatively small liberal magazine. This breaking story, however, fell into oblivion for half a decade for one reason: the Korean media are predominantly conservative, tending to ignore anything anti-establishment, including anti-American affairs.

To Oh, however, the frustration with this and similar incidents led him to his life success. 'This made me realise that we have a real imbalance in our media, 80% conservative and 20% liberal, and it needed to be corrected', Oh said in the *New York Times* (French, 2003). Resolved to 'say farewell to 20th-century Korean journalism', he started a seemingly absurd venture: an online news service operating with the motto 'Every citizen is a reporter', named OhmyNews. Less than four years later, the site had built up an army of nearly 30,000 citizen reporters, or 'news guerrillas' – ranging from housewives and schoolkids to lawyers, doctors and university professors – and was the most influential news site and the sixth most influential news outlet in Korea (Cheon, 2004). It was also credited as a, if not *the*, decisive force in the making of Roh Moo-Hyun's presidency in the 2002 election (Joyce, 2007). As of March 2009, according to its communication director, OhmyNews hosted 70,000 citizen reporters and gathered between 500,000 and one million readers with 2.5 to three million page views a day (Min, 2009). It has also been running an English-language version, OhmyNews International, with which more than 6,000 citizen reporters from about 130 countries are now registered.

Oh's 'from galley slave to prince' rise highlights the remarkable potential of the Internet in paving the way for a new news/information order via enabling what has increasingly been recognised as 'citizen journalism'. For journalists and their paymasters, OhmyNews and the rise of citizen journalism in general raise intriguing questions about their future. Some, like *Newsweek*'s Internet Executive Christopher Schroeder (2004), wonder whether this is the future of journalism. Others worry whether they will still be needed. For them, the frightening and painful fact is that many members of the public and media critics seem prepared to accept a world where their professional expertise is a thing of the past. For instance, Andrew Keen (2007) argues that 'professional journalism will die out' because in 'an increasingly personalized, chaotic and colourful environment . . . more and more people . . . will only trust their friends, not journalists'. Much of this excitement and fear, however, tends either to be inadequately informed or to overemphasise the power of citizen journalism at the same time as undervaluing and/or overlooking the crucial contribution of professional journalism to the former's success. As Robert McChesney in this volume and others, including myself (Nguyen, 2006, 2008, 2009), have argued, for citizen journalism to work well, it must be aided in one way or another by professional newspeople. Rather than focusing on which will dominate which, it would be more helpful to explore new ways in which they can work together for the better of both, and of all.

On that premise, this chapter presents a detailed case study of OhmyNews – its success story, the socio-political drivers of this success and its operation mechanism – in order to explore its implications for journalism. Moving beyond the mere statistics above, I review and re-evaluate the success of OhmyNews. Then, I examine the news production process of OhmyNews, its key editorial and administration strategies, to point out that, despite its much-touted motto, OhmyNews is essentially a hybrid news cooperative based on a cleverly, creatively managed marriage between citizen reporters and trained, skilled and experienced journalists, which is fundamental to its success. Finally, the implications of this model for the future of journalism are explored, particularly in relation to the 'journalism is dead' debate.

OhmyNews: the success story

OhmyNews is a success story that has gone beyond the expectation of anybody, including its founder. In its pre-birth days, Oh only dared to plan to run it as a weekly, not a daily, outlet for at least six months. But the two months of running its beta version brought in 727 citizen reporters, who generated a number of articles substantial enough to make the site 'automatically' function as a daily from the outset. And despite Oh's humble goal of 2,000 readers a day, citizen reporters kept coming to the site in an unprecedented manner. There have been numerous surprising moments. In 2004, for instance, in response to the National Assembly's decision to curtail funds for an encyclopaedia of pro-Japanese figures during Korea's colonial period, the site initiated a campaign to raise money to make it happen. Their plan to obtain 500 million won (roughly US$500,000) in seven months quickly turned out to be 'unrealistic': the targeted sum arrived within just eleven days from a 'frighteningly powerful bunch' of 23,000 readers (Oh, 2005). Another surprise came in 2004, shortly after the site started a semi-automatic tipping system where readers can reward writers via mobile phones or online banking. After publishing an article attacking the undemocratic nature of a decision by the Constitutional Court, a university professor ended up with a $24,000 tip from 4,500 readers. But perhaps the biggest scoop of OhmyNews so far is its widely credited decisive role in the election of the late President Roh Moo-Hyun in 2002, to which I return below.

The heyday of OhmyNews, however, seems to have passed. Korea today is no longer a 'wild west' for OhmyNews: its once unique participatory model has been adopted and adapted by, according to Oh, 'virtually every news site'. Along with intensive competition, the initial enthusiasm of citizen reporters seems to be waning. For instance, although the number of citizen reporters at OhmyNews has doubled since 2004, my data show that the daily number of stories flowing into its newsroom has remained constant at 150–200 submissions. A potentially critical problem is the lack of a sustainable business model. The site turned a profit for the first time in 2003 but, with an annual income of US$6.5 million, is still struggling. Its revenue streams – 60 per cent from advertising, 20 per cent from selling content to other websites and the rest from various other sources (e.g. direct donation, voluntary subscription) – have not proved sustainable. All this, however, should not obscure the fact that OhmyNews is still one of Korea's most important news sites and is, so far, an exemplary success in the unfolding world of citizen journalism across the globe.

A Korea-only experience?

In retrospect, Oh Yeon-Ho (2005) sees OhmyNews as 'a unique product' whose success is built on five Korea-specific factors that are generally agreed by observers (French, 2003; Cheon, 2004; Gillmor, 2004; Schroeder, 2004; Wagstaff, 2004; Allan, 2006; Joyce, 2007; Hauben, 2008; Chang, 2009).

First, as a result of the Korean government's late 1990s strategic decision to build Korea as an 'information superpower', the country enjoys an advanced Internet infrastructure. By the mid-2000s, when broadband was still a novelty for the rest of the world, it had been a daily inexpensive utility for about 80 per cent of Korean households (Allan, 2006). Second, Korea is a geographically small country, making it easy and convenient for people to travel around for news gathering and related purposes. Third, OhmyNews took advantage of Koreans' homogeneous culture – one in which people can easily be drawn into 'big fevered discussions' since their attention tends to be 'absorbed by the same kind of issues, usually at the same time' (Wagstaff, 2004) – by employing what Oh calls a 'selection and focus' strategy. That is, instead of offering a diverse 'cafeteria' news menu, the site concentrates on a few 'OhmyNews-like' issues, i.e. those resonant with its and its readers' progressive orientation (Oh, 2005). An example is the consistent and tireless coverage of Roh Moo-Hyun's escalation throughout the 2002 election.

Perhaps more critically important are the other two interrelated reasons: young Koreans' long-established distrust of and dissatisfaction with the conservative mainstream press and their strong desire for political participation. Korea is a young and vulnerable democracy. With the right to press freedom obtained in 1987, the Korean media have grown into family-run businesses that, to satisfy commercial aims, tend to provide a support structure for autocratic political interests rather than to act as a watchdog (Choi, 2003; Hauben, 2008). In seeking to 'align market profitability with political authority,' the post-authoritarianism media quickly became a 'quasi-state agency with similar functions to a governmental institution,' a 'king-maker' (Chang, 2009). This 'ChoJoongDong' system – dubbed after the three leading conservative newspapers (*Chosun Ilbo*, *JoongAng Ilbo* and *Dong-ah Ilbo*) (Hauben, 2008) – has long been a source of frustration and disillusion among young Koreans. The widespread sentiment against the right-wing mainstream newspapers has materialised in many civil attempts to boycott them and those advertising on their pages (Hauben, 2008), to abolish laws that favour their information monopoly and even to stop their symbol, *Chosun Ilbo*, from continuing (Chang, 2009).

This is especially true for the so-called '386 generation', those in their thirties (by the 1990s), university-educated in the 1980s and, obviously, born in the 1960s. These people fought hard for democracy in the 1970s and 1980s, are Internet-savvy, possess a high level of political self-efficacy and cognitive deliberation (Kang and Dyson, 2007) and, according to Chang (2009), are in the middle of a post-Confucianist transformation where non-conformity and individualistic participation are more valued than old and often abused communitarian values. And with the Internet and other news production means in hand, they quickly gather and build their own communication channels to 'change the world'. Oh – a 386 member who spent a year behind bars under dictatorship – attracted his initial investment of US$120,000 for OhmyNews from sympathetic 386 businesspeople. Thus, from the outset, he ran OhmyNews with an 'open progressivism' policy, which combines with its 'selection and focus' strategy to serve the anti-establishment and reform-hungry young Koreans, particularly those in their twenties to forties.

Perhaps nowhere did this prove to be more efficient than in the 2002 presidential election. Originally appearing as a 'political novice and maverick', Roh Moo-Hyun enjoyed no traditional party structure (Kang and Dyson, 2007). Further, being an 'anti-establishment political revolutionary', he received scant attention by the press and was defeated in the traditionally conservative Pusan province in his race for a parliament seat in 2000. For reform-minded young Koreans, however, Roh was a political icon representing their values and beliefs. They gathered on the Internet and, among other things, organised a fan club called Rohsamo ('people who love Roh') to promote his political visions, raise funds for his campaign and organise offline rallies. Along with this, OhmyNews acted as a major gathering space for Roh's supporters, assigning the 'Roh phenomenon' 95 out of 100 points on its newsworthiness scale, compared with 30 by the big newspapers (Oh, 2005). In the summer of 2002, as the press kept silent after a US Army vehicle ran over and killed two Korean schoolgirls, the aggressive coverage of the incident on OhmyNews eventually led a national movement against the American military presence, which lasted for several months and boosted the presidential candidacy of the little-known Roh (Nguyen, 2006; Chang, 2009). A professor in Korea–USA relations asserted that this sentiment, more than anything, 'made Roh Moo-Hyun the president [because] people considered him a symbol of anti-Americanism' (quoted in Joyce, 2007, p. 28).

For many, however, the defining moment of Roh's and netizens' victory was the last 24 hours of the 2002 election. All of a sudden, a few hours into election day, Roh's running mate, Chung Mong Jun, announced his withdrawal, a late godsend to the conservative press that was behind Roh's rival, Lee Hoi Chang. Roh's supporters, however, did not see this as the beginning of the end. They flocked to portal sites and electronic bulletin boards to urge people

to go to the poll and vote for their candidate. Throughout the day, they moni-
tored and reported up-to-the-minute exit poll results, sending out millions of
e-mail and SMS messages to mobilise people in their networks. This came to
a peak after 3 p.m., when the turn-out rate was still low due to the lack of
young voters (Joyce, 2007). Young citizens seemed to have followed suit and
voted significantly more for Roh, who won the day by a very narrow 2.1 per
cent lead. Kang and Dyson (2007) observe that 'the immediacy and lightning
quick responses afforded by the Internet during this election, as well as the
online deliberations and discussion generated by Rohsamo and OhmyNews,
seem to have produced significant political influence on the young which
overflowed into offline behaviours and played a huge role in the actual election'. OhmyNews was not the only place where that happened but it was
believed to be the epicentre of the whole process (Joyce, 2007; Hauben,
2008). Between 18 and 19 December, it logged more than 6.2 million unique
users with 19.1 million page views, which, according to Chang (2009), 'were
the highest volume of Internet traffic in South Korean history'. Roh gave his
first presidential interview to OhmyNews.

In a public lecture, Oh said: 'Young netizens participating voluntarily to
reform our society are really the force guaranteeing Korea's dynamic development. They may appear boisterous, anarchic and radical. [But] that spirit is
a priceless thing no Korean corporation could reproduce, no matter how
much money it threw at it.' He did not hesitate to declare that this spirit
'cannot be found in the US, Japan or anywhere else' (Oh, 2005, p. 89).

Does all this mean that the OhmyNews success cannot be replicated elsewhere? While it is too early to answer this, it is worth remembering that news
sites that follow the OhmyNews model have enjoyed only modest, if any,
success in other countries. OhmyNews itself has failed or has not succeeded
in bringing its model to non-Korean contexts. In 2006, it received US$11
million from media giant Softbank to start OhmyNews Japan, with much
fanfare, but had to close the site less than 24 months later because the
number of its active citizen reporters could be counted only in 'tens, not thousands' (Joyce, 2007, p. 32). Meanwhile, OhmyNews International, despite its
record of 6,000 citizen reporters from 130 countries, is still short of real
success. My Bloglines RSS feed of the site, for instance, shows that there were
fewer than 110 new stories posted in March 2009 (i.e. under four a day) and
these tended to be written by a small group of active reporters, including two
full-time staff reporters. Despite all this, however, it is my contention that
OhmyNews provides us with an operating mechanism that, if selectively and
creatively adopted, can improve the chances of citizen journalism succeeding
in other socio-political contexts. Indeed, in addition to the five reasons

identified by Oh, I would include this mechanism – its well managed combination of professional and non-professional expertise – as the sixth, and the most fundamental, factor that drives OhmyNews to the centre of the media landscape. Despite its seeming obviousness, this is often overlooked or blindsided amidst hype, leaving the model not always correctly understood.

The OhmyNews operation mechanism

The news production process of OhmyNews is divided into two separate camps, the editorial and the citizen (or 'news guerrilla') desks, which reflect the two key aspects of its operation mechanism. First, although the 'Every citizen is a reporter' motto leads many to think of OhmyNews as a 'pure' citizen news outlet, it is in essence a mix of professional and citizen content. The editorial desk, which consists of full-time reporters and editors, does the job of a mainstream newsroom: gathering and producing hard news, analysis, reviews, editorials and other journalistic pieces. This group, which currently contributes 30 per cent of the content, works under thorough editorial plans and strictly follows the site's 'selection and focus' strategy. OhmyNews staff reporters can follow a single event for days and weeks and cover its development hour by hour or even minute by minute, especially when the issue is deemed important for its progressively oriented readers and/or is ignored on the mainstream agenda. When necessary, citizen reporters are contacted, mobilised and organised into joint assignments with staff journalists. There is a 'news guerrilla' editor devoting all her time to liaising with the best citizen reporters (Min, 2005).

Second, in contrast to the belief of some observers (e.g. Chase, 2008), OhmyNews is not of the same type as 'publish then filter' participatory news sites such as NowPublic and WikiNews, where users' content is freely posted before being fact-checked, corrected and edited by other users. All OhmyNews citizen stories go though a thorough screening process by full-time journalists in its central Seoul newsroom, who retain the ultimate authority and right to reject or edit contributions. When a story arrives in the newsroom, it is automatically queued up in an area called 'Green Wood' (*Saengnamul*) – 'green wood' is not ready to burn, implying that *Saengnamul* submissions are not ready to publish. (OhmyNews adopts a peculiar set of copyrighted wood-cutting jargon that originates from Oh's rural forest childhood.) Then guerrilla editors screen the content, evaluate its newsworthiness, assess its currency/timeliness, probe for accuracy and other matters, identify potential legal risks, grade articles and copy-edit those that are publishable. It is only after surviving this screening that citizen contributions are formally recognised as 'articles' and moved into an area called *Ingeul*, which, in pure Korean, means 'a state when wood is burning brightly' (Oh, 2005). Despite its 70,000-strong army of 'news guerrillas', the daily inflow of content is quite manageable, fluctuating between 150 and 200 contributions. Indeed, a frequent citizen reporter at OhmyNews is defined as one who writes at least once a month (Min, 2005).

About 70 per cent of all submissions are admitted into the *Ingeul* area. The rest, according its FAQ page, are rejected for quality-related reasons such as unclear messages, poor writing with vague meaning, failure to answer the common five Ws and H (who, what, where, when, why and how), one-sidedness, advertising or self-promotion, potential defamation, plagiarism and copyright infringement. The best five or ten of these are given special editorial treatment (with catchy headlines, layout design, thumbnail pictures and so on) to be placed on the homepage while the rest are posted in section and sub-section pages. Of the criteria, accuracy is given the highest priority. If necessary, editors contact reporters to check facts and/or to make suggestions for improvement. In complicated situations, they conduct their own investigation to gain more factual information and/or further insights. Additionally, the site calls for responsible participation. The second, and the first content-related, item in its Citizen Reporters' Code of Conduct is on accuracy: 'The citizen reporter does not spread false information. He [*sic*] does not write articles based on groundless assumptions or predictions.' The key ethos, as Min (2007) puts it, is that 'personal interpretation is welcome but no factual fallacy will be tolerated'. In its nine-year existence, according to Min (2009), OhmyNews citizens' articles have incurred few – 'about five' – legal disputes and none of them was serious enough to be brought up to the court. The system, however, is not flawless. In fact, the anti-American movement following the death of the two schoolgirls in 2002 that boosted Roh Moo-Hyun's candidacy ironically stemmed from an incorrect OhmyNews citizen report, which stated that they were not accidentally but intentionally killed. However, it is fair to point out that this kind of accident has existed in our centuries-old journalism and is by no means a peculiar problem of OhmyNews.

In order to improve its overall quality, OhmyNews puts a considerable weight on training citizen reporters – a point that, again, contradicts scholars such as Atton and Hamilton (2008, p. 101), who observe 'no necessity to train … citizen reporters [at OhmyNews], since they write from personal experience and need no special, professional skills'. Coaching at OhmyNews takes a variety of online and offline forms. It can be done via detailed advice during the screening and editing process of specific articles. It can take place on a public forum embedded in OhmyNews's virtual newsroom, where staff and citizen reporters share their experience, express their views on stories and seek and/or offer tips in news gathering and writing. There is also an 'online clinic centre' where, as of October 2007, two staff reporters and ten star citizen reporters were ready to diagnose and offer treatment solutions to those who want to consult on how to improve their writing skills (Oh, 2007). Offline, OhmyNews reporters gather every month to share and evaluate each other's stories. In 2007, the organisation started its US$400,000 OhmyNews Citizen Journalism School outside Seoul, where ordinary citizens can attend short courses, like 'News writing for kids and families', to gain interviewing, writing and editing skills and understand the relevance of citizen journalism in the media environment.

What, then, is that 'citizen' in the 'citizen journalism' at OhmyNews? From the above, it seems that OhmyNews content is professionally controlled from tip to toe – so, is it just an online extension of traditional participation models such as letters to the editor? The answer is no if we note several things.

The first and most obvious is that at least in quantitative terms, OhmyNews relies mostly on user-generated content rather than on professionally produced content, with 70 per cent of its articles being written by non-professional reporters. Thus, Oh has his own reasons to distinguish OhmyNews from other news outlets in this forceful, although somewhat exaggerated, way: 'Of all the world media, OhmyNews is unique in that the editor-in-chief has no idea which article will be the lead story in the next day's edition' (Oh, 2005, p. 79).

Second, although OhmyNews applies some professional standards in editorial selection, it strategically disregards many others so that news can be presented through the lens of ordinary people. Unlike staff reporters, citizens can write about anything that might or might not fall into the 'selected and focused' areas of OhmyNews. Moreover, according to Min (2007), OhmyNews makes every effort to prioritise stories that contain a reasonable combination of eyewitness facts and personal opinion. This means, among other things, that the 'strategic ritual' of professional journalism, objectivity and its associated principles (e.g. balance, fairness, wholeness), is largely abandoned in the management of citizen content at OhmyNews. Oh (2003) did not hesitate to admit that he does 'not regard objective reporting as a source of pride'. Further, professional journalistic styles are not only disregarded but also discouraged. One of Oh's start-up strategies to make the site an authentic citizen news site is to 'destroy the [conventional] article form' (Oh, 2005, p. 52). Thus, he publicly takes pride in breaking, and teaching people to break, the stringent formula of professional journalistic writing.

A third prevailing feature of OhmyNews is a transparent 'open newsroom' structure that confers a lot of control to citizens. For one thing, access to it is not restricted to any group of citizen reporters but is open to everyone, including those against the progressivism policy of OhmyNews. As soon as a person's identity is substantiated, he or she is allocated a reporter desk, from which he or she can go anywhere in the virtual newsroom, including the *Saengnamul* list. If he or she has concerns over some editorial decisions, there is a public forum in which to share his or her views with fellow reporters and staff editors. Moreover, editors have the duty to publicly justify why they reject stories. Additionally, there is an ombudsman committee, made up of citizen reporters and external observers, to monitor OhmyNews stories every day. Combined together, these rules and procedures place the production process under constant and close public scrutiny and keep everyone at the central newsroom on their toes. If an editor ignores, for instance, a good story that happens to offend an important advertiser of OhmyNews or to be against his or her political ideologies, he or she will barely survive the fire from the community. As Oh (2005) explains when asked about commercial pressures:

> Our greatest value is as an alternative media outlet that doesn't concern itself about what certain powerful groups or capitalists think and, instead, says what it needs to say. If we were to sacrifice that, the money we'd earn would not save OhmyNews but would rather kill it.

As a trade-off for this collective power, citizen reporters are kept accountable via transparency too. Before submitting an article, a citizen reporter is asked to reveal how her article takes its shape, e.g. whether she has discovered the story herself or whether it is based on a secondary source such as a press release. Under their agreement with OhmyNews, citizen reporters from publicity industries are required to disclose this to readers. But perhaps most crucial is that all citizen reporters must post articles under their *real names*. Before admission, citizens must provide OhmyNews with adequate documented information about their identity – including basic personal data, contact details and a photograph. My own impression throughout this registration process was that its stringent procedures make it difficult to cheat and might usefully discourage from scratch those not serious enough.

Finally, the 'citizen journalism' of OhmyNews is also open to readers. In addition to the aforementioned tip jar system, Oh (2005, p. 58) asserts – probably correctly – that OhmyNews was the first news outlet 'not just in Korea but in the world' to offer a popular online service: an interactive comment facility at the bottom of each story so that readers can discuss the issue, voice their concerns and/or add further details. Right from the beginning, the amount of reader feedback went beyond expectations; one article in 2003 received a total of 85,000 comments. But it is not merely a matter of quantity. Oh (2005) observes that the usually immediate, frank, two-way, group-based and 'occasionally professional' exchanges between readers and between them and authors are instrumental to the success of OhmyNews, as they directly improve the reader's news experience, generate further content and elicit unforeseen ideas and perspectives. Even the daily look of the homepage is in part shaped by reader feedback because staff editors at OhmyNews use their votes for stories as an important basis on which to sort stories and to decide where to place them. Reader feedback also has an indirect but important effect on the long-term quality of OhmyNews because citizen reporters can learn invaluable lessons from interacting with audiences.

Concluding notes: the implications of OhmyNews for the future of journalism

Throughout the above, I have argued that OhmyNews has come to the centre stage of the Korean media landscape and of the global citizen journalism movement thanks not only to a variety of Korea-specific factors but also to a hybrid news production model that incorporates a well-managed marriage between the professional and the amateur. Although the ripe social, political and cultural conditions that fostered its rapid growth in the early twenty-first century are hard to find in other national contexts and even in the contemporary Korean press and political landscape, its working mechanism sheds some light on where professional journalism could head in a world where the power to report news is no longer its alone.

First, incorporating citizen with professional content, rather than relying solely on the former, seems to be an effective strategy. Although citizen content accounts for 70 per cent of its total content output and covers most topic categories, most of this 70 per cent takes the form of opinion-based pieces (such as essays, book and movie reviews and commentaries) and, according to Oh, the majority are devoted to life stories rather than public affairs. Hard news and analysis, the key pillars of any news outlet, are left mostly to its full-time staff reporters. The importance of professional content has been understood elsewhere. Steve Outing (2007) reported that his company's citizen news networks for mountain bikers collapsed due to an excessive belief that users' passion will generate content 'good enough to keep people's attention and keep them coming back'. Outing 'took solace' in the fact that Backfence – another citizen news network that was once hailed and much touted – shut down (after turning US$3 million into thin air) partly for a similar reason. As Bentley (2005) says, citizen reporters 'share information' rather than 'cover stories'. Thus, I would argue, OhmyNews would not have been as successful if it had been a pure civic information-sharing network.

Second, citizen content will realise its potential to the greatest extent and become real treasure if it goes through a professional filter of some types. At OhmyNews, this filter is considerably different from the traditional gatekeeping function since it takes a light-touch approach to objectivity and other established journalistic values. But a key quality of factual information, its accuracy, is guaranteed to the greatest possible extent thanks to the skills, experience and editorial eyes of the 'news guerrilla' staff. Even though most of these full-timers are recruited from citizen reporters, they are still trained, in classrooms and/or on the job, to gain a complicated and somewhat esoteric set of techniques of journalism, which is a discipline of verification in essence (Kovach and Rosenstiel, 2001). They are for the most part better than ordinary citizens in things like investigation, sceptical editing, employing circles of corroboration, probing for consistencies and inconsistencies, using accuracy checklists, examining vested interests, avoiding libel cases and many others. In my opinion, pure 'publish, then filter' news sites such as WikiNews have met with no great success to date due at least in part to the absence of such professional filters. And if we look at the blogosphere, it is clear that many, if not most, successful blogs are owned and run by journalists or pundits used to verification, or a combination of citizens and these people.

Both of these points, in the end, contradict the many 'journalism is dead' prophecies mentioned earlier. At the least, OhmyNews, as the world's most successful citizen news venture so far, shows that the 'will this kill that?' debate is quite irrelevant. If anything, it provides an excellent case against such authors as Keen (2007), who contends that the professional, or at least the full-time and paid, journalist will lose authority and 'die out' in the process of journalism being democratised by citizen networks. OhmyNews suggests that this authority is, or at least can be, further promoted and is instrumental in citizen news cultivating public trust and attracting large followings. Thus, instead of wasting time wondering whether they will be needed, journalists should devote their energy and creative talents to inventing new methods that help them to fulfil their public duties in the changing news environment. They need to reinvent themselves.

How, then, could journalists reinvent themselves to catch this new thing called citizen journalism? This requires much more space to answer than this chapter allows. However, the OhmyNews experience suggests two things.

First, professional newspeople must abandon their long-held 'we publish, you accept' mindset and stop turning a blind eye to the public's concerns over their standards (Nguyen, 2006). OhmyNews generates trust among its citizen reporters and keeps them doing their job because it gives them remarkable, although not absolute, control over its own production process. By creating a kind of conversational journalism based on a transparent mutual check system for citizens and journalists, its open newsroom structure is perhaps the most crucial contributor to its success as a genuine 'for the people and by the people' public space. Second, some of journalism's most established and cherished professional principles and ideals might have to be redefined. At OhmyNews, staff journalists are not totally 'professional' in the traditional sense: they are serious and rigorous in doing journalistic verification but, to keep citizen content as what it literally means, they are ready to play down conventional journalistic forms and, more importantly, objective reporting.

This second point needs further discussion. By disregarding objective reporting and putting forth a 'selection and focus' agenda that serves primarily to promote its liberal ideologies, OhmyNews has induced a large movement – a 'Fifth Estate' – against the predominantly conservative press and political system and thereby generated a more balanced political order that the somewhat vulnerable democracy in Korea needs to develop healthily and sustainably. Like others (Allan, 2006; Chang, 2009), I value and welcome OhmyNews as a healthy addition to democracy because it can at least act against the vested interest of the elite media. However, this is not the same as calling for a future in which professional journalism is overwhelmed by the partisan journalism of OhmyNews. Whatever ideologies are involved, such a world might lead us to an increasingly fragmented and even polarised public sphere rather than a healthy *agora* where consensus is reached via scientific reasoning. In reality, OhmyNews has shown signs of this problem. Chase (2008) found from an analysis of its coverage of the North Korean nuclear test in 2006 that despite professional editorial oversight, 'important gains in news diversity have been offset by … the prevalence of extreme or polemical commentary unsupported by sound reasoning' and even by 'the tendency to demonize differences'. Its close relationship with President Roh's government, which it was 'reluctant to criticize … on matters of unemployment, the ailing economy, and its diplomacy with North Korea' (Veale, 2007, p. 96), has been under much pressure. The citizen journalism enabled by the Internet, therefore, is self-limiting. Objectivity, the 'strategic ritual' of the news profession is too important to be allowed to disappear. A future dominated by journalism without journalists is a dangerous future.

REFERENCES

Allan, Stuart (2006) *Online News: Journalism and the Internet* (Maidenhead: Open University Press).

Atton, Chris and Hamilton, James (2008) *Alternative Journalism* (London: Sage).

Bentley, Clyde (2005) 'Reconnecting with the audience: what they say – not what they think – is what counts', *Nieman Reports*, Winter, http://www.nieman.harvard. edu/reportsitem.aspx?id=100566, accessed 29 March 2009.

Chang, Woo-Young (2009) 'OhmyNews: citizen journalism in South Korea', in Stuart Allan and Einar Thorsen (eds), *Citizen Journalism: Global Perspectives* (New York: Peter Lang).

Chase, Thomas (2008) 'How new is online news? Online news services in China and South Korea', Paper presented at the 17th Biannual Conference of the Asian Studies Association of Australia. Melbourne, 1–3 July, http://arts.monash.edu.au/ mai/asaa/thomaschase.pdf, accessed 29 March 2009.

Cheon, Young-Cheol (2004) 'Internet newspapers as alternative media: the case of OhmyNews', http://waccglobal.org/en/20041-media-reform/611-Internet-news-papers-as-Alternative-Media-The-Case-of-OhmyNews-in-South-Korea.html, accessed 29 April 2006.

Choi, Jinbong (2003) 'Public journalism in cyberspace: a Korean case study', *Global Media Journal*, 2: 3, http://lass.calumet.purdue.edu/cca/gmj/fa03/graduatefa03/ gmj-fa03-choi.htm, accessed 24 April 2005.French, Howard (2003) 'Online newspaper shakes up Korean politics', *New York Times*, 6 March.

Hauben, Ronda (2008) 'S. Korea: new media vs. conservative press', *OhmyNews International*, 24 July, http://english.ohmynews.com/articleview/article_view.asp? menu=c10400&no=383090&rel_no=1, accessed 10 January 2009.

Joyce, Mary (2007) 'The citizen journalism website OhmyNews and the 2002 South Korean presidential election', Berkman Centre Research for Internet and Society Publication No. 2007-15, http://papers.ssrn.com/sol3/papers.cfm?abstract_id= 1077920, accessed 24 September 2008.

Kang, Daniel Jisuk and Dyson, Lauren Evelyn (2007) 'Internet politics in South Korea: the case of Rohsamo and OhmyNews', in *Proceedings of the Eighteenth Australasian Conference on Information Systems*, 5–7 December, http://www. acis2007.usq.edu.au/assets/papers/179.pdf, accessed 20 January 2009.

Keen, Andrew (2007) *The Cult of the Amateur: How Today's Internet Is Killing Our culture and Assaulting our Economy* (New York: Nicholas Brealey Publishing).

Kovach, Bill and Rosenstiel, Tom (2001) *The Elements of Journalism* (New York: Three Rivers Press).

Min, Jean K. (2005) 'OhmyNews editorial process explained', 12 July, OhmyNews Reporters' BBS, accessed 14 March 2009.

Min, Jean K. (2007) 'OhmyNews: every citizen is a reporter. Q&A with the Center for Citizen Media, Harvard University', http://www.kcnn.org/principles/ ohmynews, accessed 8 March 2009.

Min, Jean K. (2009) Personal interview with An Nguyen, via telephone and e-mail, between 19 February and 10 March.

Nguyen, An (2006) 'Journalism in the wake of participatory publishing', *Australian Journalism Review*, 28: 1, 143–55.

Nguyen, An (2008) *The Penetration of Online News: Past, Present and Future* (Saarbrücken: VDM Publishing House).

Nguyen, An (2009) 'Globalisation, citizen journalism and the nation-state: a Vietnamese perspective', in Stuart Allan and Einar Thorsen (eds), *Citizen Journalism: Global Perspectives* (New York: Peter Lang).

Oh, Yeon-ho (2003) 'OhmyNews makes every citizen a reporter', Interview by *Japan Media Review*, http://www.ohmynews.com/NWS_Web/company/01_introduction_04.aspx#a_10, accessed 12 June 2007.

Oh, Yeon-Ho (2005) *OhmyNews: A Unique Product of Korea*, draft memoirs provided to the author by Jean K. Min in February 2009.

Oh, Yeon-ho (2007) 'OhmyNews, Wikinews: two of a kind?', Interview by Cynthia Yoo, http://english.ohmynews.com/articleview/article_view.asp?article_class=8&no=380730&rel_no=1, accessed 29 January 2009.

Outing, Steve (2007) 'An important lesson about grassroots media', *Editor and Publisher*, 26 November, http://www.editorandpublisher.com/eandp/columns/stopthepresses_display.jsp?vnu_content_id=1003677395, accessed 28 August 2008.

Schroeder, Christopher (2004) 'Is this the future of journalism?', *Newsweek*, 18 June, http://www.newsweek.com/id/53873/output/print, accessed 11 September 2005.

Veale, Jennifer (2007) 'Seoul searching', *Foreign Policy*, January/February, 94–6.

Wagstaff, Jeremy (2004) 'Korea's news crusaders', *Far Eastern Economic Review*, 7 October, http://blogs.law.harvard.edu/dowbrigade/koreas-new-crusaders/, accessed 22 April 2007.

Conclusion

GUY REDDEN AND GRAHAM MEIKLE

This book is organised around change and continuity. Online news is a terrain of ongoing transformation, building upon innovations in technologies and the uses to which they can be put. It is also a terrain dominated by established institutions, and by many decades of cultural, social and political experience, which continue to shape our assumptions and expectations about what news is. Our introduction mapped the contours of some of these processes, proposing a framework of convergence as a tool for understanding them. In addition to the underlying technological developments that allow news to have an increasingly multimedia character, flows of digital information across networks involve new interrelationships between production and consumption, the professional and the popular, the public and the personal. The chapters have examined in greater detail phenomena – from user generation of content to ambient news – that articulate these issues.

Using convergence as an organising idea comes with certain risks. For instance, it could fetishise 'the very latest' in technology above other kinds that are widely used – broadband over broadcast, podcasts over print, Facebook over photos – and it might easily suggest both a linear logic of development from the less to the more convergent and an unproblematic coming together of things that were previously separate. These are features present in many popular commentaries that hype the possibilities of new media. However, the range of approaches taken and concerns expressed by the authors here indicates that change is far from being monological, and it can only really be understood as a relation to established practices, forms and conventions. New interrelationships unsettle concepts through which we (citizens, practitioners and scholars) have come to understand what news is, and why it matters.

Unless one takes a strong technological determinist view that technology compels change (see Curran, 2008, for a critique of this view in relation to the Internet), other factors are involved in the shaping of online news, and users may be able to influence them in practice. The texts through which it is disseminated are fashioned by media institutions that operate as they do for numerous reasons, including political legislation, economics, popular demand and cultural expectations surrounding the professional standards of journalism. As McChesney has noted above, online journalism makes its appearance in a news milieu that is already changing in ways that have generated tensions over the status of news as a public good. One of the affordances of an edited collection like this is that, as the analyses present different sets of relations in case studies, such contested lines of emergence can be discussed as they play out in contexts, setting up something of a comparative frame for their consideration.

The professional and the non-professional

Over recent decades cultural studies scholars have developed the idea that audiences are active in their responses to media messages. The signal moment in this tradition was David Morley's study *The Nationwide Audience* (1980), in which he presented the argument that television viewers respond to the framing of current affairs with diverse interpretations that cannot be fully predicted from their social identities. The Internet promises to radically enfranchise users by extending their active roles to the publication of their views in public spaces. Indeed, to repeat Bruns's term, they may become 'produsers', consumers of news whose published responses constitute further production of it, bringing the very dichotomy of production and consumption into question.

There is little doubt that some of Rosen's 'people formerly known as the audience' have taken up (inter)active roles, but what are the broader implications of this? Dan Gillmor (2004) writes hopefully about ordinary people themselves becoming the media because of this new possibility to organise and produce, and in the process transforming news into a conversation, in contrast with an old model in which professional journalists lecture the rest of us. For Gillmor:

> Blogs and other modern media are feedback systems. They work in something close to real time and capture – in the best sense of the word – the multitude of ideas and realities each of us can offer. On the Internet, we are defined by what we know and share. Now, for the first time in history, the feedback system can be global and nearly instantaneous. (Gillmor, 2004, p. 236)

This vision of the many talking to the many may articulate a technological potential, but it is pertinent to ask whether it can be realised.

There are of course exemplary citizen journalism initiatives such as OhmyNews. However, as Nguyen argues in his chapter, the success of that venture may depend more on the existence of a set of convivial factors to do with Korean traditions of participation and a political climate in which many younger citizens have felt politically disenfranchised to the extent of committing to alternative forums for expression. These are arguably social movement dynamics that cannot easily be replicated. And, as Nguyen shows, the operations are based upon well thought-out cooperation between amateurs, a core of professional staff and readers, a dimension of which is a culture of training through which professionals pass on their skills. In providing suggestions for how pro-am models might work, Bruns also attests to this simple fact that fruitful collaboration between citizen journalists and professionals is no foregone conclusion but requires effort and organisational design.

At the same time it is important to acknowledge that not all opportunities that users have to participate in organised news production constitute citizen journalism. Most are examples of interactivity being channelled into responses to professionally produced content through feedback and comment functions, and message boards of news sites. As the move of the British *Independent* to reduce reader feedback shows, the role of amateurs in established outlets is contested. In her interviews with US news site producers, Chung (2007) found varying levels of enthusiasm for the incorporation of interactive features, suggesting that a majority of 'cautious traditionalists' are caught between innovators (often located in independent news organisations) and those who resist interactivity. In practice, publication staff are most cautious about facilitating human-to-human interactivity, as opposed to human–machine interactions such as online polls. Thurman (2008) finds that the great majority of user-generated content in news sites is subject to professional editing or pre-moderation. His interviews with British editors found considerable reticence about the quality of user contributions when judged by the professional standards of journalism – although those standards may not be the ones by which this new phenomenon should, in fact, be judged.

Economies of news

As established news providers adapt to the new environment there are no guarantees as to models that will work, and it appears unlikely that one size will fit all. The key here is that, as agents, those who implement and realise any interactive potential seek to square it with established institutional norms that may be as specific to the organisation as they are to journalism in general.

Of course, as Thurman notes, the values that may ultimately determine the extent to which amateur content is incorporated are economic. Interestingly, some professionals' perceptions that consumers still want 'one-way top-down news' online (Chung 2007, p. 58) is one of their justifications for their caution in ceding power over production. Meanwhile, user-generated content is free, or if costs related to professional filtering and presentation of it are added, cheap, and vast swathes are available in the blogosphere, where it is produced independently.

It is an ongoing challenge for news organisations to discern a viable role in this attention economy. As Kim and Hamilton (2006, p. 543) point out, 'Despite the localized benefits of internet distribution (negating physical distribution costs), the costs of information gathering, publicizing the new media organization and administration remain', and the content produced must cover these costs, in most cases by generating advertising revenue. On the one hand, as Deuze and Fortunati argue in their contribution to this book, there is an economic incentive for media owners (whose interests are not identical to those of their employees) to embrace the cheaper amateur content over maintenance of a highly skilled professional workforce. On the other, as Fenton and Witschge observe in their chapter, any trend away from professional journalism in the name of embracing the popular could diminish the ability of news organisations to produce news to standards that only they can. This in turn could have potentially self-defeating consequences, if, as seems reasonable, significant demand for content created in line with professional news values persists.

McNair predicts in his chapter that professional journalism will survive and flourish in combination with content-generating users. Indeed, few amateur or independent sites have the resources to present a wide range of reporting. Those that can do this often rely upon gifted labour and money, plus previously published sources (such as Wikinews), activist networks (such as Indymedia) or both (such as Alternet). Nonetheless, this broader ecology of news, especially when millions of bloggers are included, presents a radical challenge to news hierarchies in that users have the ability to filter and select from multiple sources.

In the aggregate, a greater number of definitions of, and providers of, news is a characteristic of its form online. Newsworthiness is less determined by gatekeepers and more by those who seek and find. Websites, as Manovich (2001, p. 219) argues, are built around the capacity to 'view, navigate, search', reshaping the experience of the user from reading to exploring. Burnett and Marshall (2003, p. 160), refer to 'informational news': flows of 'information exchange via news sites, newsgroups, email, chatrooms, from institutional sites to alternative media sites, resource centre sites, search engines, portals' that allow the development of 'different news registers' (ibid., p. 163). In these terms the mass media forms that have characterised news over the past century start to look like historically specific genres. Now blogs allow current affairs commentary to overlap with personal journal-keeping practices and, as Bogost et al., Crawford and Goggin have shown in their contributions to this collection, news discourses can be combined with game play, social networking and personal mobile communications respectively. Is it possible that news as a 'standalone' textual mode has passed its zenith? Indeed, Cassidy (2007) finds that online journalists have an expanded view of what constitutes news compared to their offline peers. And a recent survey of journalism students at the Queensland University of Technology in Australia found that the vast majority are personally not interested in reading newspapers. Instead they expect to get their news online in portals where it is accessible alongside their other interests (*ABC News*, 2009).

The politics of expression

The form in which news circulates is also a political issue. News matters because it is a social good through which members of communities share information about the world they inhabit together. News values such as objectivity, balance, accuracy and fairness represent civic ideals about the kinds of information that are available to citizens. One of the themes of Western scholarship about journalism has been this concern with its democratic credentials (Carlsson, 2007, p. 1014). It is often construed as society's 'Fourth Estate' that ensures that the operations of all social institutions are subject to the scrutiny of citizens. Democratisation has also been a recurring theme in new media scholarship, with communications that allow greater participation of and interaction between citizens generally being seen as more democratic (Hacker, 1996). Benjamin (1936) famously celebrated the advent of 'letters to the editor', predicting that 'the distinction between author and public [was] about to lose its basic character'.

The empowerment of users through the ability to participate in communications can be seen as a good in its own right, consistent with values of free speech and a self-organising citizenry. However, we also have to question how the democratisation of access to expression relates to use of new media to enhance political democracy. Habermas (1974, 1989) is the most influential theorist in this regard. His conception of a healthy democratic sphere is modelled on an ancient Athenian *agora*, free of distortions of money and power, in which information necessary for collective decision-making is available and citizens, in turn, have the ability to engage in deliberation towards collective consensus making (Carlsson, 2007, p. 1026).

Although the many-to-many communications enabled by the Internet are often viewed as realising this ideal to some extent, Habermas has rejected this view (Millioni, 2009, p. 410). Instead, he sees the net as effecting the fragmentation of the public sphere because it promotes publics that form around isolated issues. This is consistent with other criticisms of online democracy that question the powers of the individual user. Cass Sunstein (2001) criticises Negroponte's notion of the 'daily me', the customised intake of an empowered online information consumer who tailors their personal consumption. For Sunstein, this customisation promotes the individual's ability to retreat into sectional communities and personal interests, rather than be exposed to news discourses about issues that affect us all.

Along these lines, McChesney (1999) has argued that commentaries on online democracy often conflate individual liberty with democratic deliberation, and vanguard new media uses such as activism with general usage. However, this is not to be confused with a technological determinist argument that the net has no democratic potential. In this volume McChesney suggests that a free online citizen commentariat is worth fighting for as a component of a layered democratic communications sphere that has civic journalism, with a rigorous focus on quality of information, at its core.

In weighing up the political significance of the fact that citizens' voices can carry further than ever before, it is necessary to critically appraise actual information flows. For example, the particular value of citizen journalism may be at its highest in cases where institutional journalism fails in its Fourth Estate role. Although it may also have the character of celebrity scandal, the most famous instance of online political exposé so far centred on no less than the potential abuse of power by the world's most powerful public office holder: the President of the United States. It is notable that when Matt Drudge (1998) broke the news of Clinton's affair with Monika Lewinsky on his site, central to his claim was that the story had just been suppressed by *Newsweek*.

The ongoing incorporation of citizen reportage and commentary also has the potential to counter 'helicopter journalism' (Allan, 2006, p. 7), the superficial reporting of events on the ground and weak contextual research by media organisations that is all too common given low levels of investment in correspondents. Even when citizens are only responding to public sources and provided news, one of the key features of popular 'redactional' current affairs discourse is that citizen-users are able not only to undertake online research about issues, but also to publish their findings. Bloggers' incessant criticisms of the media framing of the Second Gulf War and their search for alternative sources of information was an illustrative case (Redden et al., 2003).

Ultimately, how the political significance of online news is determined depends on both theoretical presuppositions and contextual factors. Certain websites may be seen to have something of an ideal mix of democratic communications forms and roles. As Allan and Thorsen show in their chapter, the BBC is at the cutting edge of innovations in online news, including the incorporation of citizen perspectives into its site alongside meticulous journalism. But this level of performance is perhaps wired into the conditions of its very existence. It has a public service remit in exchange for which it is generously funded by the public, based on a consensus that could break down or be overturned at any time depending upon political will.

The social and political conditions that shape online news are not always the same. In some places the technological bias towards free expression is curtailed by censorship or the bias of the media establishment. As Xin argues in her contribution to this book, independent campaigning online journalism in China treads a careful line in relation to the political authorities. And Lugo-Ocando and Cañizález note in their chapter that in Latin America private media corporations hostile to popular left-wing governments have little focus on online news. It is government supporters, somewhat ironically, who are driven onto the net to pursue a self-organised alternative public sphere.

In conclusion, online news is a variable phenomenon, an emergent property shaped by multiple factors in socio-historical contexts. Although the Internet has now been around for decades, the communications platforms that operate through it change rapidly. At the time of writing, one cutting edge is probably the integration of social media functions such as collaborative bookmarking into news sites and news functions into social networking sites. Five years ago it might have been blogs, and a future reader might find all of these to be decidedly old news. Yet amid the change, continuities persist. The institutions and textual forms of news are not, of course, reducible to technology alone. Conventions and traditions that predate digital networks continue to have force. Similarly, broad affordances of new media, such as the possibility of active roles for users, work out in different ways.

The social significance of news is open to interpretation, and continually calls into question the concepts and distinctions through which news has been known and managed. The news is changing – that's always true. But it remains fundamental to our understandings of media, of politics, of culture and of ourselves. News affects and is used by us all. It's too important to be left only to journalists. The ongoing task of scholars and reflective practitioners is to continue to track and make sense of developments that define what is possible in news culture.

REFERENCES

ABC News (2009) 'Journalism students "don't read papers"', *ABC News*, 11 March, http://www.abc.net.au/news/stories/2009/03/11/2513424.htm, accessed 10 October 2009.

Allan, Stuart (2006) *Online News* (Maidenhead: Open University Press).

Benjamin, Walter (1936) *The Work of Art in the Age of Mechanical Reproduction*, http://www.marxists.org/reference/subject/philosophy/works/ge/benjamin.htm, accessed 10 October 2009.

Burnett, Rob and Marshall, P. David (2003) *Web Theory* (London: Routledge).

Carlsson, Matt (2007) 'Order versus access: news search engines and the challenge to traditional journalistic roles', *Media, Culture and Society*, 29: 6, 1014–30.

Cassidy, William P. (2007) 'Online news credibility: examination of the perceptions of newspaper journalists', *Journal of Computer-Mediated Communication*, 12: 2, http://jcmc.indiana.edu/vol12/issue2/cassidy.html, accessed 10 October 2009.

Chung, Deborah Soun (2007) 'Profits and perils: online news producers' perceptions of interactivity and uses of interactive features', *Convergence: The International Journal of Research into New Media Technologies*, 13: 1, 43–61.

Curran, James (2008) 'Communication and history', in Barbie Zelizer (ed.), *Explorations in Communications and History* (Abingdon and New York: Routledge), pp. 46–59.

Drudge, Matt (1998) 'Newsweek kills story on White House intern. Blockbuster report: 23-year old, former White House intern, sex relationship with President', *The Drudge Report*, 17 January, http://www.drudgereportarchives.com/data/2002/01/17/20020117_175502_ml.htm, accessed 12 April 2010.

Gillmor, Dan (2004) *We the Media: Grassroots Journalism by the People, for the People* (Sebastopol, CA: O'Reilly Media).

Habermas, Jürgen (1974) 'The public sphere: an encyclopedia article', *New German Critique*, 1: 3, 49–55.

Habermas, Jürgen (1989) *The Structural Transformation of the Public Sphere* (Cambridge, MA: MIT Press).

Hacker, Kenneth L. (1996) 'Missing links in the evolution of electronic democratization', *Media, Culture and Society*, 18: 2, 213–32.

Kim, Eun-Gyoo and Hamilton, James W. (2006) 'Capitulation to capital? OhmyNews as alternative media', *Media, Culture and Society*, 28: 4, 541–60.

McChesney, Robert W. (1999) *Rich Media, Poor Democracy: Communication Politics in Dubious Times* (Urbana: University of Illinois Press).

Manovich, Lev (2001) *The Language of New Media* (Cambridge, MA: MIT Press).

Millioni, Dimitria (2009) 'Probing the online counterpublic sphere: the case of Indymedia Athens', *Media, Culture and Society*, 31: 3, 409–31.

Morley, David (1980) *The Nationwide Audience: Structure and Decoding* (London: BFI).

Redden, Guy, Nick Caldwell and Nguyen, An (2003) 'Warblogging as critical social practice', *Southern Review*, 36: 2, 68–79.

Sunstein, Cass (2001) *Republic.com* (Princeton, NJ: Princeton University Press).

Thurman, Neil (2008) 'Forums for citizen journalists? Adoption of user generated content initiatives by online news media', *New Media and Society*, 10: 1, 139–57.

Index

24-hour news 6, 23, 121, 137, 144
About.com 91
accuracy 20, 34, 46, 48, 57, 105, 119, 141, 156, 160, 201, 202, 206, 214
activist media 213
advertising 4, 39, 40, 49, 50, 55, 60–1, 66, 73, 84, 91, 94, 95, 135, 143, 145, 159, 197, 213
agenda-setting 43, 71, 78, 137, 166
aggregators of news 5, 10, 38, 40, 50
  see also Google News
Agha-Soltan, Neda 1, 99
Alierakieron 122
Al Jazeera 7, 11
Allan, Stuart 2, 27, 179, 204, 215
Alternet 152, 213
Andrejevic, Mark 151, 159
Apple 8, 73, 102,
aporrea.org 78
Argentina 71, 74, 75, 77, 79
Associated Press 56, 76, 195
AT&T 62–3
Atlanta Constitution 59
Atlanta News 59
Atlantic, The 122
Atton, Chris 151–2, 202
audiences 2–3, 24, 118, 164–79
  active 211
  critical 150–1, 155,
  fragmented 148, 170,
  Latin American 74–5
  networked 174
  participatory 10–12, 29–36, 42, 153–4
  'the people formerly known as the audience' 2, 36, 133, 164–5, 211
Australian, The
Axel Springer publishing group 50

babble 123–4, 127
balance 151–3
Balkam, Stephen 108

Bambuser 108
Barth-Nilsen 107
BBC (British Broadcasting Corporation) 1, 5, 11, 23, 51, 65, 66, 118, 119, 121, 151, 222,
BBC Chinese service website 180
BBC homepage 27
BBC News 23, 30
BBC News 24 (TV channel) 28
BBC News Interactive 21
BBC News Online 21–37, 134, 145
BBC UCG Hub 6, 30–2
BBC World Service 5
Beckett, Charlie 31, 106, 159,
Beijing Olympics 180, 186, 187–8
Belam, Martin 27, 29–30
Benjamin, Walter 214
bias 42–3, 87–8, 92, 136, 152, 155–6, 179, 206
Bingham, Matthew 26
Bird, S. Elisabeth 51
Blackberry 102
Blair, Jayson 43
blogs 9, 11, 34, 42–3, 54, 144, 152–2, 156, 211, 216
  breaking news 10, 23, 24–7, 29, 90, 118, 119
  and mobile phones 102, 106
Boaden, Helen 33–4
Boczkowski, Pablo 103, 151,
Bolivia 71, 75, 77, 79
Bowman, Shayne 118–19
boyd, danah 116, 124, 125
BNO News 119, 125
Brewer, Dave 24
broadband internet 40, 62–3, 198
broadcast news 4, 12, 22, 35, 39, 42, 47, 51, 55–6, 65–6, 89, 100, 103, 108, 111, 118, 128
  Twitter and 121–6
Bruns, Axel 134, 138, 168, 211
Bucks, Simon 48

Bulletin, The 145
bulloggers.com 181
Buncefield fuel explosion December 2005
  30–1
business models for news
  see economics of news
Burnett, Rob 213–14
Bush, George W. 27, 57, 61
bushfires in South Australia, 2008 117
Butterworth, Brendan 26–7

Capital Times 63–4
Carey, James 116, 120
Casa Editorial El Tiempo 74
Castells, Manuel 9, 78, 116
celebrity news 38, 44, 50, 59, 66, 116,
  127
cell phones
  see mobile phones
censorship 1, 45, 216
  in China 61, 181, 184,
  in Latin America 77–8
  self-censorship of journalists 167
Center for Public Integrity 57
Chang, Woo-Young 175, 199, 200
China 178–91
  Sanlu milk scandal 2008 186–8
  fengqing 'angry youth' phenomenon
    118–90
  nail house issue 182–4
  nationalism online 188–90
China Internet Network Information
  Centre 179
Chávez, Hugo 71, 77, 787
Chester, Jeff 63
Chunlong, Sun 184, 185
Chung, Deborah Soun 212, 213
Chung, Mong Jun 199
Cisco Systems 140
citizen journalism 2, 11, 28, 42, 118–19,
  212, 214
  and mobile news 104–7, 109
  and Twitter 121–4
  relationship with professional journalism
    6, 10–12, 14, 48, 65, 111, 132–45,
    151–2, 156, 178–91, 195–207
  see also user-generated content
CityTV 74
Clarín 74
Clifton, Pete 21
Clinton, Bill 215
climate change 57

CNN 2, 11, 23, 40, 46, 75, 177, 178,
  119
CNNfail 2, 121–3
co-creation of content 14, 101, 167
  see also user-generated content
Columbia Journalism Review 127
consumption of news 5, 11, 174, 213,
  215
  and mobile phones 100–4
  in relation to production 41–4, 46,
    111, 170
  see also produsage
Comcast 63
commercialised media 53–67
communities of interest 116, 125
community 4–5
  and Twitter 127–8
  and newsgames 93–6
  collaborative 139–45
  online 174, 180
community media 65–7, 151
ComScore 70
convergence 35, 41, 73–4, 148, 210
  and forms of news 7–8
Couldry, Nick 12, 157
Craigslist 91
Creative Commons licensing 139, 164
crisis of journalism 4, 39–41, 53–8, 64,
  65, 67, 159

Dahong, Min 188
Daily Dish, The 42
Daily Mail, The 11
Daily Show, The 136, 145
Daily Telegraph, The (UK) 11, 154
Data.gov 86
Delicious 12
democracy and news 5, 6, 9, 13, 51, 53,
  55, 66–7, 106, 119, 161, 179–81,
  214–16
democratisation of news 13, 29, 33,
  42–3, 86, 106, 153–4, 157, 167,
  206
depth of coverage 12, 24, 29, 50, 76,
  79, 133, 137, 138, 159
Deuze, Mark 14, 104, 118, 119, 165
Diana (Princess of Wales) 20–1
Dickinson, Andy 110
Digg 12
Digital Britain report 40
digital divide 64, 180

digital communication technology   2, 4,
    11, 39–42, 46, 51, 60–5, 84–5, 148,
    210, 216
Dispatches (TV documentary series)   46
Doctorow, Cory   12
Donner, Jonathan   105
Döpfner, Mathias   50
Downie, Len   54
Drudge Report, The   47, 75
Dyson, Lauren Evelyn   199, 200

eBay   91
economics of news   3–4, 39–40, 50, 51,
    53–67, 140, 145, 149, 159, 164–75,
    197, 212–14
editing   12, 46, 48, 51, 109–10, 134,
    140–1, 148, 154, 165–70, 173, 201–7,
    212
    self-editing   25
    online editors   76
    see also preditors
Eggington, Bob   22–3, 26–9
election coverage   1–2, 26–30, 99, 121–2,
    136, 140, 196–200
Eltringham, Matthew   5–6, 28, 31
El Comercio   73
El Diario del Lago   77
El Diario de Los Andes   73
El Mercurio   73
El Nacional   73
El Tiempo   74
ElTiempo.com   74, 76
El Universal   72, 74, 77
Encyclopædia Britannica   139
e-readers   102–3
ethics of journalism   38, 105, 148–61,
    166, 167, 203
    see also accuracy, balance, facts and
        fact-checking, fairness, objectivity
Euronews   23
eyewitness reports   20–36, 42, 45, 46,
    109, 117–21, 120, 179, 203
    see also citizen journalism

Facebook   1, 2, 9, 10, 11, 32, 39, 99,
    100, 108, 181, 210
facts and fact-checking   7, 27, 44, 57,
    143, 148–61, 206
    see also accuracy
fairness   34, 203
Fairness & Accuracy in Reporting (FAIR)
    66

fair.org   152
fantasy sports   95
Faris, Robert   107
Fawkes, Guido   38, 42
Financial Times, The   4, 47, 50
Flash (Adobe software)   88
Flickr   1, 34, 121, 179, 181
Folha de São Paulo   74
Foreign Intelligence Surveillance Act   61
foreign news   76, 180
Fourth Estate   10, 13, 42, 191, 214
Fox Interactive Media   72
Fox News   7
Franco, Guillermo   76
Freedman, Des   159
free speech   62, 214
freedom of the press   54, 59–64, 78, 92,
    106, 167, 173, 181, 198
Fulton, Nic   110

gatekeeping   48, 134–5, 206
    also see editing, gatewatching, social
        filtering
gatewatching   134–47
Gans, Herbert   8
Garton Ash, Timothy   100
Gee, James   92–3
Generación Y   74
Germany   143, 145
Gillmor, Dan   164, 179, 211
Gizmodo   74
Glass, Stephen   43, 44
GlobalMojo   107
Greenslade, Roy   50
Goggin, Gerard   9–10
Gomez, Ricardo   74
Google   4, 72, 108
Google News   10, 12, 38, 134
    see also aggregators of news
gossip   20, 43, 127–8, 156–7
Guardian, The   1, 6, 38, 44, 47, 50, 102,
    103

Habermas, Jürgen   3, 214
Half-Life game engine   95, 96
Hall, Tony   23
Hamilton, James   151–2, 202, 213
hard news   72, 201, 205
Hargreaves, Ian   151, 153
Hartley, John   12
Harvard Berkman Center for Internet and
    Society   107

helicopter journalism 215
Herald, The (Scotland) 49
Hermida, Alf 25
Herrmann, Steve 32
Holmes, Stephanie 32
Horrocks, Peter 5, 32, 35, 47–8
Huffington Post, The 38, 144
Hurricane Katrina, USA August 2005 179
Hussein, Saddam 27, 31
Human Development Index 70

IBM 86
IndyMedia 11, 74, 152, 213
infographics 85–6
informational news
Information Week 62
interactivity 21–9, 47, 151, 153–9, 170, 212
  'dissociated' 165
Inter American Press Association 75
International Federation of Journalists 168
International Game Developers Association 91
investigative journalism 75, 89, 137, 156
iPhone 8, 91, 100, 102, 103, 108
iTunes 73, 103
Iranian election protests June 2009 1–2, 45–6, 117, 121–3
Iraq war 27–8, 57–8, 90

Jackson, Michael 50
  death of 38, 44, 116, 127
Jakarta bombings July 2009 117
JasmineNews 105–6
Jarvis, Jeff 6
Jiabao, Wen 185
Jianfeng, Fu 187
Jing, Jin 189
Johnston Press 49
journalism
  'bad' 152
  destructuring of 166–8
  education 60, 65, 92
  mainstream 9, 28, 58, 7–25, 77, 78, 122, 125–8, 135–7, 144, 151–5, 178–87, 198, 201
  specialist 54, 174, 137
  traditional 42
  see also citizen journalism, crisis of journalism, ethics of journalism

journalists 10
  as employees 171
  deskilling of 169

Kaiser, Robert 54
Kamm, Oliver 42
Kang, Daniel Jisuk 199–200
Keane, Fergal 20
Keen, Andrew 136, 172, 196, 206
Kelly, Ryan 123–4
Kim, Eun-Gyoo 213
Kindle e-reader 103
  see also e-readers
Kongregate 91
Koskinen, Timo 109
Kovach, Bill 58, 206
Krums, Janis 117–20

labour 164–75, 213
  audiences as unpaid labour 170–1, 173
  immaterial 171–2
  precarious 169
La Nación 74
Lanzhou Morning Post 187
Lasica, J. D. 10, 133
Latin America 69–80
Leadbeater, Charles 15, 139–40
Lee, Hoi Chang 199
Le Monde 64
Lewinsky, Monika 215
local news 40, 66, 94, 135, 143
London Bombings July 2005 30, 33, 106, 179
Loufan landslide 184–6

Madrid bombings 2004 87
ManyEyes project 186
Márquez, Gabriel García 69, 76, 79
McBride, Damian 38
McChesney, Robert 215
McLellan, John 149
McLuhan, Marshall 115, 128
Manovich, Lev 170, 213
Markey, Edward 62–3
Marshall, P. David 213
mass media model 11, 214
Mattelart, Armand 41
mediachannel.org 152
media ownership
  see ownership of news media
media policy 59–62, 65, 149
Meikle, Graham 111

MercadoLibre   72
message or discussion boards   28, 199,
    212
Mexico   74, 78–9
Microsoft   72
Miel, Persephone   107
Miller, Paul   15, 139–40
Miller, Vincent   126
mobile journalism   107–10
mobile media   100
mobile news   99–104, 111
    and citizen journalism   104–7
mobile phones   1, 10, 28, 40, 71, 73, 74,
    99–111
    video and image capture   28–32, 99
modding   95
Mogulus   108
Molecular news   127
mojo   107–9
    see also mobile journalism
Mojo Evolution   107
monopolies of media   55–6, 60, 61, 62–3,
    70, 198
    see also ownership of news media
Morley, David   211
MSNBC   23, 121
Muchacho, Eladio   73
multimedia   25, 33, 41, 45, 47–8, 76, 85,
    103, 89, 110, 155, 210
Mumbai terror attacks November 2008
    34–6, 46, 117
Murdoch, Rupert   4, 48, 49, 103
    see also News Corporation
Myanmar unrest 2007   32
myHeimat   142–3, 145
MySpace   179

National Forum   140
National People's Congress   184
Negroponte, Nicholas   12, 215
networked publics   174–5
network neutrality   63–5
New Republic   184
News Corporation   4, 23, 49, 51
    see also Murdoch, Rupert
Newgrounds   97
news
    free   4, 73
    paid-for   49–50, 73, 105–6
News.com.au   11
news cycle   12, 137
    see also 24–hour news

Newsnight   45
Newsnight Scotland   49
Newsquest   49
newsrooms   46, 65, 75, 119, 148, 165,
    169, 180
newsgames   84–96
newsgathering   33, 45, 48, 76, 106, 108,
    158–9
newsworthiness   116, 199, 201, 213
Newspoll   136
news values   3, 55, 34, 46, 156, 158, 159,
    213, 214
New Yorker, The   91, 189
New York Times, The   1, 11, 43, 57, 86, 90,
    91, 102, 116, 118, 121, 134, 174, 195
New Zealand earthquake July 2009   125
Nietzsche, Friedrich   173
Nintendo Wii   8, 95
Nogeun-ni massacre July 1950   95
Nokia   100, 102, 109–10
Nokia Research Labs   109
Nokia-Reuters mobile journalism kit
    109–10
Norris, Pippa   174, 180
NowPublic   201
Nyirubugara, Olivier   106

Oakland Tribune   91
Obama, Barack   134
Oriental Outlook   184
Örnebring, Henrik   154, 159
objectivity   9, 38, 43, 87, 127, 149,
    150–3, 155, 157, 160, 203, 206,
Ofcom (Office of Communications, UK)
    153, 155
O Globo   74
Oh, Yeon Ho   195–9, 200, 201, 202, 203,
    204, 205
OhmyNews   11, 14–15, 195–207, 133,
    141, 142, 145
    Citizen Reporters' Code of Conduct
    202
online communities   174
    see also community
Online Journalism Blog   108
open source software   138, 145
Oriental Morning Post   187
Oriental Outlook   184
Outing, Steve   205–6
ownership of news media   3, 54, 58,
    60–1, 65, 165, 170, 172
    see also monopolies

participatory journalism
  see citizen journalism
PBS (Public Broadcasting Service)   66,
  123
Pear Analytics   123–4
Perez Hilton   74
personalisation of news   11, 12, 66, 104,
  111, 126, 127, 196
Peru   71
Pew Project For Excellence in Journalism
  3
photographs   26, 30–4, 92, 106, 121,
  171, 182
Phillips, Angela   150, 154, 158
political economy
  see economics of news
professional values of journalism
  see ethics of journalism
podcasting   164
PopCap   91
preditors   140–2
production of news
  merging with consumption   41–4
produsage   138–40
propaganda   57, 187
psephology   136, 137
Public Affairs Monitor Omnibus Survey   55
public relations   57, 155
public service media   21–4, 29, 59, 65–6,
  156–8, 216
puzzles in newspapers   90–1
Patriot Games (puzzle)   90

Qik   108
quality of news   30, 42, 51, 60, 65, 70,
  79, 102, 110, 140, 142, 144, 173,
  202, 205, 212
Quiggin, John   135–6
Quinn, Stephen   107

Rangel, Jose Vicente   77
Reforma   74
regulation
  see media policy
reportage   20, 43, 108, 149
  newsgames   87–8, 92
Reuters   45, 76, 109–10
Robins, Jane   25
Roh, Moo-Hyun   196, 197, 198,
  199–200, 202, 207
rolling news
  see 24-hour news

Rorty, James   61
Rosen, Jay   2, 36, 133, 164, 168, 211
RSS   12, 40, 188, 200
rumour   43, 44, 116, 126

Salon.com   47, 54
Sambrook, Richard   30, 45
Sánchez, Yoani   74, 77–8
Sanlu infant milk scandal, China 2008
  186–8
SBS (Special Broadcasting Service)   140
Scardino, Marjorie   50
Schudson, Michael   9, 54–5, 174
Scott, C. P.   149
Scott, Mark   119
Sennett, Richard   172
September 11 terror attacks USA, 2001
  89
Shirky, Clay   5, 127, 133, 135, 139, 164,
  165
Shortz, Will   91
Sicart, Miguel   87
Sigal, Leon. V.   153
Sky News   38, 48
slander   156–7
Slashdot   12
Slate.com   47
smartphones   100, 103, 110
Smartt, Mike   24, 27
social network media   5, 9–10, 32, 34,
  38–9, 46, 64, 95, 100, 115–29, 173–4,
  179
Southern Metropolitan Daily   182, 183,
  187
South Florida Sun Sentinel   85
Southern Weekend   187
South Korea   101, 195–209
Sri Lanka   105–6
Stam, Robert   7
Stone, Biz   115
Stewart, Kathleen   127
student media   60, 65
StumbleUpon   12
Sullivan, Andrew   42, 122, 151
Sun, The   4
Sunday World   90
Sunstein, Cass   65–6, 215
Sydney Morning Herald, The   102
syndication   21, 141

Tiananmen Square protests Beijing June
  1989   121, 181

Taylor, Vicky   29, 31, 32
technological determinism   210
technophilic discourse   108
Terra Networks   72
Thurman, Neil   212–13
Torvalds, Linus   139
Troedsson, Hans   186
Times, The (London)   23
TMZ.com   38, 44, 50
Tsunami in the Indian Ocean 2004   5,
   28, 30, 134, 179
Tufte, Edward   85
Twitter   1, 2, 9, 10, 11, 15, 34–5, 39, 48,
   99, 100, 108, 115–29

US Airways Flight 1549 2009   128
user-generated content   30–1, 144, 164,
   171, 174, 179, 203
   unreliability of   43–4, 46
   see also co-creation of content,
      produsage

Venezuela   71, 73, 75, 77, 78, 79
Verizon   63
video news   25–32, 49, 99–100, 105, 106,
   108, 111
videogames and news   8
   9/11 Survivor   89
   Beyond Good & Evil   92
   and community   93–5
   Cutthroat Capitalism   87
   Dead Rising   92
   docugames   89–90
   editorial   87–9
   Escape From Woomera   89, 95
   Fallout 3   92
   Global Conflict: Latin America   92
   Global Conflict: Palestine   92
   Global Conflict series   92
   Grand Theft Auto   96
   Gravitation   90
   infographics   85–6
   Kuma\War games   89, 95–6
   Madrid   87

Massively Multiplayer Online Games
   94
So you think you can drive, Me!?   87
September 12th   87
Sims, The game   94
Six Days in Fallujah   90
Super Mario Bros   94
Super Mario Land   96
tabloid   87–8
Tetris   91
World Without Oil   94
Zuma   91
Voices of Africa Media Foundation
   106
Voices of Africa project   106

Wagstaff, Jeremy   198
Wall Street Journal, The   49, 118
Wang, Grace   186
Washington Post   54, 57
web 2.0   154, 179–81
Webb, Gary   58
weblogs
   see blogs
Web Ecology Project   127
Whitworth, Damian   23
Wikinews   11, 201, 206, 213
Wikipedia   38, 72, 137, 138, 139, 170
Williams, Evan   115
Williams, Raymond   127
Willis, Chris   118–19
Wilson, Jason   140, 142
Wired magazine   87
World Association of Newspapers   39–40

Xinhua News Agency   182

Yahoo!   72
Youdecide2007.org   140
YouTube   1, 10, 94 99, 100, 125, 179,
   181, 189

Zapatistas   78–9
Zhou, Zola   183